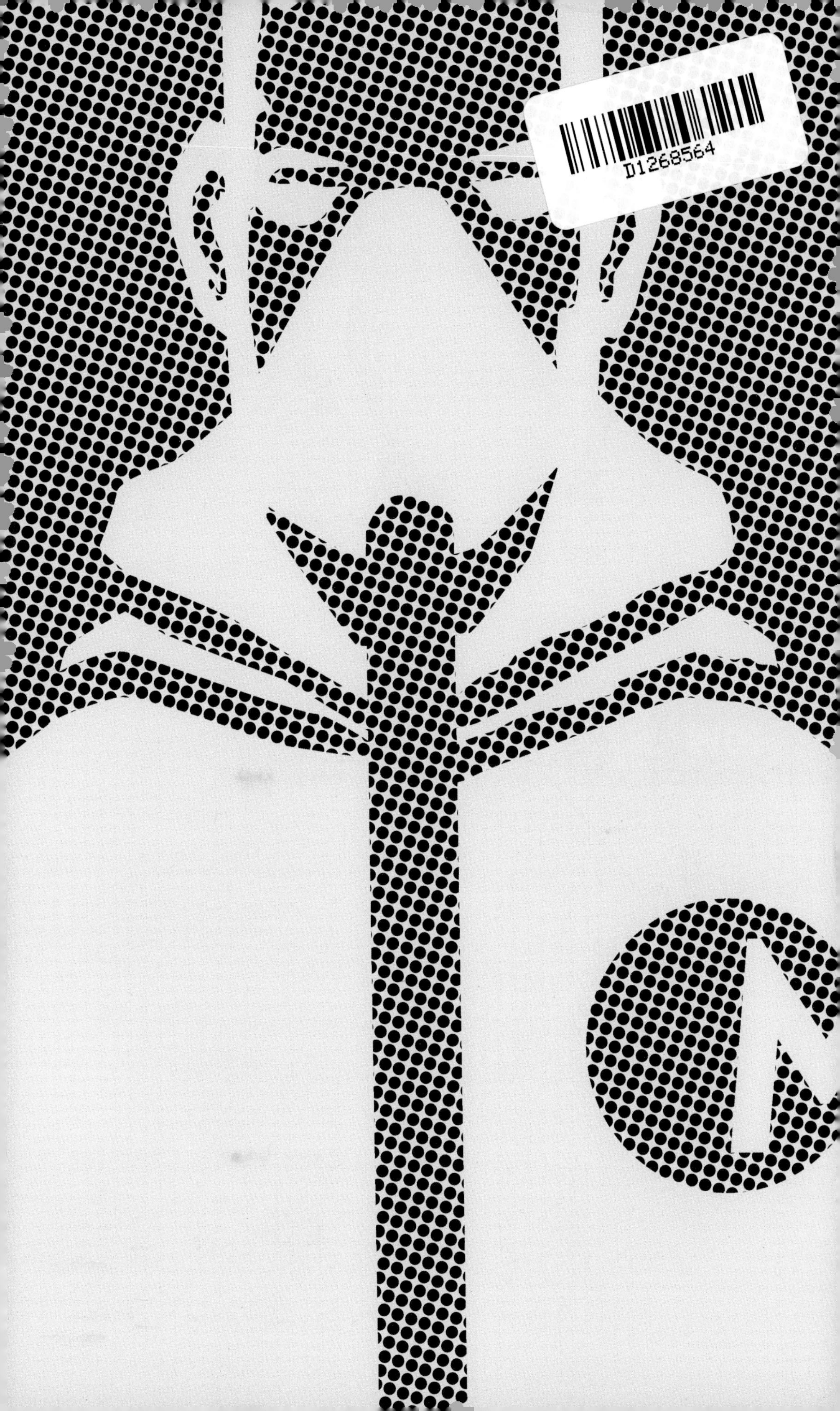

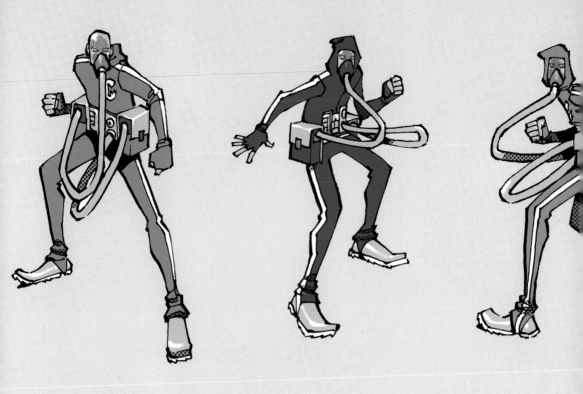

Facebook: **facebook.com/idwpublishing**
Twitter: **@idwpublishing**
YouTube: **youtube.com/idwpublishing**
Tumblr: **tumblr.idwpublishing.com**
Instagram: **instagram.com/idwpublishing**

COVER ART BY
ASHLEY WOOD

COLLECTION EDITS BY
JUSTIN EISINGER
AND ALONZO SIMON

PUBLISHER
TED ADAMS

COLLECTION DESIGN BY
JEFF POWELL

978-1-63140-560-0   19 18 17 16   1 2 3 4

Originally published as STRING DIVERS issues #1–5.

Ted Adams, CEO & Publisher
Greg Goldstein, President & COO
Robbie Robbins, EVP/Sr. Graphic Artist
Chris Ryall, Chief Creative Officer/Editor-in-Chief
Matthew Ruzicka, CPA, Chief Financial Officer
Dirk Wood, VP of Marketing
Lorelei Bunjes, VP of Digital Services
Jeff Webber, VP of Digital and Subsidiary Rights
Jerry Bennington, VP of New Product Development

STRING DIVERS

EFFECT REQUIRES CAUSE

CREATOR/ART DIRECTOR
ASHLEY WOOD

STORYTELLERS
CHRIS RYALL
AND NELSON DÁNIEL

LETTERS
NEIL UYETAKE

EDITORIAL ASSIST
MICHAEL BENEDETTO

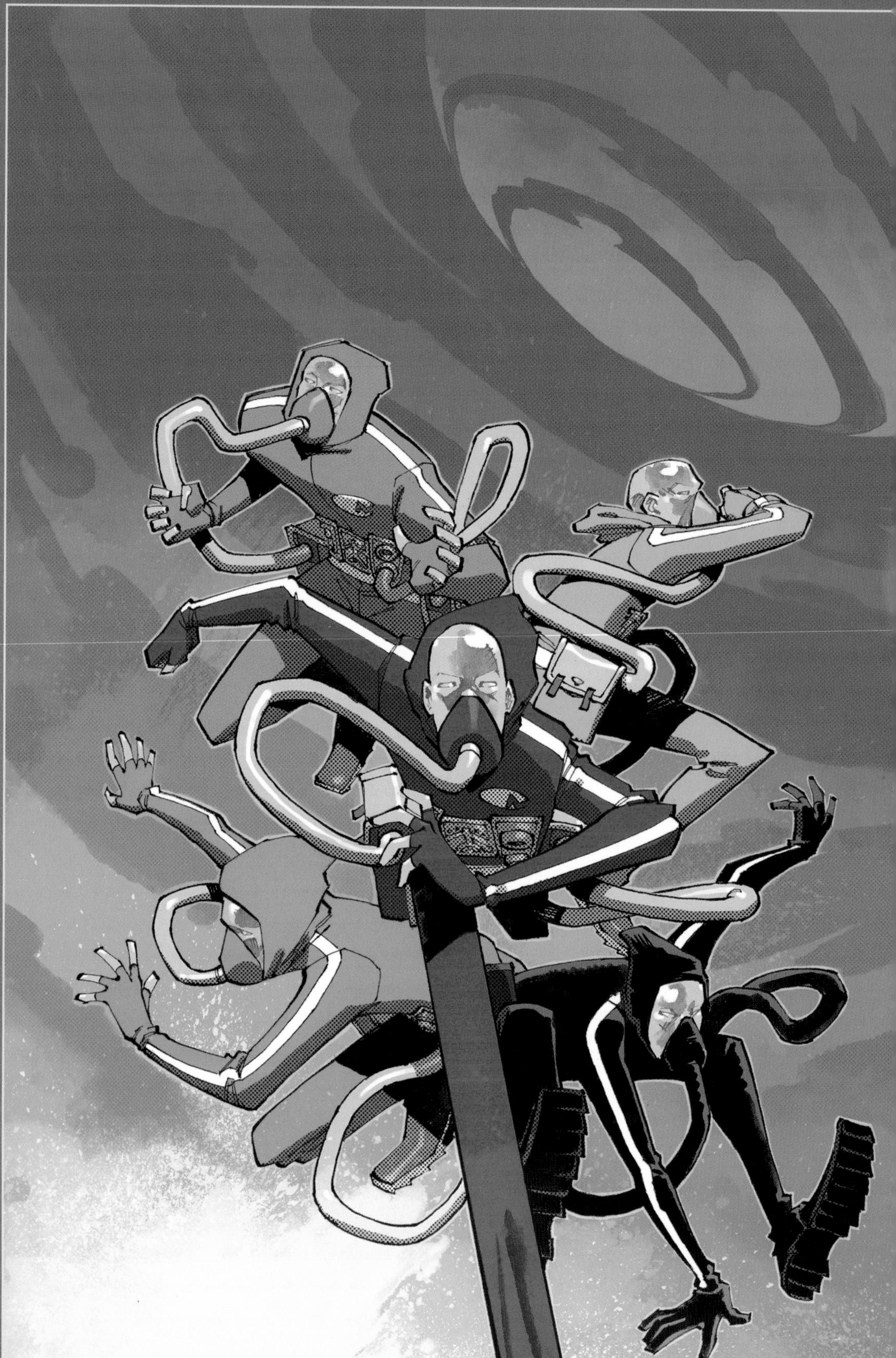

01 | ART BY NELSON DÁNIEL

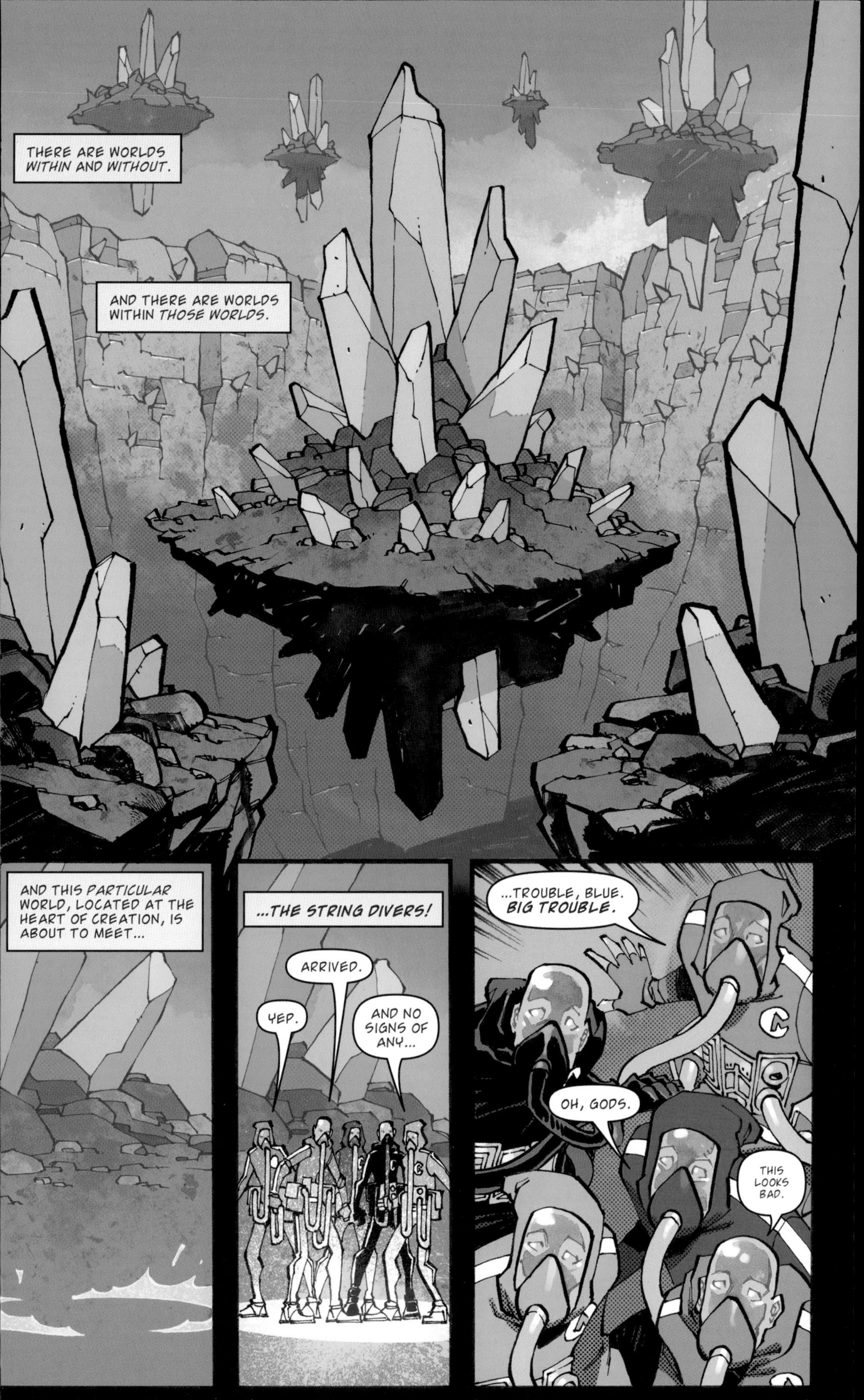
THERE ARE WORLDS WITHIN AND WITHOUT.
AND THERE ARE WORLDS WITHIN *THOSE* WORLDS.
AND THIS *PARTICULAR* WORLD, LOCATED AT THE HEART OF CREATION, IS ABOUT TO MEET...
...THE STRING DIVERS!
YEP.
ARRIVED.
AND NO SIGNS OF ANY...
...TROUBLE, BLUE. BIG TROUBLE.
OH, GODS.
THIS LOOKS BAD.

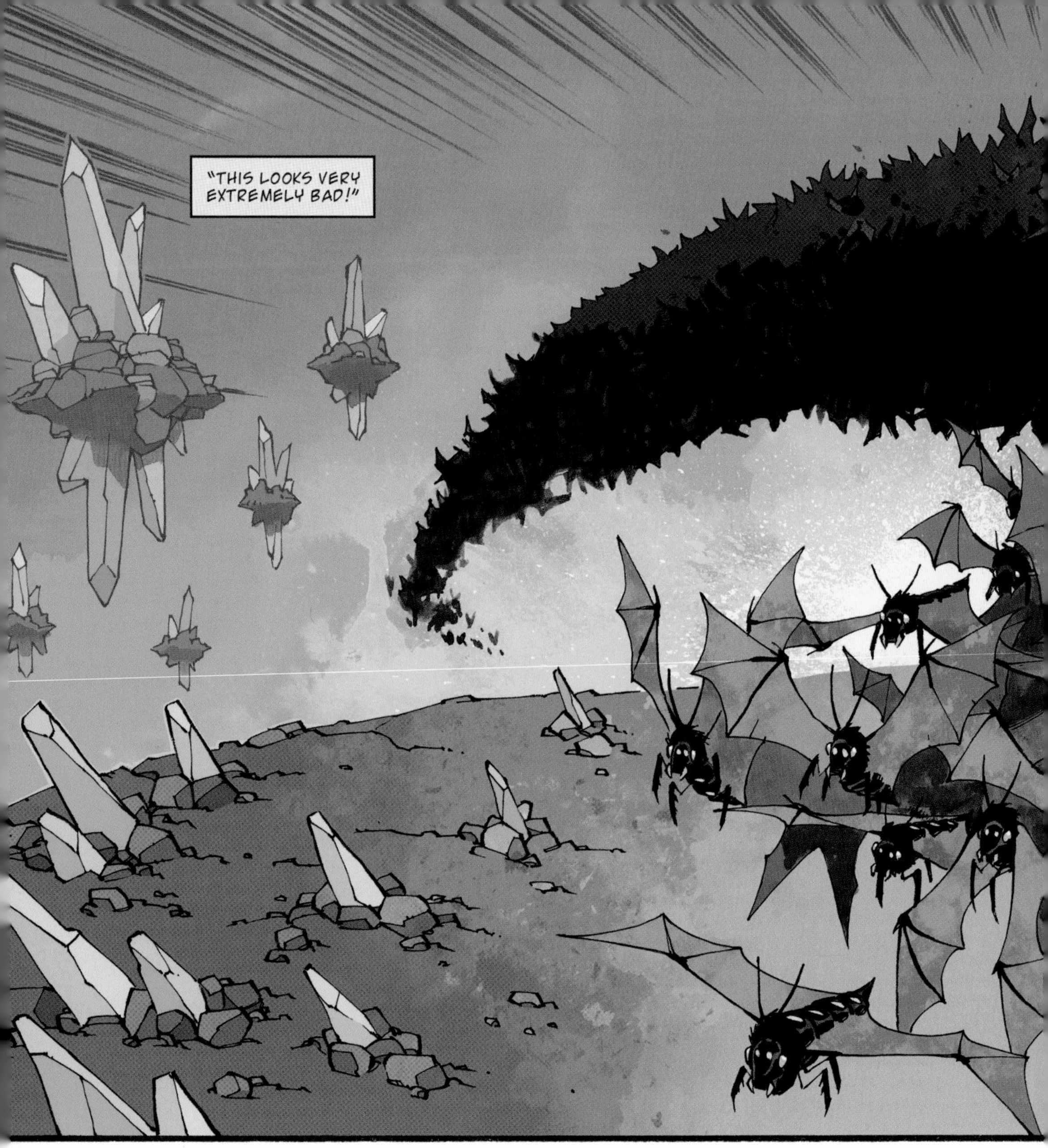
"THIS LOOKS VERY EXTREMELY BAD!"

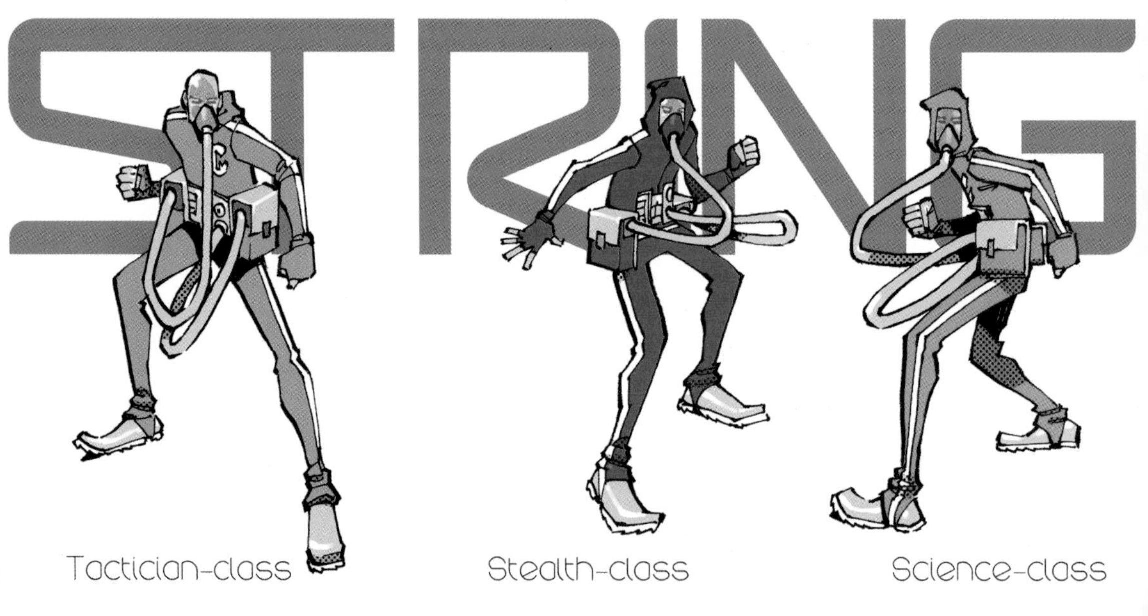
STRING
Tactician-class
Stealth-class
Science-class

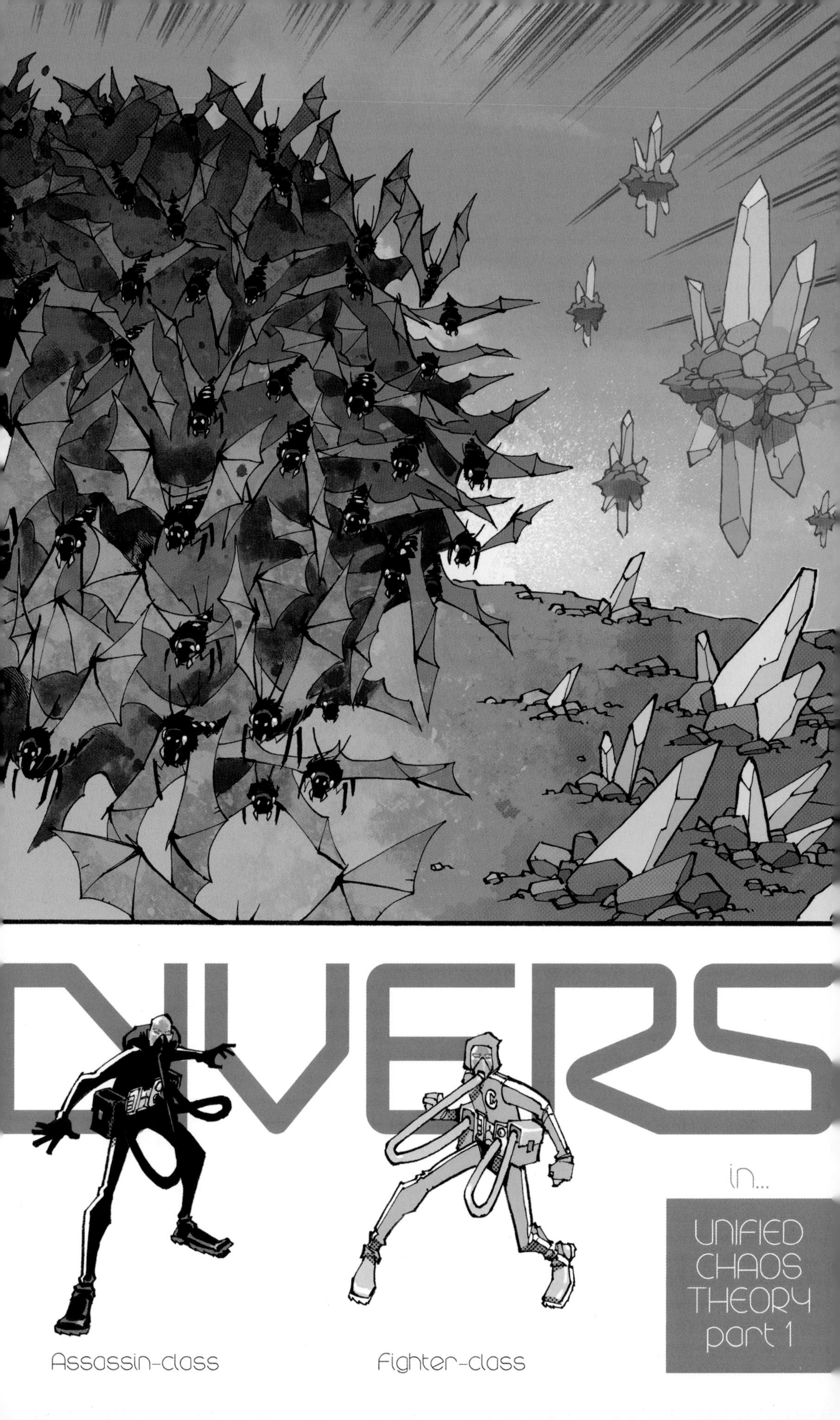
in...
UNIFIED CHAOS THEORY part 1
Assassin-class
Fighter-class

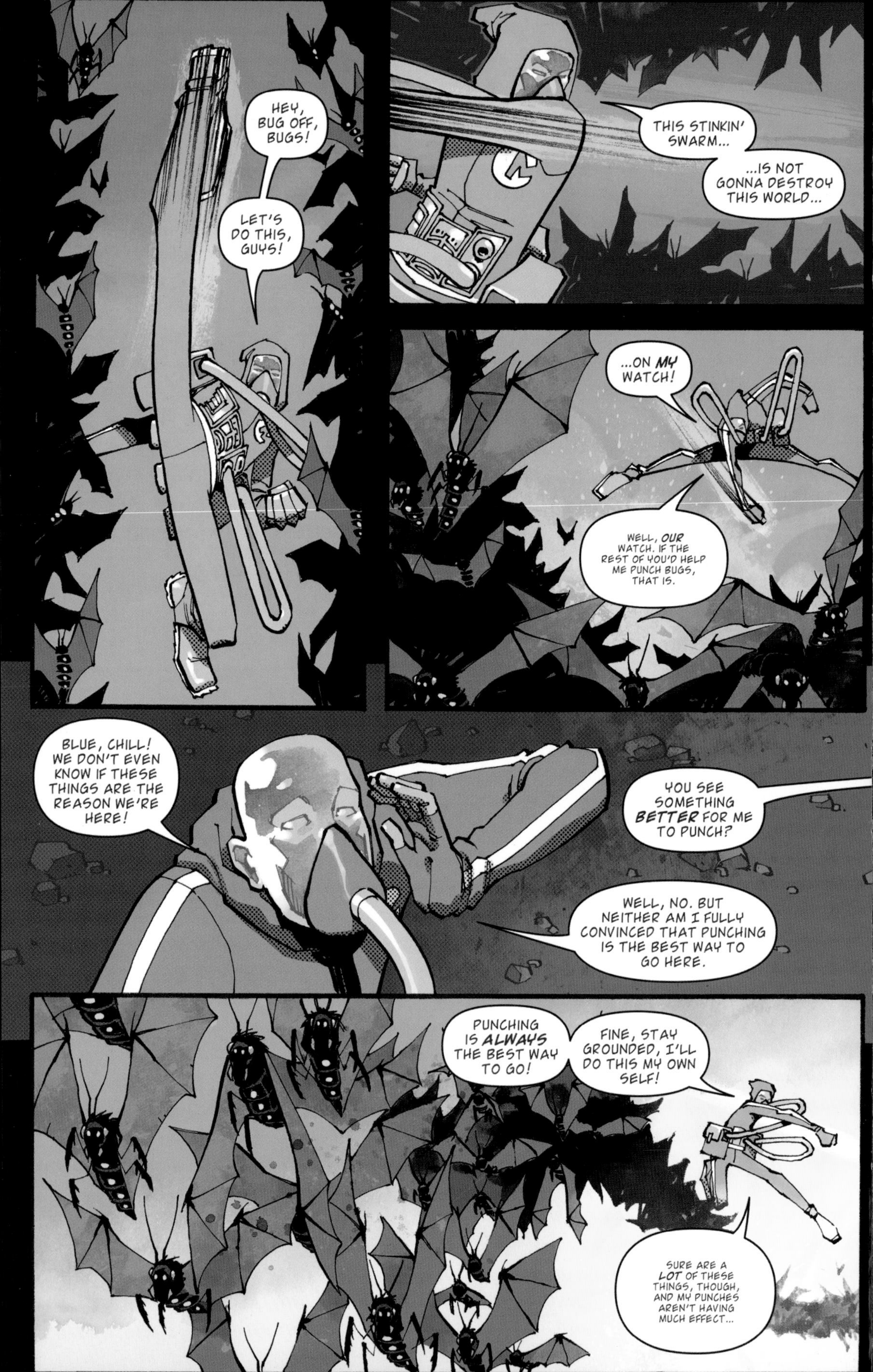
HEY, BUG OFF, BUGS!
LET'S DO THIS, GUYS!
THIS STINKIN' SWARM...
...IS NOT GONNA DESTROY THIS WORLD...
...ON MY WATCH!
WELL, OUR WATCH. IF THE REST OF YOU'D HELP ME PUNCH BUGS, THAT IS.
BLUE, CHILL! WE DON'T EVEN KNOW IF THESE THINGS ARE THE REASON WE'RE HERE!
YOU SEE SOMETHING BETTER FOR ME TO PUNCH?
WELL, NO. BUT NEITHER AM I FULLY CONVINCED THAT PUNCHING IS THE BEST WAY TO GO HERE.
PUNCHING IS ALWAYS THE BEST WAY TO GO!
FINE, STAY GROUNDED, I'LL DO THIS MY OWN SELF!
SURE ARE A LOT OF THESE THINGS, THOUGH, AND MY PUNCHES AREN'T HAVING MUCH EFFECT...

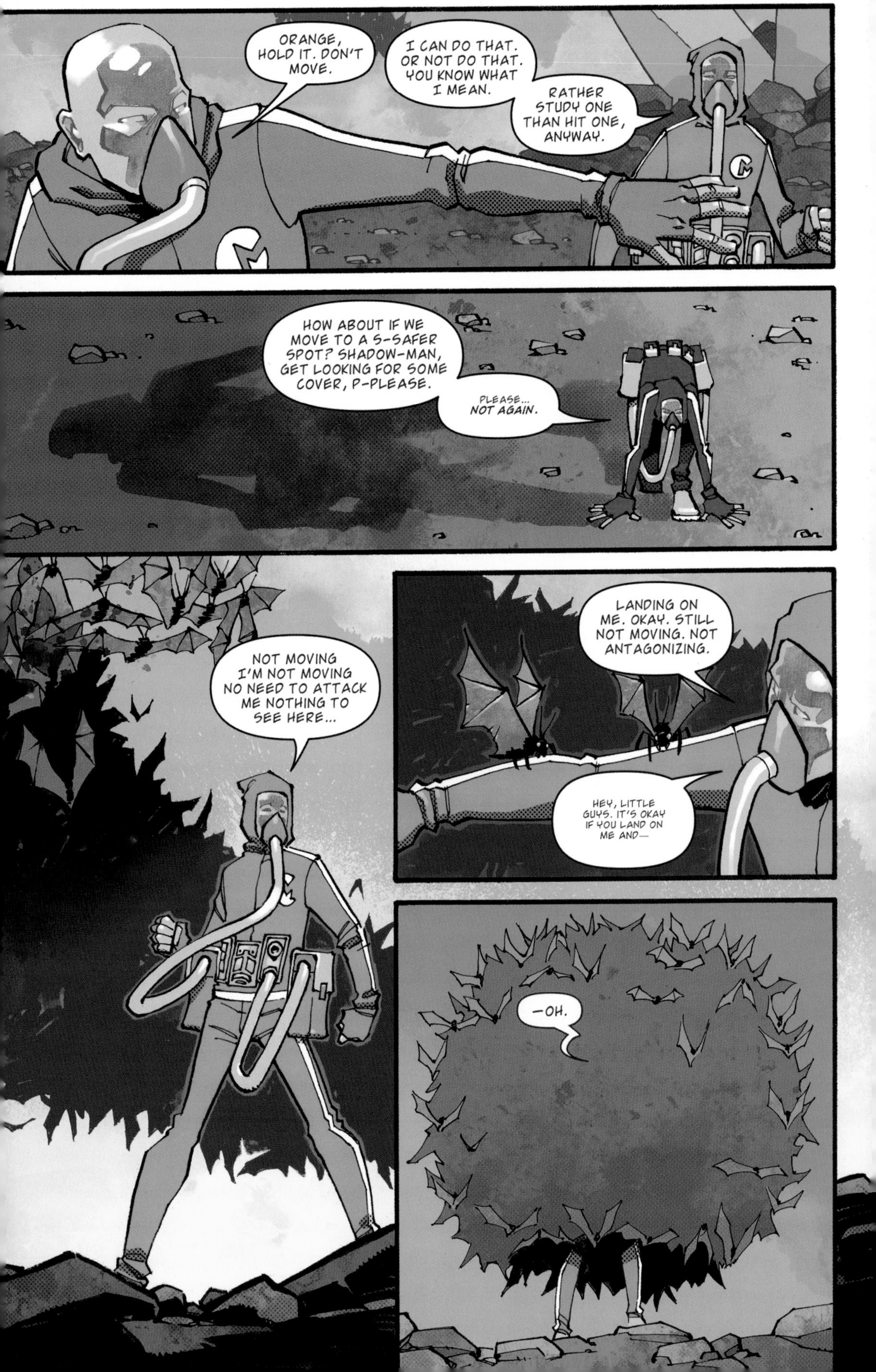
ORANGE, HOLD IT. DON'T MOVE.
I CAN DO THAT. OR NOT DO THAT. YOU KNOW WHAT I MEAN.
RATHER STUDY ONE THAN HIT ONE, ANYWAY.
HOW ABOUT IF WE MOVE TO A S-SAFER SPOT? SHADOW-MAN, GET LOOKING FOR SOME COVER, P-PLEASE.
PLEASE... NOT AGAIN.
NOT MOVING I'M NOT MOVING NO NEED TO ATTACK ME NOTHING TO SEE HERE...
LANDING ON ME. OKAY. STILL NOT MOVING. NOT ANTAGONIZING.
HEY, LITTLE GUYS. IT'S OKAY IF YOU LAND ON ME AND—
—OH.

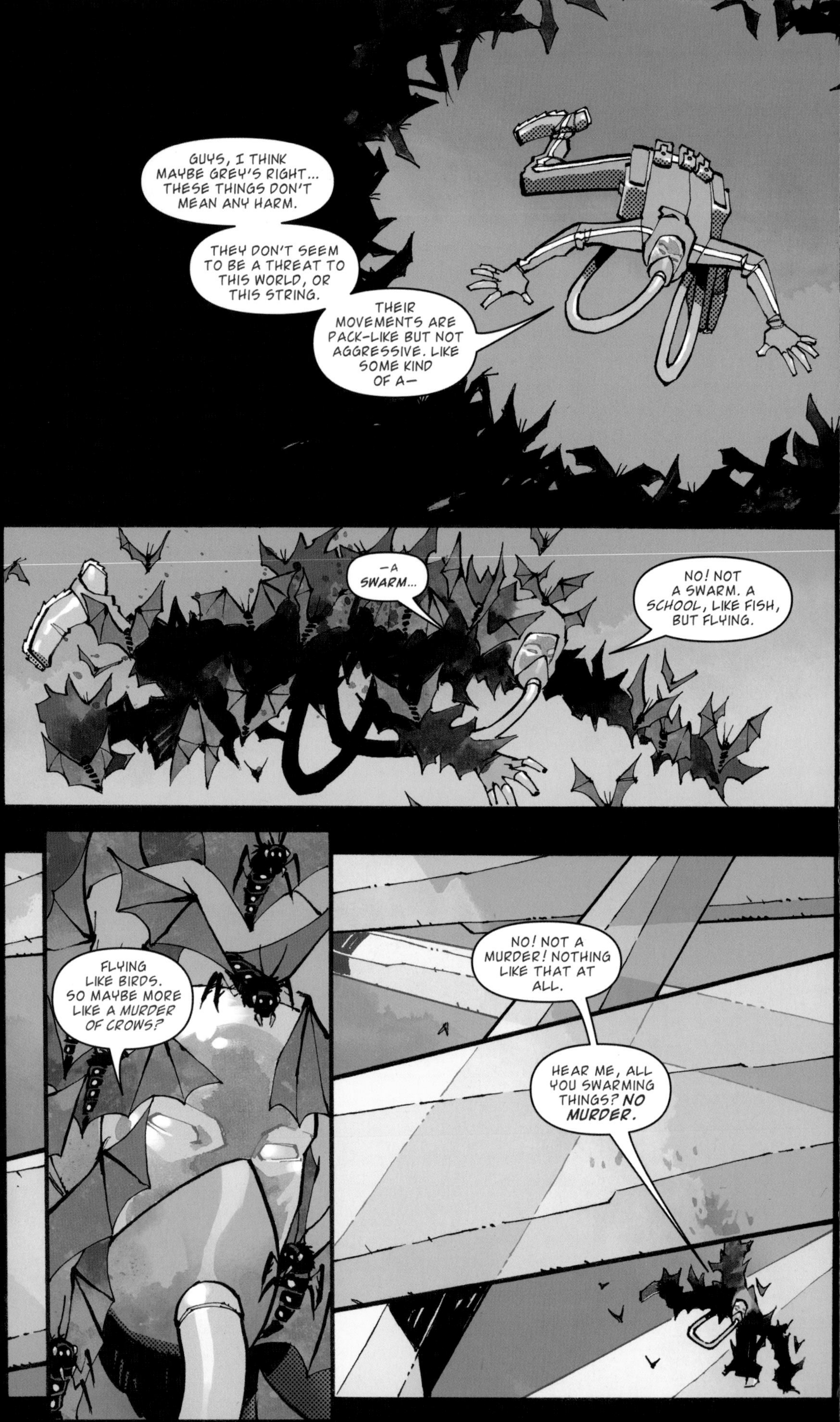
GUYS, I THINK MAYBE GREY'S RIGHT... THESE THINGS DON'T MEAN ANY HARM.
THEY DON'T SEEM TO BE A THREAT TO THIS WORLD, OR THIS STRING.
THEIR MOVEMENTS ARE PACK-LIKE BUT NOT AGGRESSIVE. LIKE SOME KIND OF A—
—A SWARM...
NO! NOT A SWARM. A SCHOOL, LIKE FISH, BUT FLYING.
FLYING LIKE BIRDS. SO MAYBE MORE LIKE A MURDER OF CROWS?
NO! NOT A MURDER! NOTHING LIKE THAT AT ALL.
HEAR ME, ALL YOU SWARMING THINGS? NO MURDER.

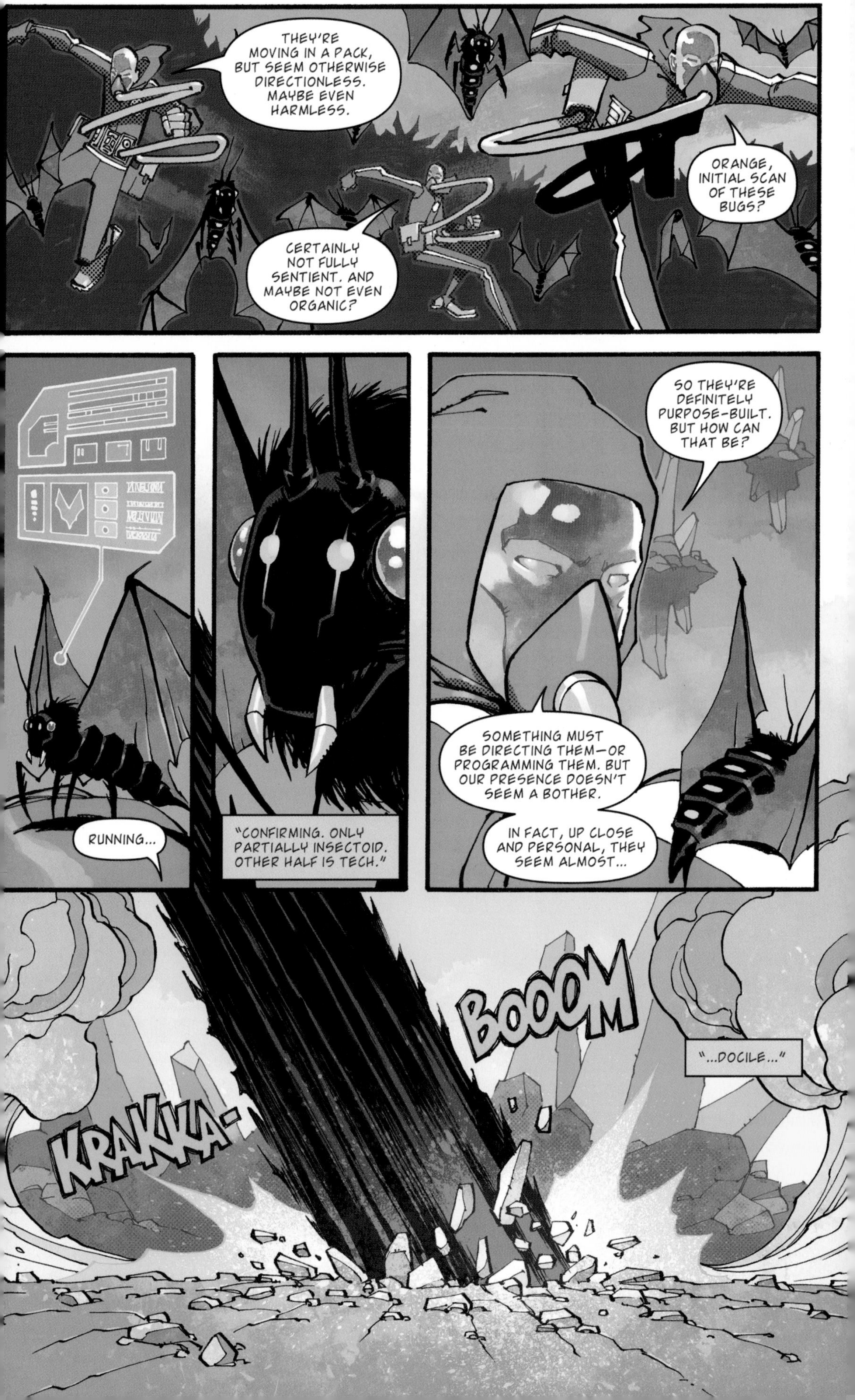
THEY'RE MOVING IN A PACK, BUT SEEM OTHERWISE DIRECTIONLESS. MAYBE EVEN HARMLESS.
ORANGE, INITIAL SCAN OF THESE BUGS?
CERTAINLY NOT FULLY SENTIENT. AND MAYBE NOT EVEN ORGANIC?
RUNNING...
"CONFIRMING. ONLY PARTIALLY INSECTOID. OTHER HALF IS TECH."
SO THEY'RE DEFINITELY PURPOSE-BUILT. BUT HOW CAN THAT BE?
SOMETHING MUST BE DIRECTING THEM—OR PROGRAMMING THEM. BUT OUR PRESENCE DOESN'T SEEM A BOTHER.
IN FACT, UP CLOSE AND PERSONAL, THEY SEEM ALMOST...
BOOOM
"...DOCILE..."
KRAKKA-

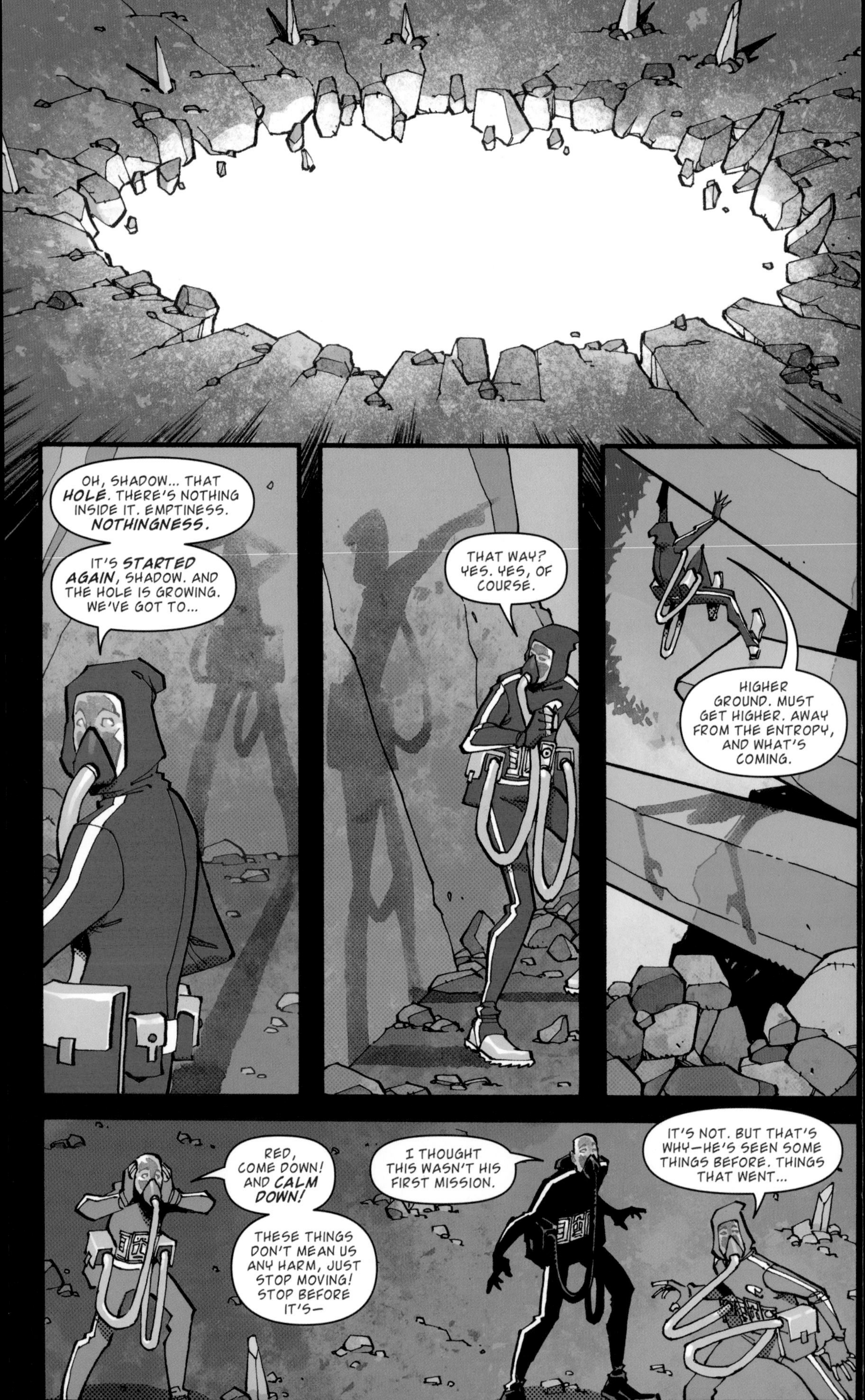
OH, SHADOW... THAT HOLE. THERE'S NOTHING INSIDE IT. EMPTINESS. NOTHINGNESS.
IT'S STARTED AGAIN, SHADOW. AND THE HOLE IS GROWING. WE'VE GOT TO...
THAT WAY? YES. YES, OF COURSE.
HIGHER GROUND. MUST GET HIGHER. AWAY FROM THE ENTROPY, AND WHAT'S COMING.
RED, COME DOWN! AND CALM DOWN!
THESE THINGS DON'T MEAN US ANY HARM, JUST STOP MOVING! STOP BEFORE IT'S—
I THOUGHT THIS WASN'T HIS FIRST MISSION.
IT'S NOT. BUT THAT'S WHY—HE'S SEEN SOME THINGS BEFORE. THINGS THAT WENT...

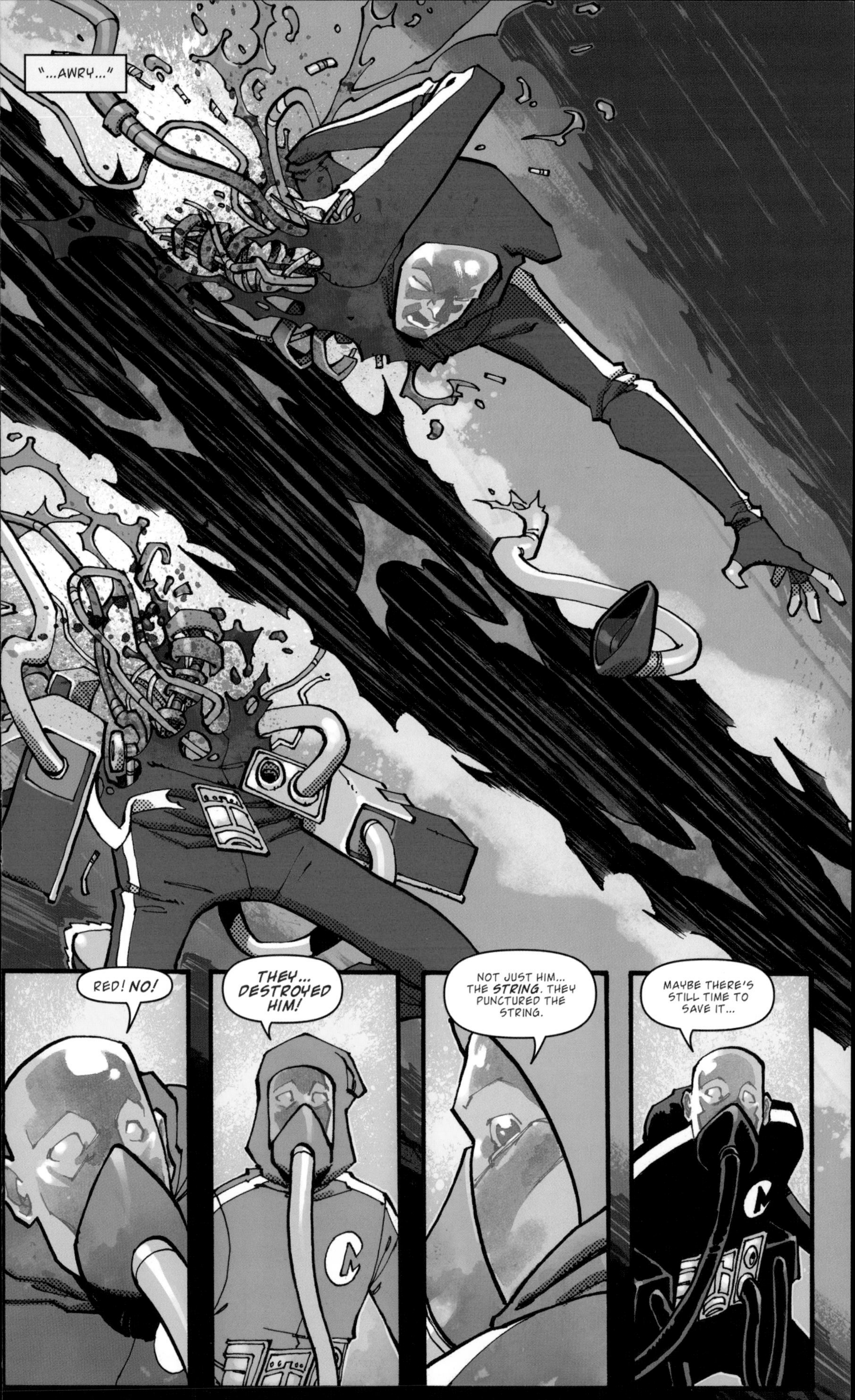
"...AWRY..."
RED! NO!
THEY... DESTROYED HIM!
NOT JUST HIM... THE STRING. THEY PUNCTURED THE STRING.
MAYBE THERE'S STILL TIME TO SAVE IT...

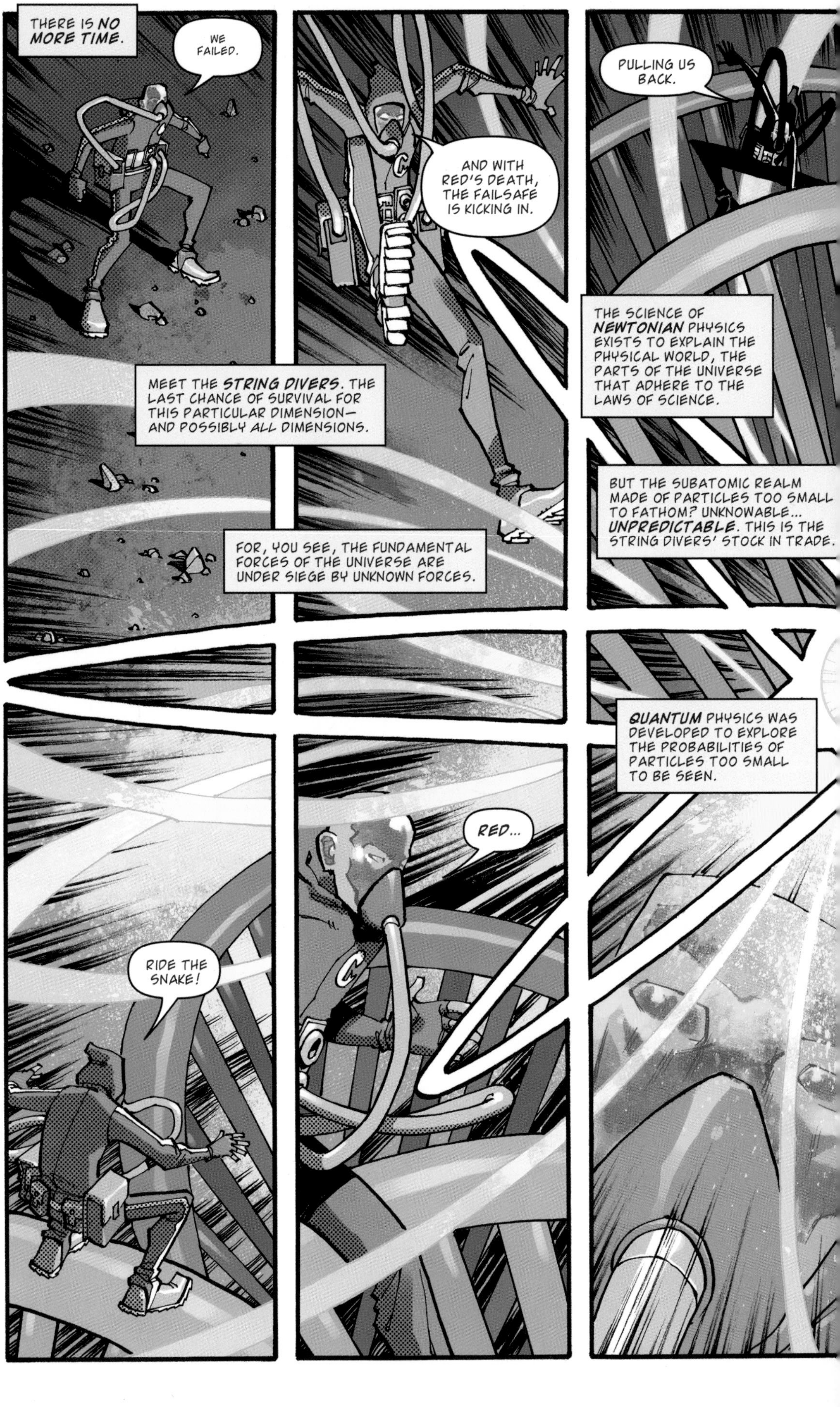
THERE IS NO MORE TIME.
WE FAILED.
AND WITH RED'S DEATH, THE FAILSAFE IS KICKING IN.
PULLING US BACK.
MEET THE STRING DIVERS. THE LAST CHANCE OF SURVIVAL FOR THIS PARTICULAR DIMENSION— AND POSSIBLY ALL DIMENSIONS.
THE SCIENCE OF NEWTONIAN PHYSICS EXISTS TO EXPLAIN THE PHYSICAL WORLD, THE PARTS OF THE UNIVERSE THAT ADHERE TO THE LAWS OF SCIENCE.
FOR, YOU SEE, THE FUNDAMENTAL FORCES OF THE UNIVERSE ARE UNDER SIEGE BY UNKNOWN FORCES.
BUT THE SUBATOMIC REALM MADE OF PARTICLES TOO SMALL TO FATHOM? UNKNOWABLE... UNPREDICTABLE. THIS IS THE STRING DIVERS' STOCK IN TRADE.
QUANTUM PHYSICS WAS DEVELOPED TO EXPLORE THE PROBABILITIES OF PARTICLES TOO SMALL TO BE SEEN.
RED...
RIDE THE SNAKE!

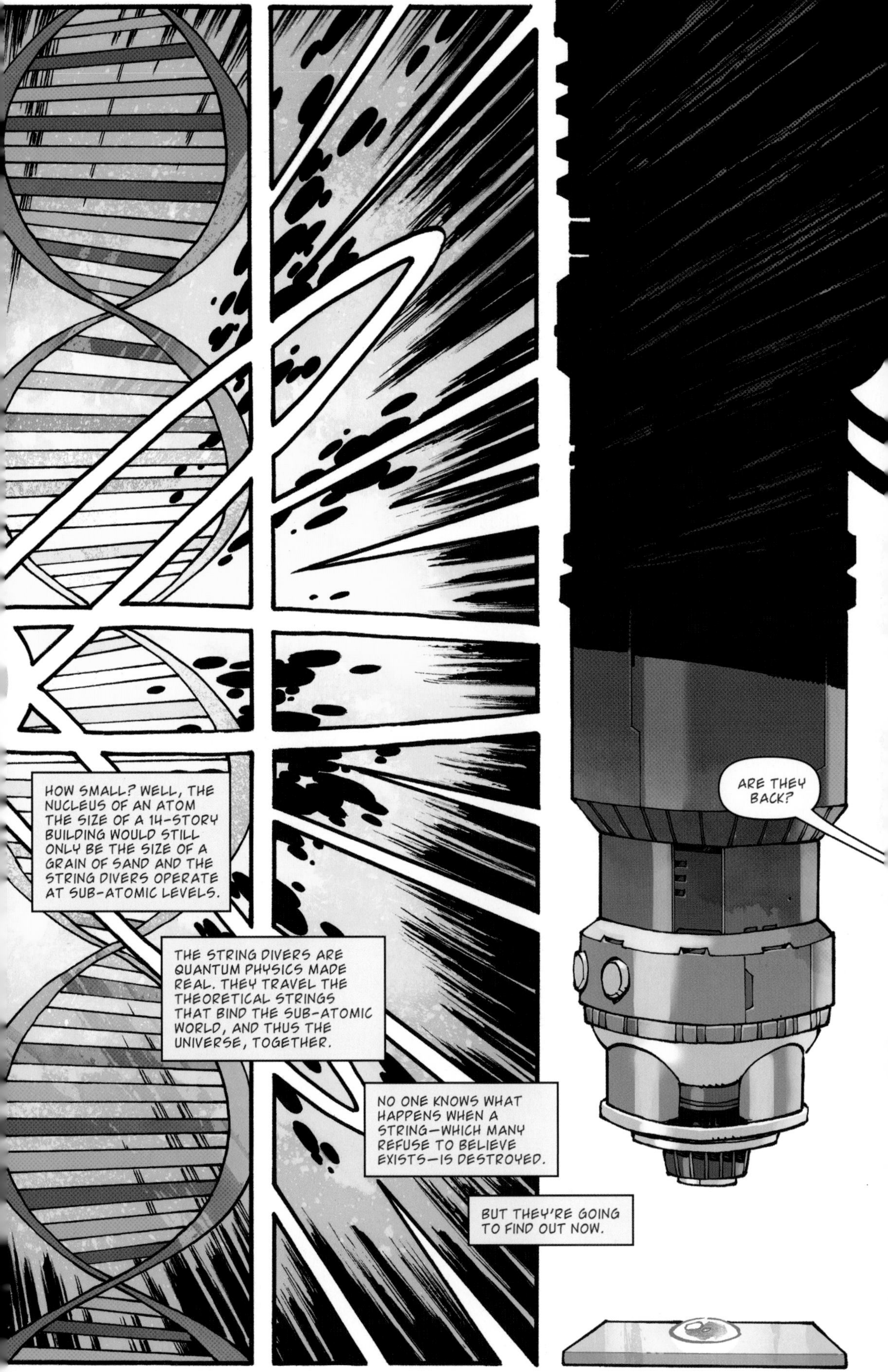
HOW SMALL? WELL, THE NUCLEUS OF AN ATOM THE SIZE OF A 14-STORY BUILDING WOULD STILL ONLY BE THE SIZE OF A GRAIN OF SAND AND THE STRING DIVERS OPERATE AT SUB-ATOMIC LEVELS.
THE STRING DIVERS ARE QUANTUM PHYSICS MADE REAL. THEY TRAVEL THE THEORETICAL STRINGS THAT BIND THE SUB-ATOMIC WORLD, AND THUS THE UNIVERSE, TOGETHER.
NO ONE KNOWS WHAT HAPPENS WHEN A STRING—WHICH MANY REFUSE TO BELIEVE EXISTS—IS DESTROYED.
BUT THEY'RE GOING TO FIND OUT NOW.
ARE THEY BACK?

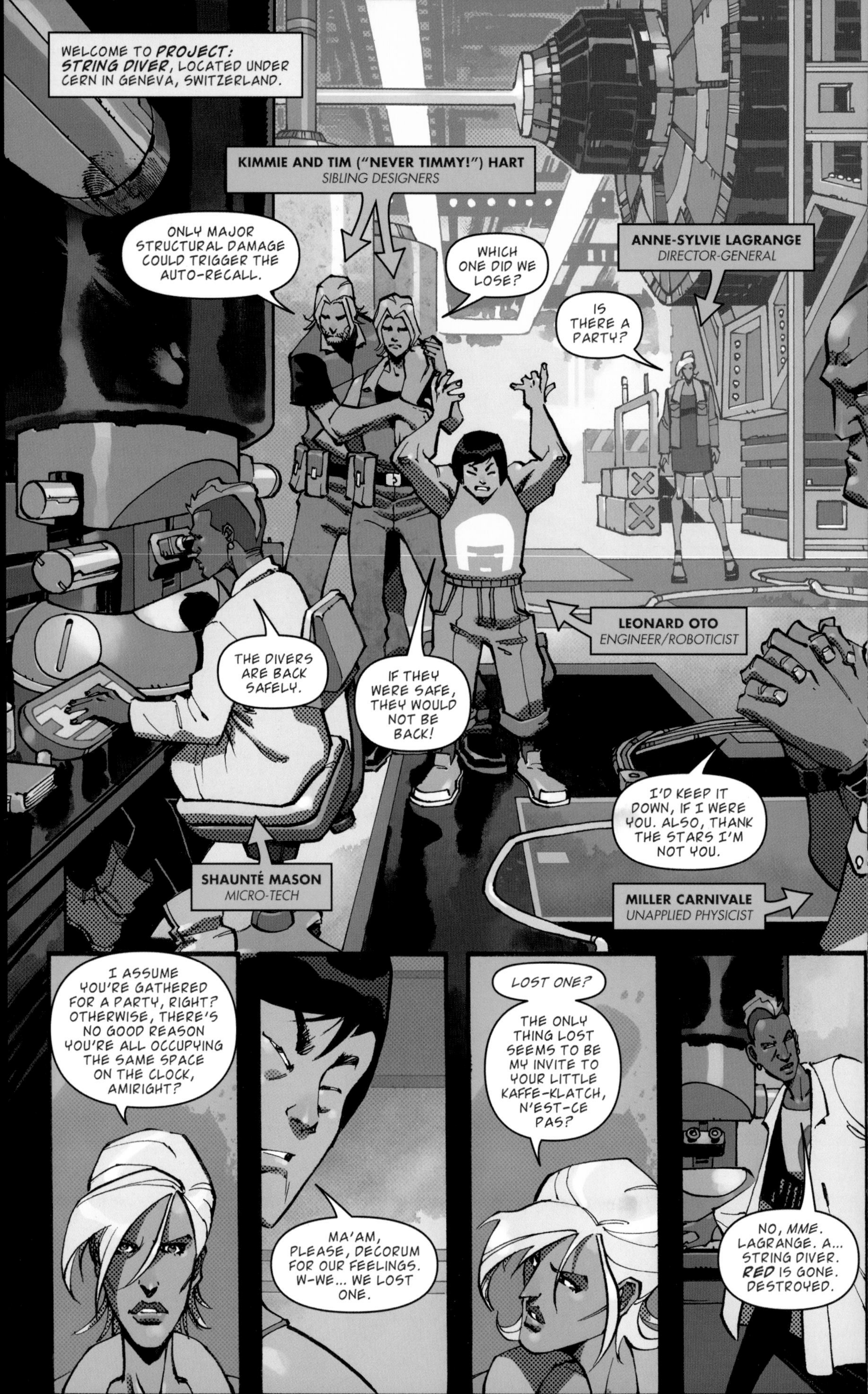
WELCOME TO PROJECT: STRING DIVER, LOCATED UNDER CERN IN GENEVA, SWITZERLAND.
KIMMIE AND TIM ("NEVER TIMMY!") HART
SIBLING DESIGNERS
ONLY MAJOR STRUCTURAL DAMAGE COULD TRIGGER THE AUTO-RECALL.
WHICH ONE DID WE LOSE?
ANNE-SYLVIE LAGRANGE
DIRECTOR-GENERAL
IS THERE A PARTY?
LEONARD OTO
ENGINEER/ROBOTICIST
THE DIVERS ARE BACK SAFELY.
IF THEY WERE SAFE, THEY WOULD NOT BE BACK!
I'D KEEP IT DOWN, IF I WERE YOU. ALSO, THANK THE STARS I'M NOT YOU.
SHAUNTÉ MASON
MICRO-TECH
MILLER CARNIVALE
UNAPPLIED PHYSICIST
I ASSUME YOU'RE GATHERED FOR A PARTY, RIGHT? OTHERWISE, THERE'S NO GOOD REASON YOU'RE ALL OCCUPYING THE SAME SPACE ON THE CLOCK, AMIRIGHT?
MA'AM, PLEASE, DECORUM FOR OUR FEELINGS. W-WE... WE LOST ONE.
LOST ONE?
THE ONLY THING LOST SEEMS TO BE MY INVITE TO YOUR LITTLE KAFFE-KLATCH, N'EST-CE PAS?
NO, MME. LAGRANGE. A... STRING DIVER. RED IS GONE. DESTROYED.

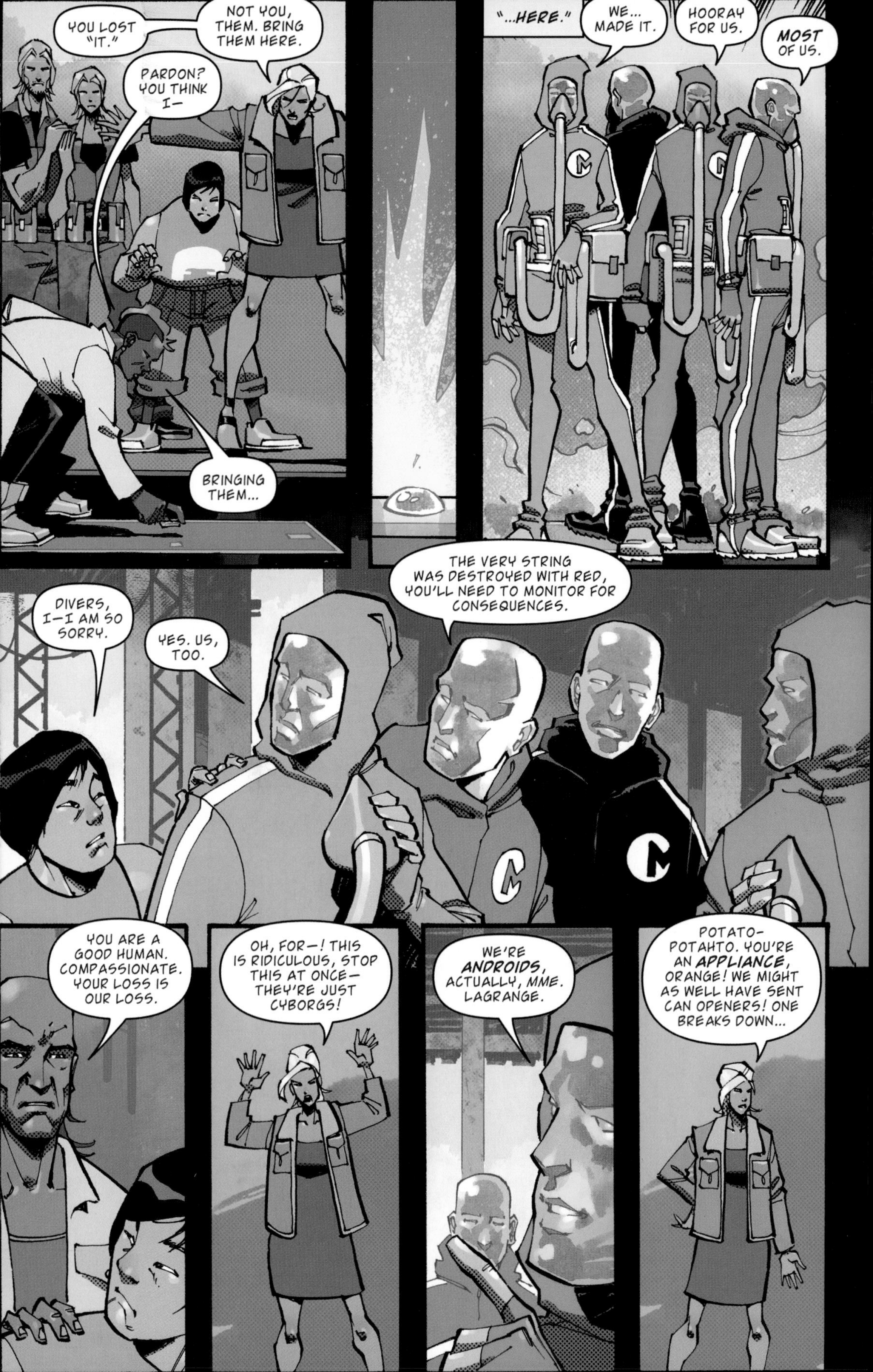

YOU LOST "IT."
NOT YOU, THEM. BRING THEM HERE.
PARDON? YOU THINK I—
BRINGING THEM...
"...HERE."
WE... MADE IT.
HOORAY FOR US.
MOST OF US.
DIVERS, I—I AM SO SORRY.
YES. US, TOO.
THE VERY STRING WAS DESTROYED WITH RED, YOU'LL NEED TO MONITOR FOR CONSEQUENCES.
YOU ARE A GOOD HUMAN. COMPASSIONATE. YOUR LOSS IS OUR LOSS.
OH, FOR—! THIS IS RIDICULOUS, STOP THIS AT ONCE— THEY'RE JUST CYBORGS!
WE'RE ANDROIDS, ACTUALLY, MME. LAGRANGE.
POTATO-POTAHTO. YOU'RE AN APPLIANCE, ORANGE! WE MIGHT AS WELL HAVE SENT CAN OPENERS! ONE BREAKS DOWN...

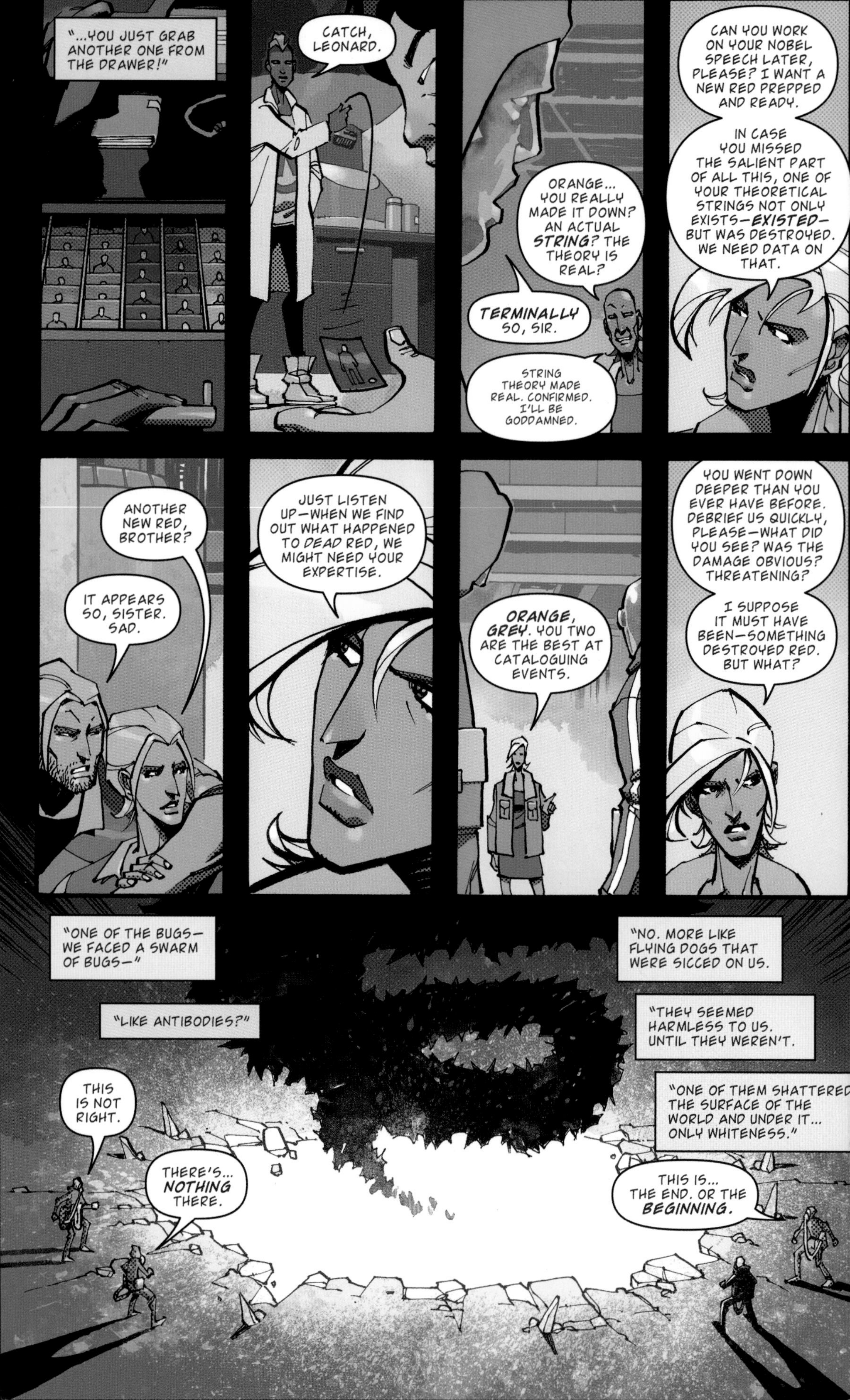
"...YOU JUST GRAB ANOTHER ONE FROM THE DRAWER!"
CATCH, LEONARD.
ORANGE... YOU REALLY MADE IT DOWN? AN ACTUAL STRING? THE THEORY IS REAL?
TERMINALLY SO, SIR.
STRING THEORY MADE REAL. CONFIRMED. I'LL BE GODDAMNED.
CAN YOU WORK ON YOUR NOBEL SPEECH LATER, PLEASE? I WANT A NEW RED PREPPED AND READY.
IN CASE YOU MISSED THE SALIENT PART OF ALL THIS, ONE OF YOUR THEORETICAL STRINGS NOT ONLY EXISTS—EXISTED—BUT WAS DESTROYED. WE NEED DATA ON THAT.
ANOTHER NEW RED, BROTHER?
IT APPEARS SO, SISTER. SAD.
JUST LISTEN UP—WHEN WE FIND OUT WHAT HAPPENED TO DEAD RED, WE MIGHT NEED YOUR EXPERTISE.
ORANGE, GREY. YOU TWO ARE THE BEST AT CATALOGUING EVENTS.
YOU WENT DOWN DEEPER THAN YOU EVER HAVE BEFORE. DEBRIEF US QUICKLY, PLEASE—WHAT DID YOU SEE? WAS THE DAMAGE OBVIOUS? THREATENING?
I SUPPOSE IT MUST HAVE BEEN—SOMETHING DESTROYED RED. BUT WHAT?
"ONE OF THE BUGS— WE FACED A SWARM OF BUGS—"
"LIKE ANTIBODIES?"
"NO. MORE LIKE FLYING DOGS THAT WERE SICCED ON US.
"THEY SEEMED HARMLESS TO US. UNTIL THEY WEREN'T.
"ONE OF THEM SHATTERED THE SURFACE OF THE WORLD AND UNDER IT... ONLY WHITENESS."
THIS IS NOT RIGHT.
THERE'S... NOTHING THERE.
THIS IS... THE END. OR THE BEGINNING.

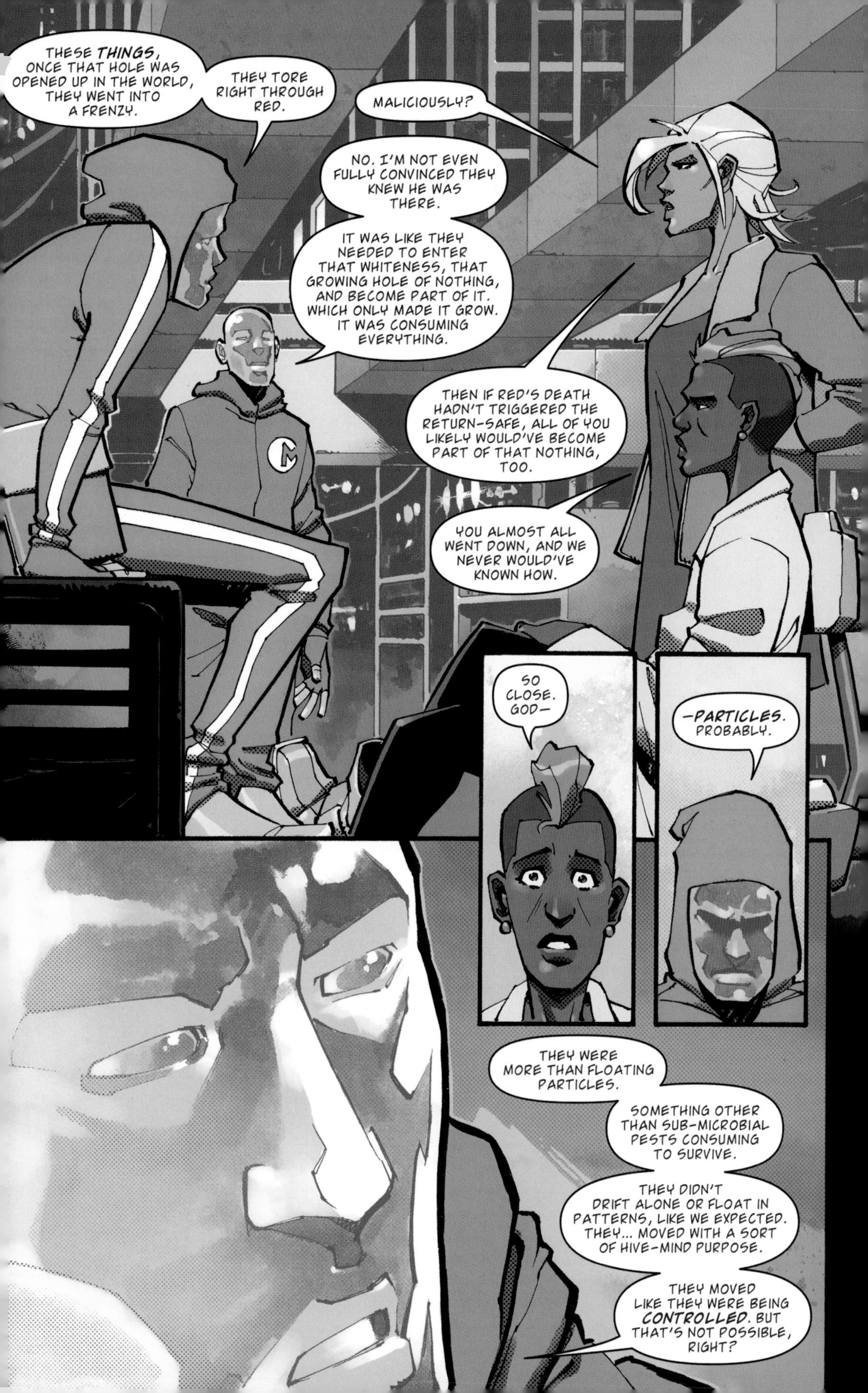
THESE THINGS, ONCE THAT HOLE WAS OPENED UP IN THE WORLD, THEY WENT INTO A FRENZY.
THEY TORE RIGHT THROUGH RED.
MALICIOUSLY?
NO. I'M NOT EVEN FULLY CONVINCED THEY KNEW HE WAS THERE.
IT WAS LIKE THEY NEEDED TO ENTER THAT WHITENESS, THAT GROWING HOLE OF NOTHING, AND BECOME PART OF IT. WHICH ONLY MADE IT GROW. IT WAS CONSUMING EVERYTHING.
THEN IF RED'S DEATH HADN'T TRIGGERED THE RETURN-SAFE, ALL OF YOU LIKELY WOULD'VE BECOME PART OF THAT NOTHING, TOO.
YOU ALMOST ALL WENT DOWN, AND WE NEVER WOULD'VE KNOWN HOW.
SO CLOSE. GOD—
—PARTICLES. PROBABLY.
THEY WERE MORE THAN FLOATING PARTICLES.
SOMETHING OTHER THAN SUB-MICROBIAL PESTS CONSUMING TO SURVIVE.
THEY DIDN'T DRIFT ALONE OR FLOAT IN PATTERNS, LIKE WE EXPECTED. THEY... MOVED WITH A SORT OF HIVE-MIND PURPOSE.
THEY MOVED LIKE THEY WERE BEING CONTROLLED. BUT THAT'S NOT POSSIBLE, RIGHT?

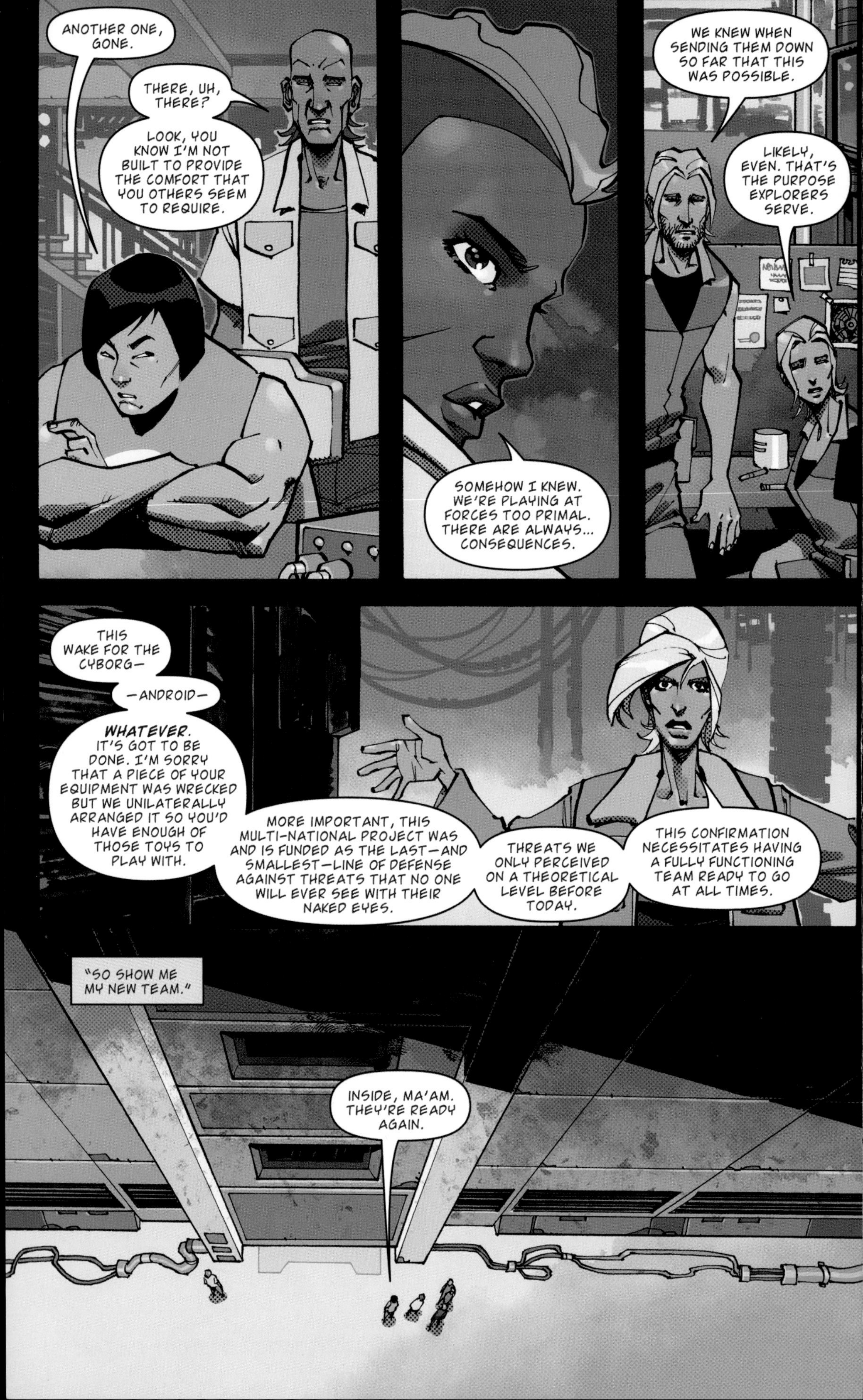
ANOTHER ONE, GONE.
THERE, UH, THERE?
LOOK, YOU KNOW I'M NOT BUILT TO PROVIDE THE COMFORT THAT YOU OTHERS SEEM TO REQUIRE.
SOMEHOW I KNEW. WE'RE PLAYING AT FORCES TOO PRIMAL. THERE ARE ALWAYS... CONSEQUENCES.
WE KNEW WHEN SENDING THEM DOWN SO FAR THAT THIS WAS POSSIBLE.
LIKELY, EVEN. THAT'S THE PURPOSE EXPLORERS SERVE.
THIS WAKE FOR THE CYBORG—
—ANDROID—
WHATEVER. IT'S GOT TO BE DONE. I'M SORRY THAT A PIECE OF YOUR EQUIPMENT WAS WRECKED BUT WE UNILATERALLY ARRANGED IT SO YOU'D HAVE ENOUGH OF THOSE TOYS TO PLAY WITH.
MORE IMPORTANT, THIS MULTI-NATIONAL PROJECT WAS AND IS FUNDED AS THE LAST—AND SMALLEST—LINE OF DEFENSE AGAINST THREATS THAT NO ONE WILL EVER SEE WITH THEIR NAKED EYES.
THREATS WE ONLY PERCEIVED ON A THEORETICAL LEVEL BEFORE TODAY.
THIS CONFIRMATION NECESSITATES HAVING A FULLY FUNCTIONING TEAM READY TO GO AT ALL TIMES.
"SO SHOW ME MY NEW TEAM."
INSIDE, MA'AM. THEY'RE READY AGAIN.

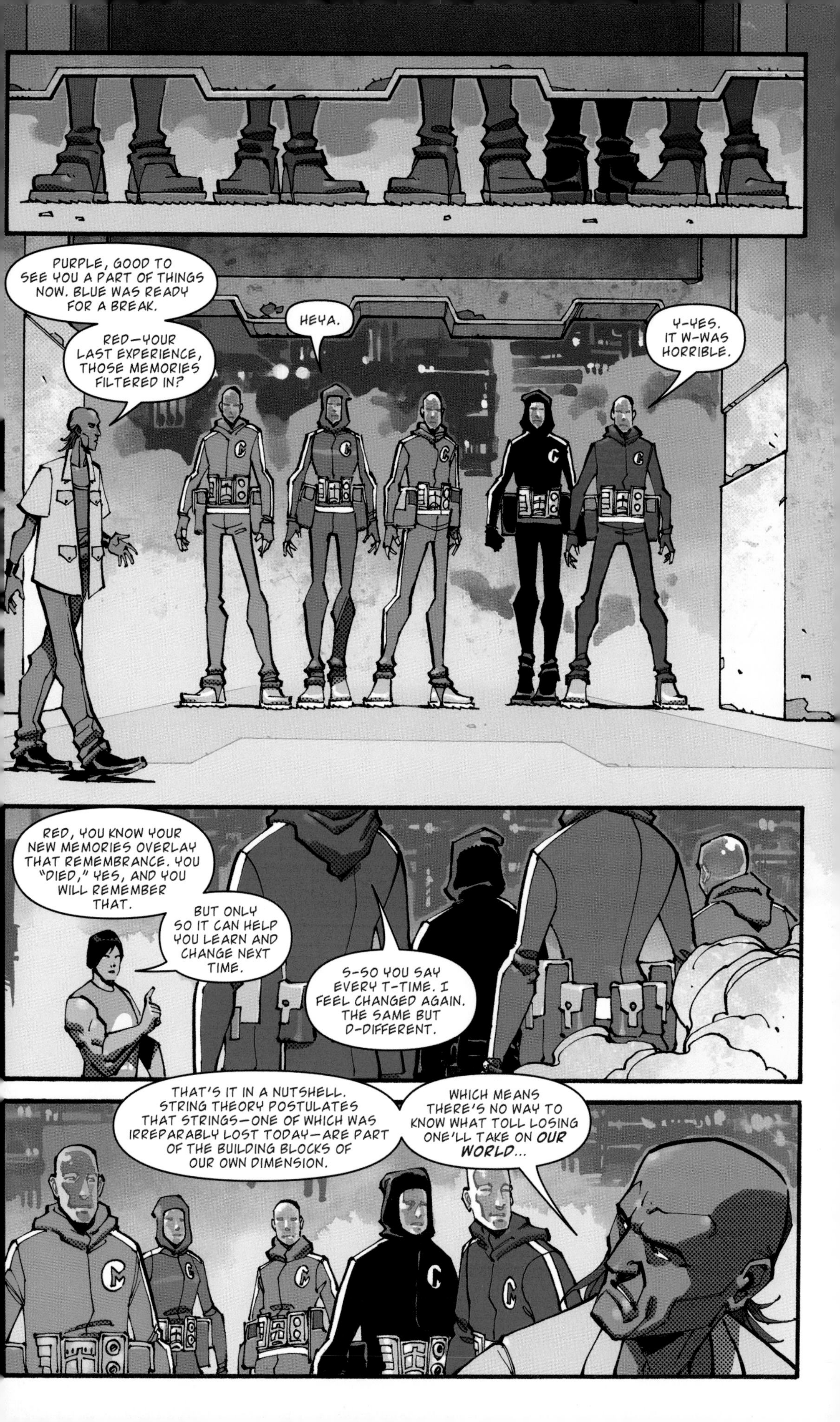
PURPLE, GOOD TO SEE YOU A PART OF THINGS NOW. BLUE WAS READY FOR A BREAK.
HEYA.
RED—YOUR LAST EXPERIENCE, THOSE MEMORIES FILTERED IN?
Y-YES. IT W-WAS HORRIBLE.
RED, YOU KNOW YOUR NEW MEMORIES OVERLAY THAT REMEMBRANCE. YOU "DIED," YES, AND YOU WILL REMEMBER THAT.
BUT ONLY SO IT CAN HELP YOU LEARN AND CHANGE NEXT TIME.
S-SO YOU SAY EVERY T-TIME. I FEEL CHANGED AGAIN. THE SAME BUT D-DIFFERENT.
THAT'S IT IN A NUTSHELL. STRING THEORY POSTULATES THAT STRINGS—ONE OF WHICH WAS IRREPARABLY LOST TODAY—ARE PART OF THE BUILDING BLOCKS OF OUR OWN DIMENSION.
WHICH MEANS THERE'S NO WAY TO KNOW WHAT TOLL LOSING ONE'LL TAKE ON *OUR WORLD*...

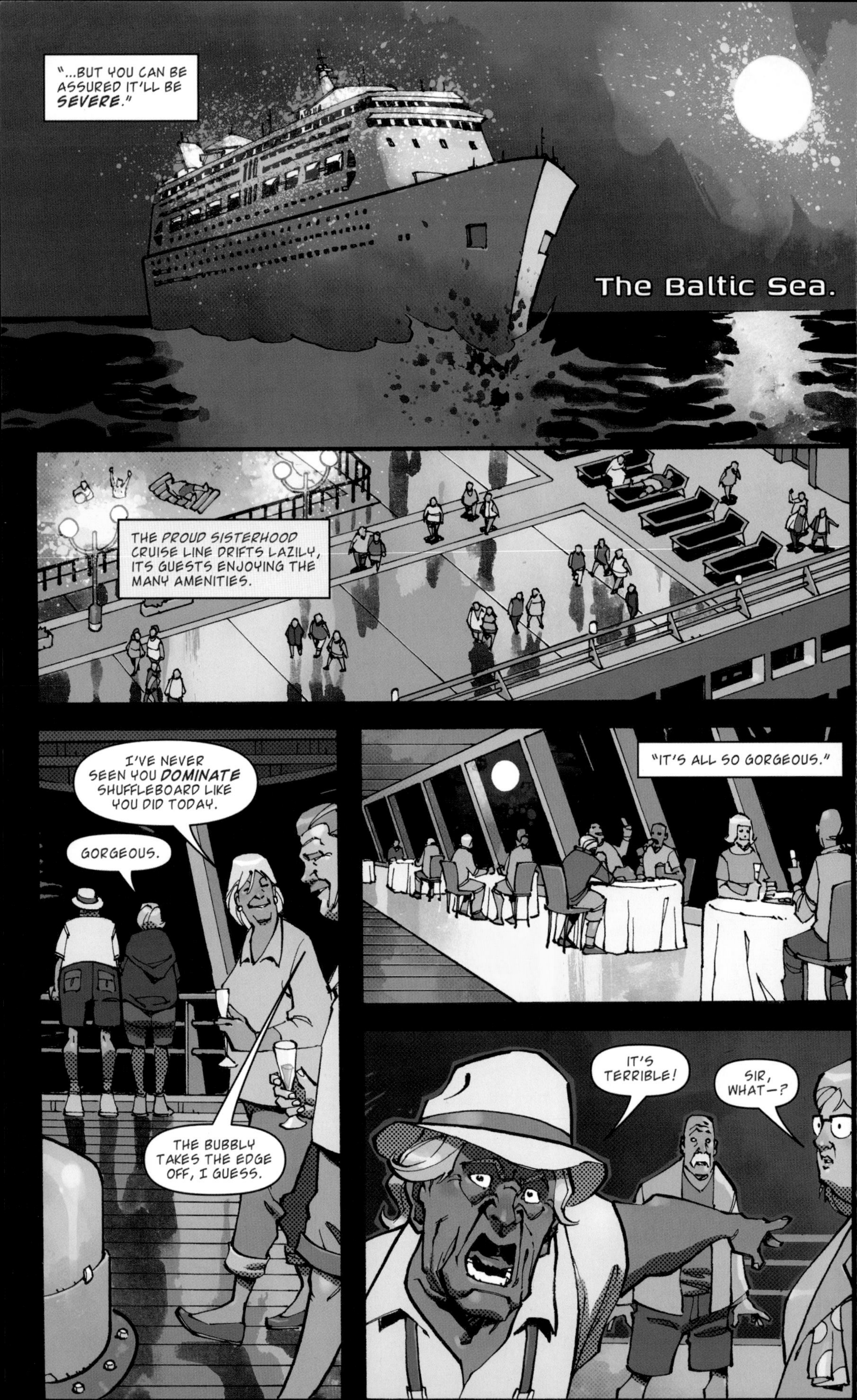
"...BUT YOU CAN BE ASSURED IT'LL BE SEVERE."
The Baltic Sea.
THE PROUD SISTERHOOD CRUISE LINE DRIFTS LAZILY, ITS GUESTS ENJOYING THE MANY AMENITIES.
I'VE NEVER SEEN YOU DOMINATE SHUFFLEBOARD LIKE YOU DID TODAY.
GORGEOUS.
THE BUBBLY TAKES THE EDGE OFF, I GUESS.
"IT'S ALL SO GORGEOUS."
IT'S TERRIBLE!
SIR, WHAT—?

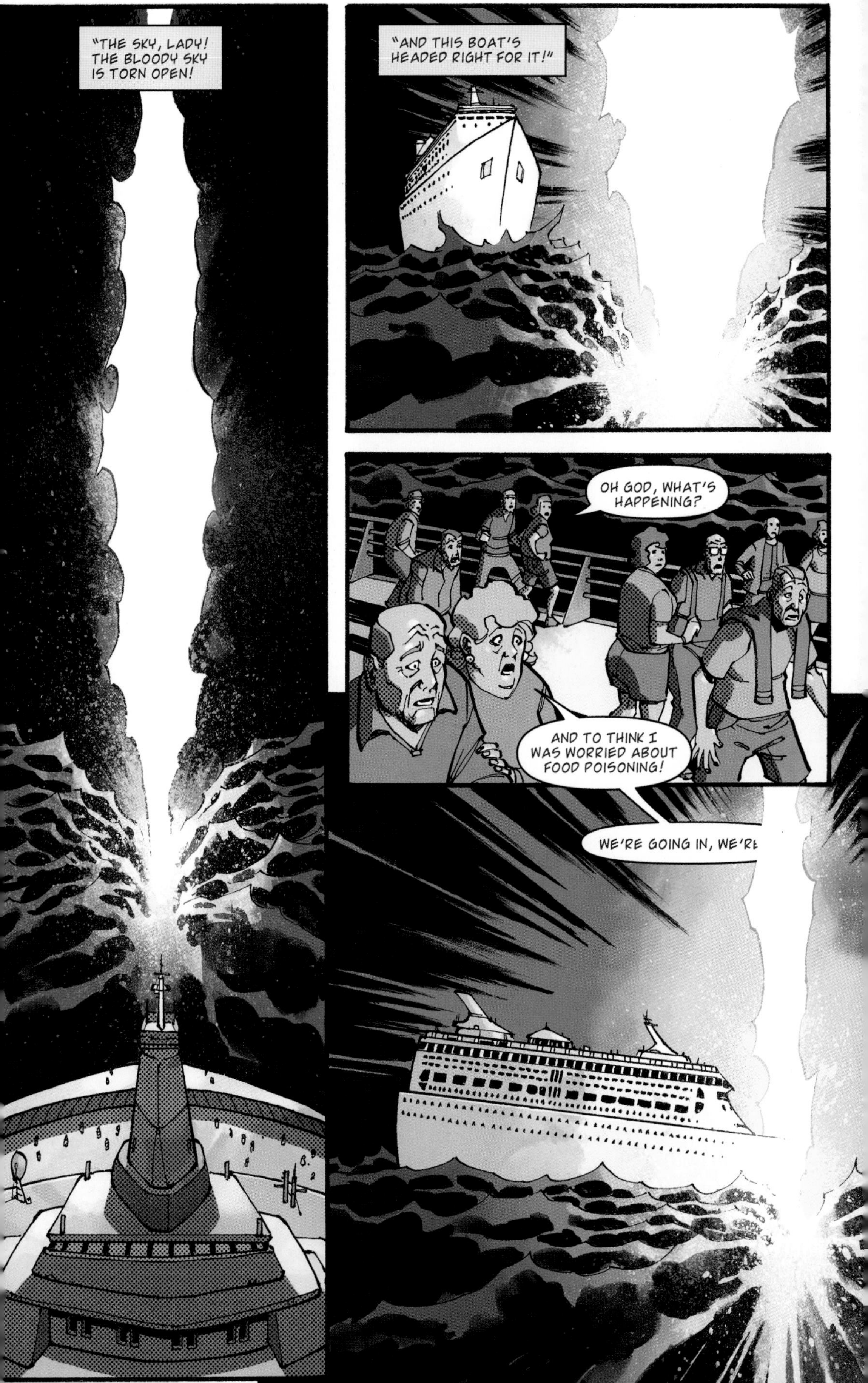
"THE SKY, LADY! THE BLOODY SKY IS TORN OPEN!
"AND THIS BOAT'S HEADED RIGHT FOR IT!"
OH GOD, WHAT'S HAPPENING?
AND TO THINK I WAS WORRIED ABOUT FOOD POISONING!
WE'RE GOING IN, WE'RE

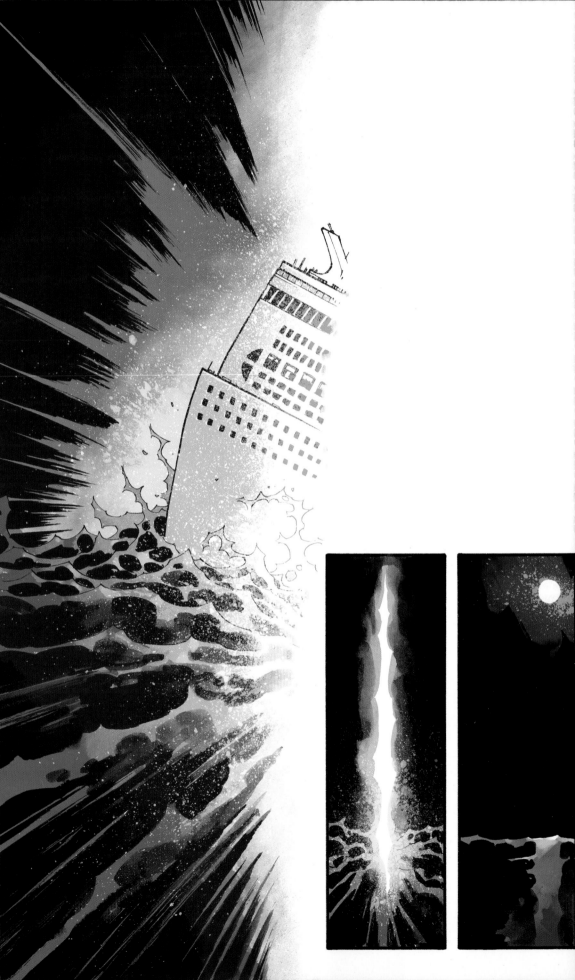

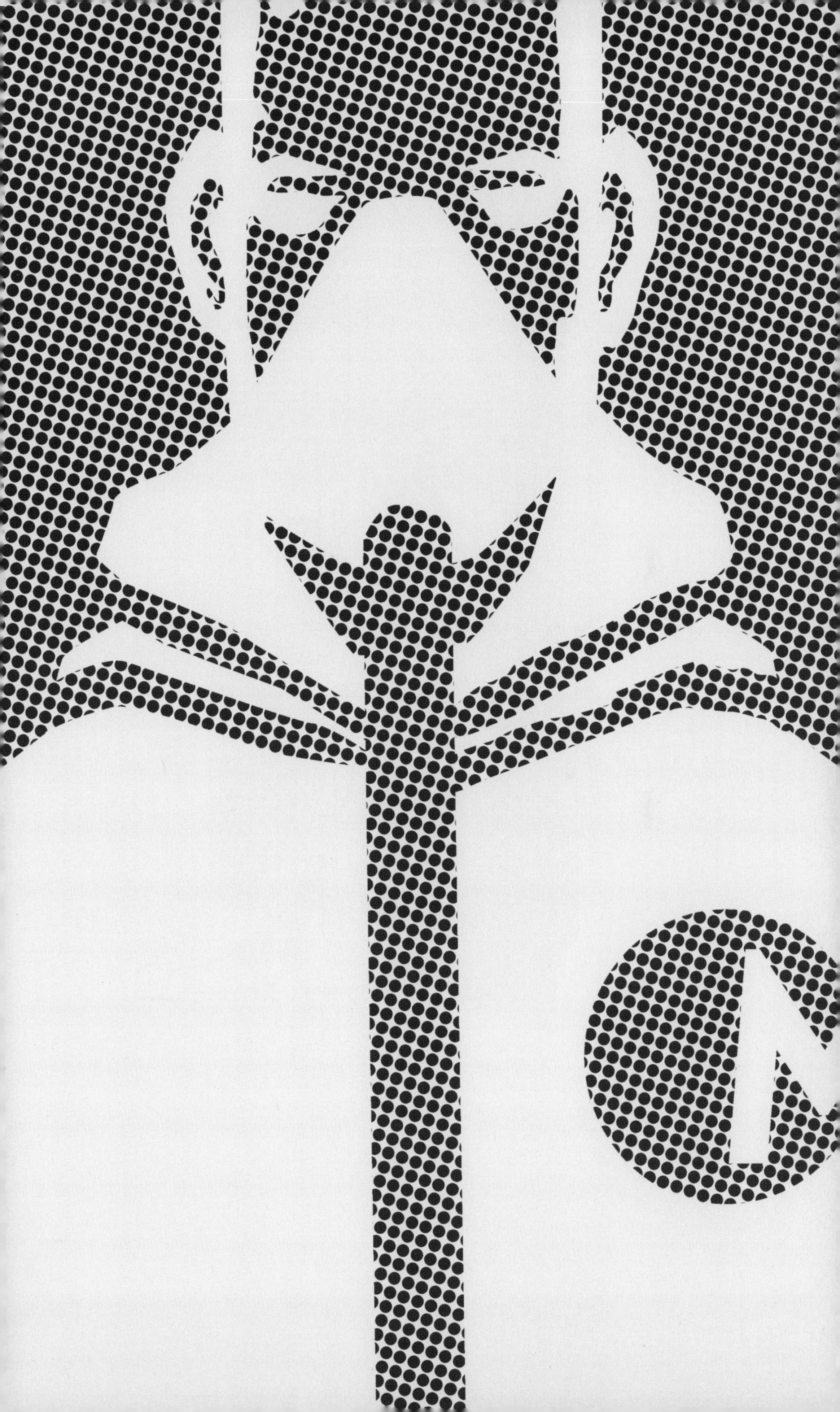

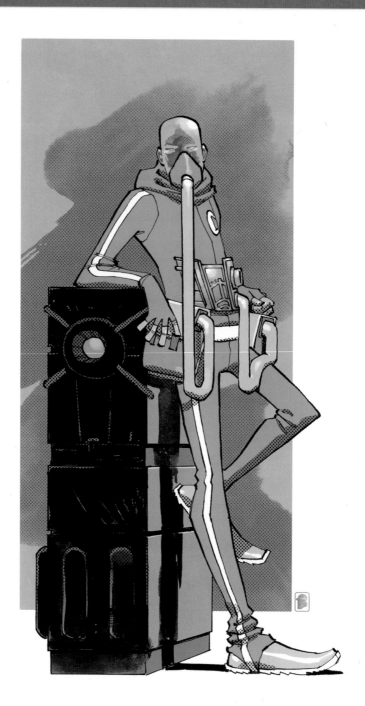

| ART BY NELSON DÁNIEL

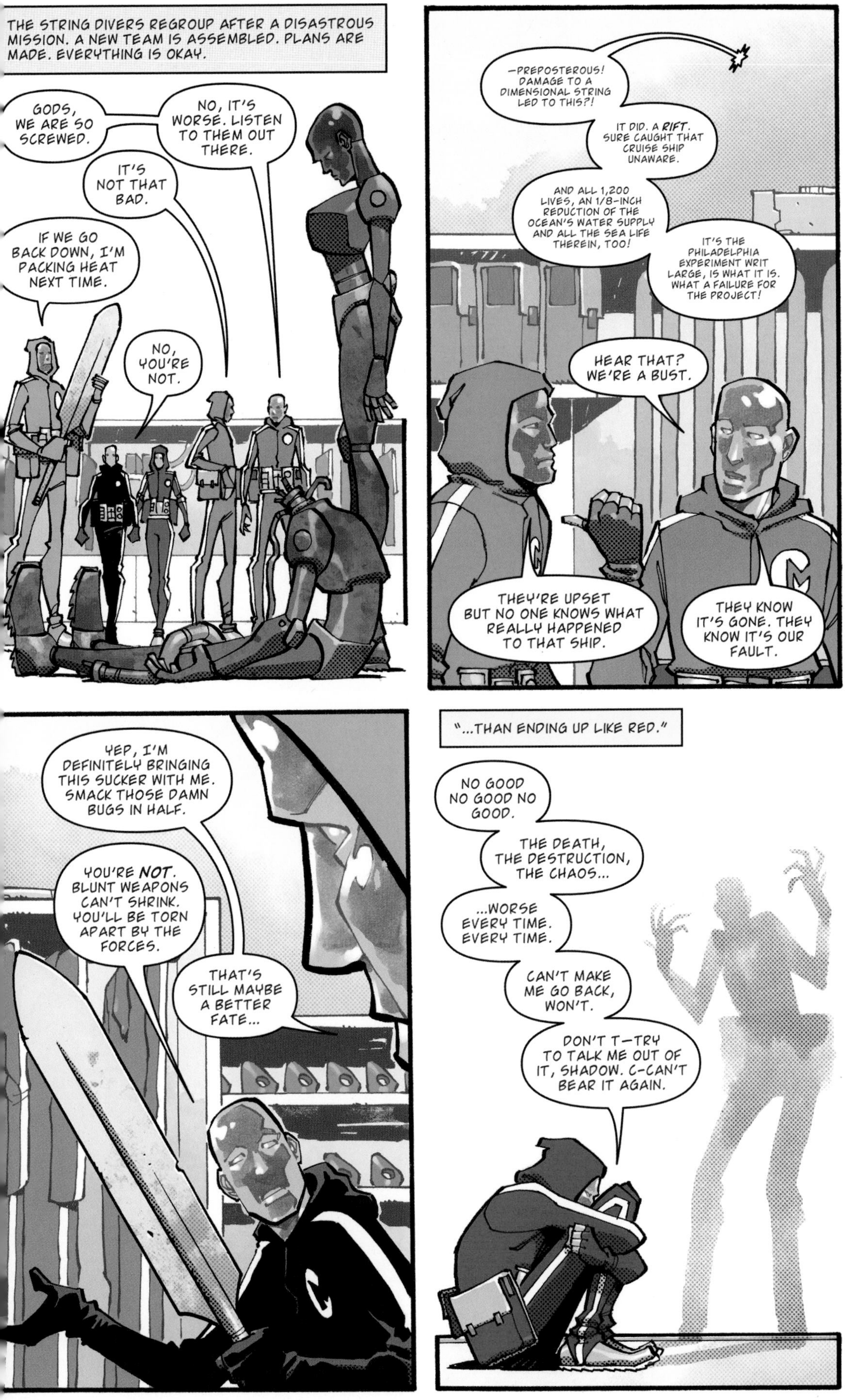
THE STRING DIVERS REGROUP AFTER A DISASTROUS MISSION. A NEW TEAM IS ASSEMBLED. PLANS ARE MADE. EVERYTHING IS OKAY.
GODS, WE ARE SO SCREWED.
NO, IT'S WORSE. LISTEN TO THEM OUT THERE.
IT'S NOT THAT BAD.
IF WE GO BACK DOWN, I'M PACKING HEAT NEXT TIME.
NO, YOU'RE NOT.
—PREPOSTEROUS! DAMAGE TO A DIMENSIONAL STRING LED TO THIS?!
IT DID. A RIFT. SURE CAUGHT THAT CRUISE SHIP UNAWARE.
AND ALL 1,200 LIVES, AN 1/8-INCH REDUCTION OF THE OCEAN'S WATER SUPPLY AND ALL THE SEA LIFE THEREIN, TOO!
IT'S THE PHILADELPHIA EXPERIMENT WRIT LARGE, IS WHAT IT IS. WHAT A FAILURE FOR THE PROJECT!
HEAR THAT? WE'RE A BUST.
THEY'RE UPSET BUT NO ONE KNOWS WHAT REALLY HAPPENED TO THAT SHIP.
THEY KNOW IT'S GONE. THEY KNOW IT'S OUR FAULT.
YEP, I'M DEFINITELY BRINGING THIS SUCKER WITH ME. SMACK THOSE DAMN BUGS IN HALF.
YOU'RE NOT. BLUNT WEAPONS CAN'T SHRINK. YOU'LL BE TORN APART BY THE FORCES.
THAT'S STILL MAYBE A BETTER FATE...
"...THAN ENDING UP LIKE RED."
NO GOOD NO GOOD NO GOOD.
THE DEATH, THE DESTRUCTION, THE CHAOS...
...WORSE EVERY TIME. EVERY TIME.
CAN'T MAKE ME GO BACK, WON'T.
DON'T T-TRY TO TALK ME OUT OF IT, SHADOW. C-CAN'T BEAR IT AGAIN.

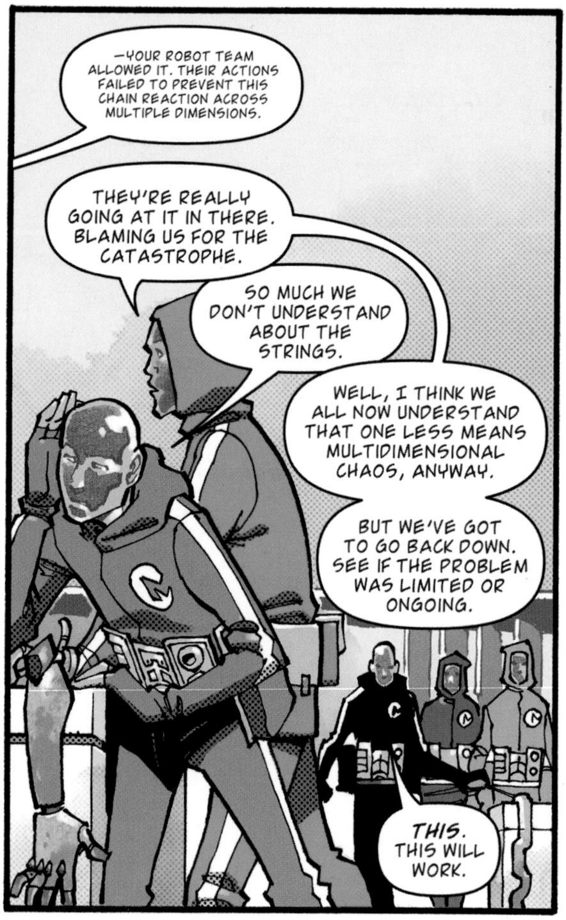
—YOUR ROBOT TEAM ALLOWED IT. THEIR ACTIONS FAILED TO PREVENT THIS CHAIN REACTION ACROSS MULTIPLE DIMENSIONS.
THEY'RE REALLY GOING AT IT IN THERE. BLAMING US FOR THE CATASTROPHE.
SO MUCH WE DON'T UNDERSTAND ABOUT THE STRINGS.
WELL, I THINK WE ALL NOW UNDERSTAND THAT ONE LESS MEANS MULTIDIMENSIONAL CHAOS, ANYWAY.
BUT WE'VE GOT TO GO BACK DOWN. SEE IF THE PROBLEM WAS LIMITED OR ONGOING.
THIS. THIS WILL WORK.

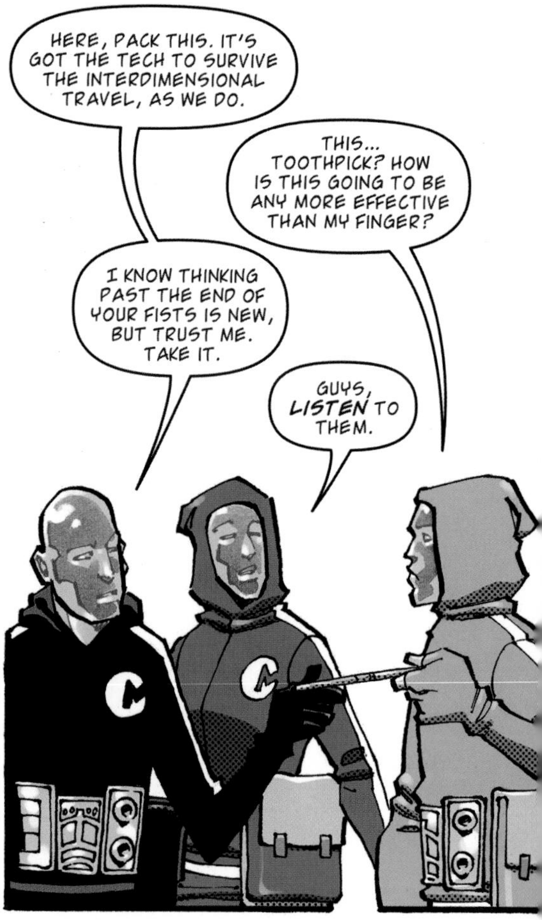
HERE, PACK THIS. IT'S GOT THE TECH TO SURVIVE THE INTERDIMENSIONAL TRAVEL, AS WE DO.
THIS... TOOTHPICK? HOW IS THIS GOING TO BE ANY MORE EFFECTIVE THAN MY FINGER?
I KNOW THINKING PAST THE END OF YOUR FISTS IS NEW, BUT TRUST ME. TAKE IT.
GUYS, LISTEN TO THEM.

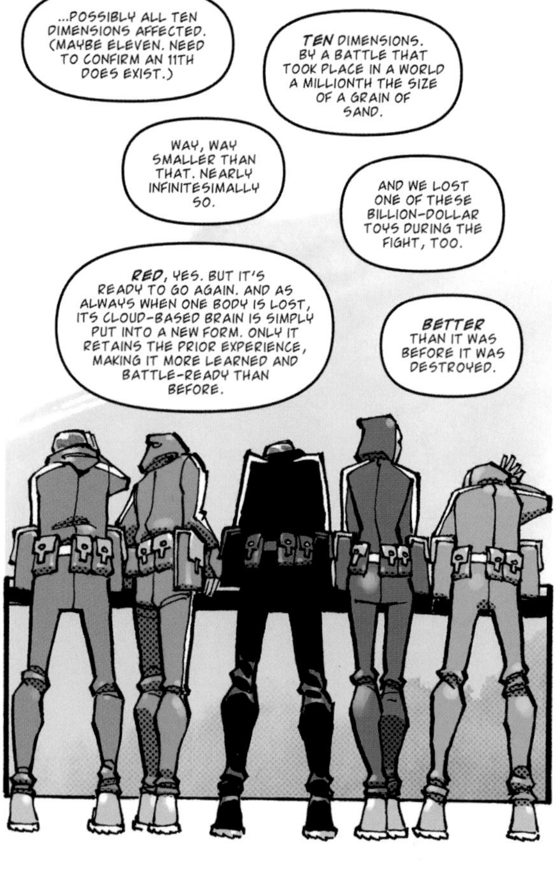
...POSSIBLY ALL TEN DIMENSIONS AFFECTED. (MAYBE ELEVEN. NEED TO CONFIRM AN 11TH DOES EXIST.)
TEN DIMENSIONS. BY A BATTLE THAT TOOK PLACE IN A WORLD A MILLIONTH THE SIZE OF A GRAIN OF SAND.
WAY, WAY SMALLER THAN THAT. NEARLY INFINITESIMALLY SO.
AND WE LOST ONE OF THESE BILLION-DOLLAR TOYS DURING THE FIGHT, TOO.
RED, YES. BUT IT'S READY TO GO AGAIN. AND AS ALWAYS WHEN ONE BODY IS LOST, ITS CLOUD-BASED BRAIN IS SIMPLY PUT INTO A NEW FORM. ONLY IT RETAINS THE PRIOR EXPERIENCE, MAKING IT MORE LEARNED AND BATTLE-READY THAN BEFORE.
BETTER THAN IT WAS BEFORE IT WAS DESTROYED.

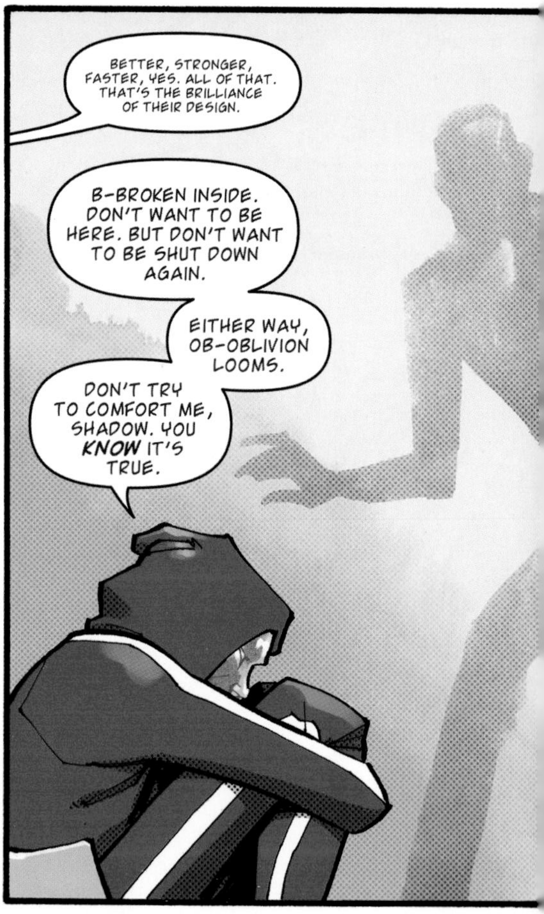
BETTER, STRONGER, FASTER, YES. ALL OF THAT. THAT'S THE BRILLIANCE OF THEIR DESIGN.
B-BROKEN INSIDE. DON'T WANT TO BE HERE. BUT DON'T WANT TO BE SHUT DOWN AGAIN.
EITHER WAY, OB-OBLIVION LOOMS.
DON'T TRY TO COMFORT ME, SHADOW. YOU KNOW IT'S TRUE.

STRING DIVERS

UNIFIED CHAOS THEORY, part 2

INTRODUCING

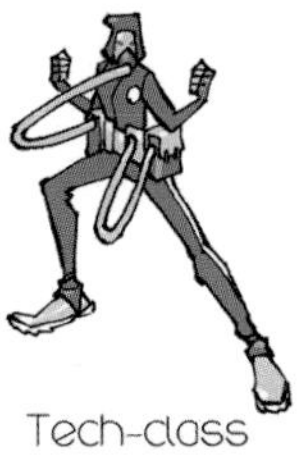

Tech-class

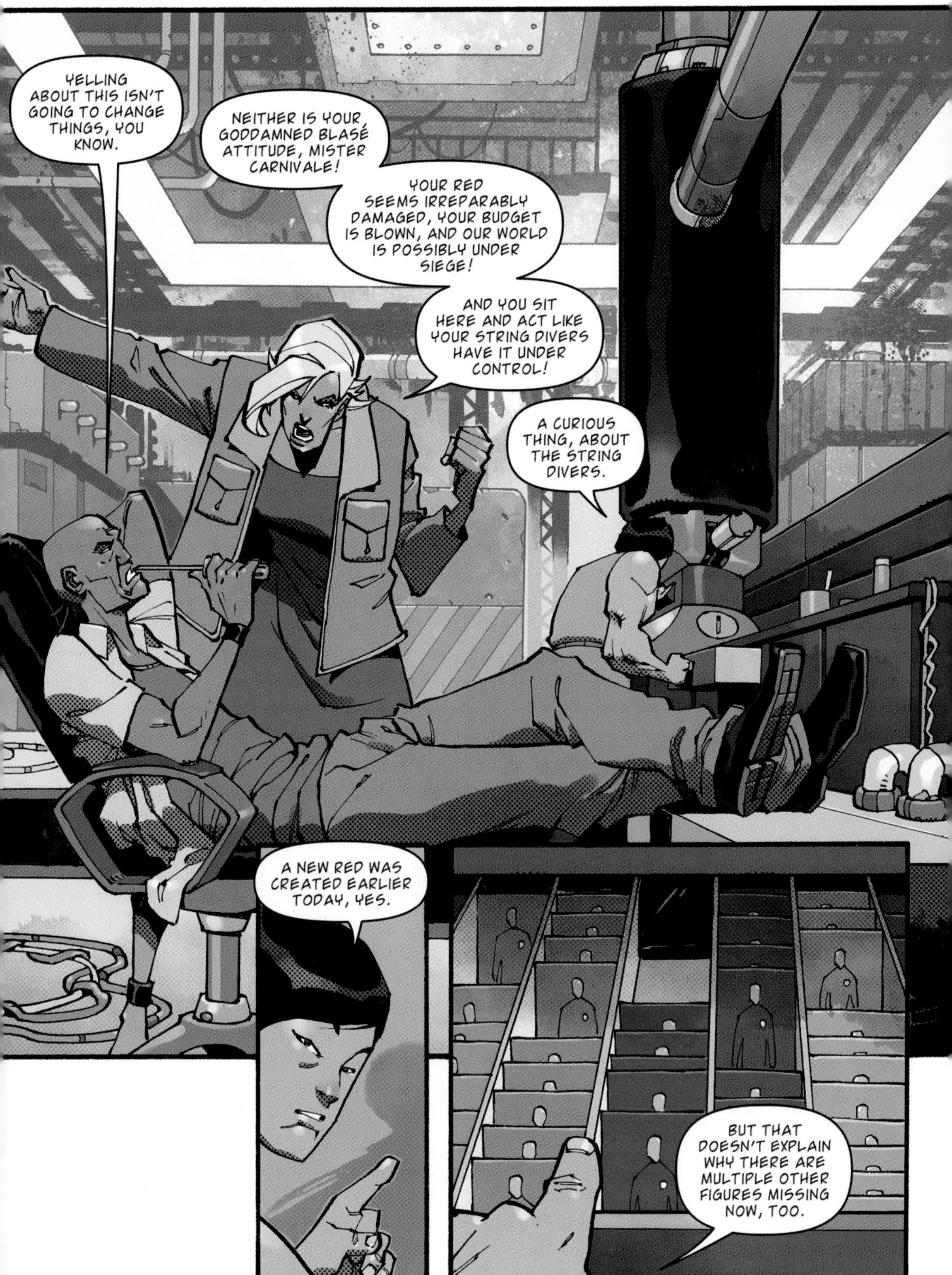

YELLING ABOUT THIS ISN'T GOING TO CHANGE THINGS, YOU KNOW.
NEITHER IS YOUR GODDAMNED BLASÉ ATTITUDE, MISTER CARNIVALE!
YOUR RED SEEMS IRREPARABLY DAMAGED, YOUR BUDGET IS BLOWN, AND OUR WORLD IS POSSIBLY UNDER SIEGE!
AND YOU SIT HERE AND ACT LIKE YOUR STRING DIVERS HAVE IT UNDER CONTROL!
A CURIOUS THING, ABOUT THE STRING DIVERS.
A NEW RED WAS CREATED EARLIER TODAY, YES.
BUT THAT DOESN'T EXPLAIN WHY THERE ARE MULTIPLE OTHER FIGURES MISSING NOW, TOO.

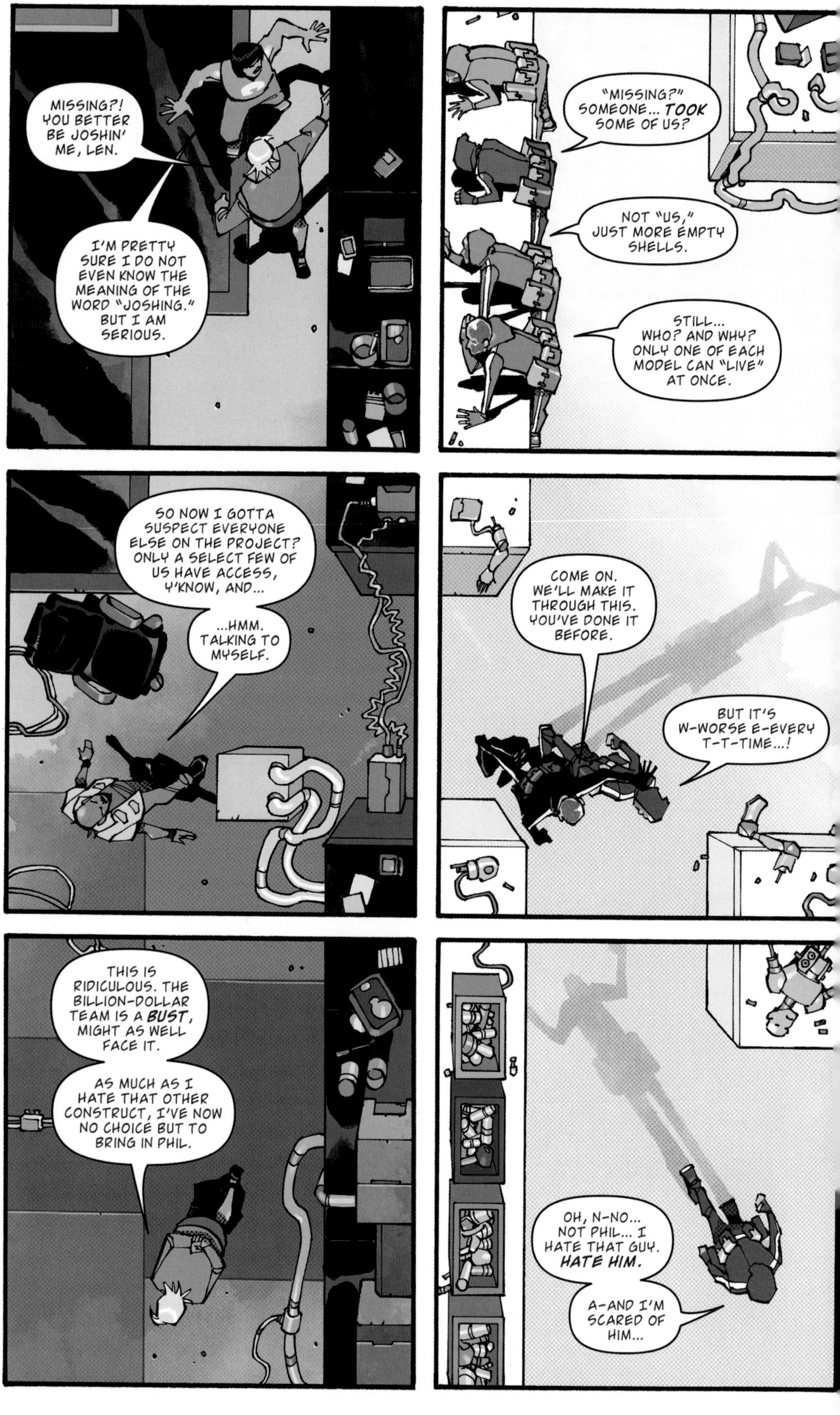
MISSING?! YOU BETTER BE JOSHIN' ME, LEN.
I'M PRETTY SURE I DO NOT EVEN KNOW THE MEANING OF THE WORD "JOSHING." BUT I AM SERIOUS.
"MISSING?" SOMEONE... TOOK SOME OF US?
NOT "US," JUST MORE EMPTY SHELLS.
STILL... WHO? AND WHY? ONLY ONE OF EACH MODEL CAN "LIVE" AT ONCE.
SO NOW I GOTTA SUSPECT EVERYONE ELSE ON THE PROJECT? ONLY A SELECT FEW OF US HAVE ACCESS, Y'KNOW, AND...
...HMM. TALKING TO MYSELF.
COME ON. WE'LL MAKE IT THROUGH THIS. YOU'VE DONE IT BEFORE.
BUT IT'S W-WORSE E-EVERY T-T-TIME...!
THIS IS RIDICULOUS. THE BILLION-DOLLAR TEAM IS A BUST, MIGHT AS WELL FACE IT.
AS MUCH AS I HATE THAT OTHER CONSTRUCT, I'VE NOW NO CHOICE BUT TO BRING IN PHIL.
OH, N-NO... NOT PHIL... I HATE THAT GUY. HATE HIM.
A-AND I'M SCARED OF HIM...

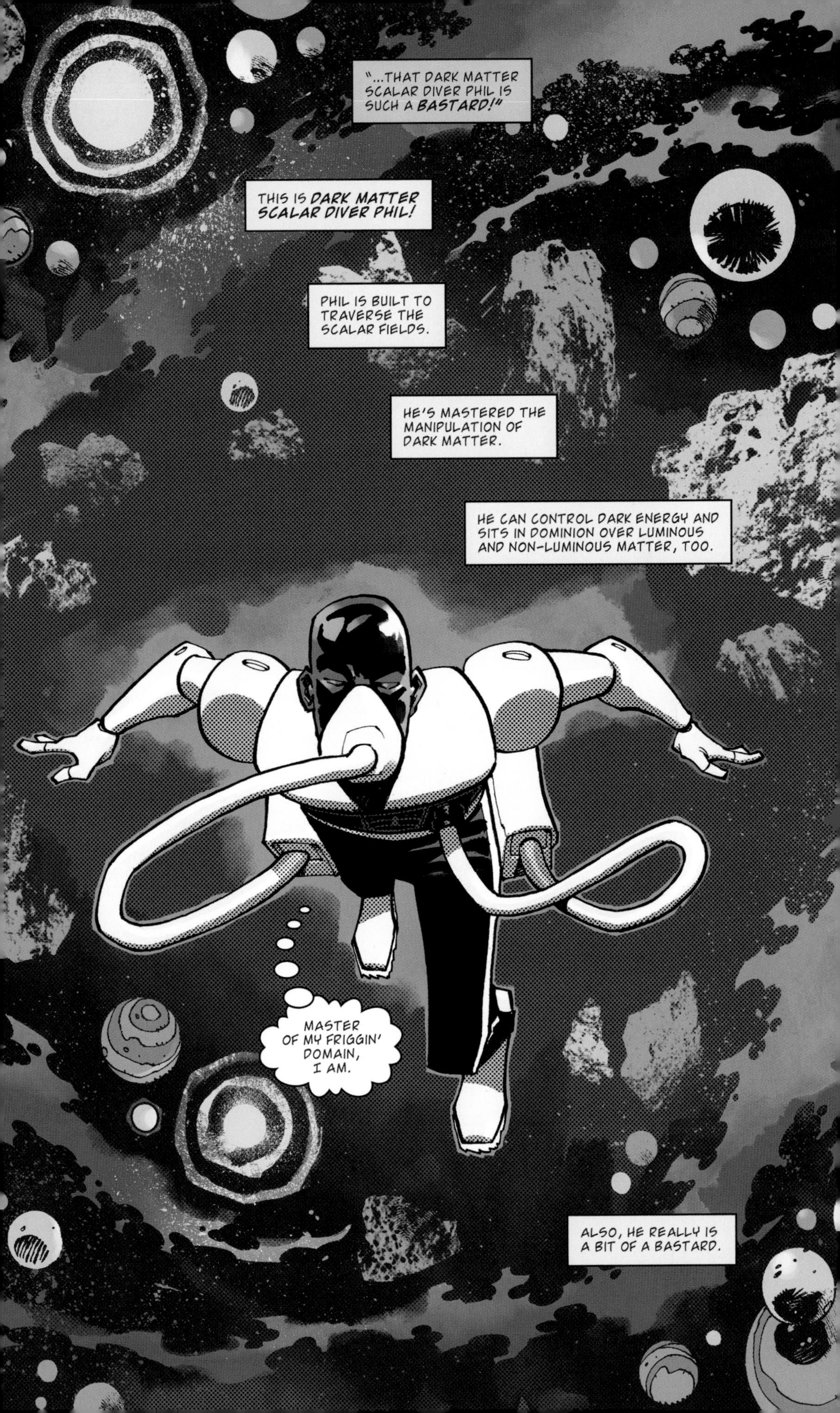
"...THAT DARK MATTER SCALAR DIVER PHIL IS SUCH A *BASTARD!*"
THIS IS *DARK MATTER SCALAR DIVER PHIL!*
PHIL IS BUILT TO TRAVERSE THE SCALAR FIELDS.
HE'S MASTERED THE MANIPULATION OF DARK MATTER.
HE CAN CONTROL DARK ENERGY AND SITS IN DOMINION OVER LUMINOUS AND NON-LUMINOUS MATTER, TOO.
MASTER OF MY FRIGGIN' DOMAIN, I AM.
ALSO, HE REALLY IS A BIT OF A BASTARD.

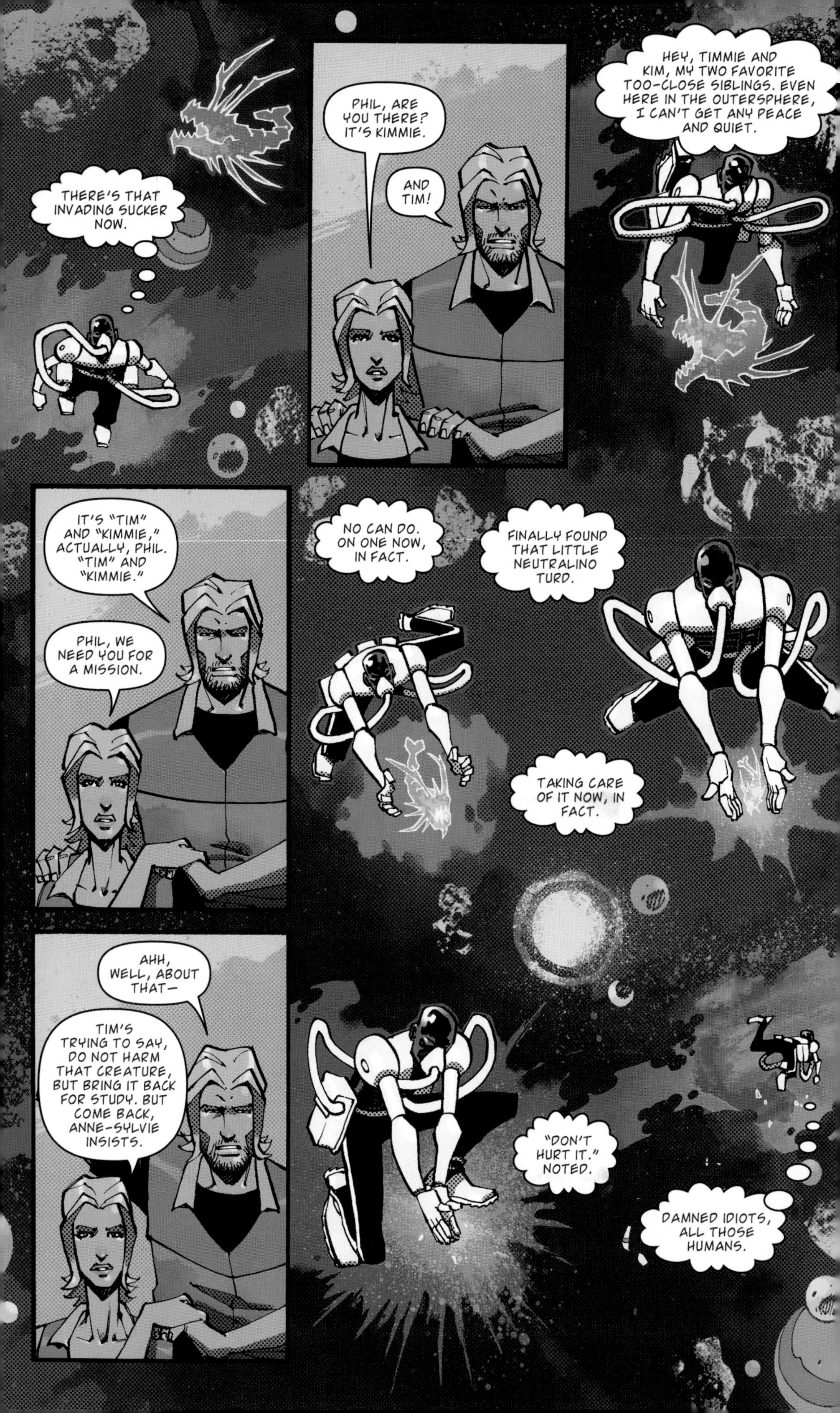
PHIL, ARE YOU THERE? IT'S KIMMIE.
AND TIM!
THERE'S THAT INVADING SUCKER NOW.
HEY, TIMMIE AND KIM, MY TWO FAVORITE TOO-CLOSE SIBLINGS. EVEN HERE IN THE OUTERSPHERE, I CAN'T GET ANY PEACE AND QUIET.
IT'S "TIM" AND "KIMMIE," ACTUALLY, PHIL. "TIM" AND "KIMMIE."
PHIL, WE NEED YOU FOR A MISSION.
NO CAN DO. ON ONE NOW, IN FACT.
FINALLY FOUND THAT LITTLE NEUTRALINO TURD.
TAKING CARE OF IT NOW, IN FACT.
AHH, WELL, ABOUT THAT—
TIM'S TRYING TO SAY, DO NOT HARM THAT CREATURE, BUT BRING IT BACK FOR STUDY. BUT COME BACK, ANNE-SYLVIE INSISTS.
"DON'T HURT IT." NOTED.
DAMNED IDIOTS, ALL THOSE HUMANS.

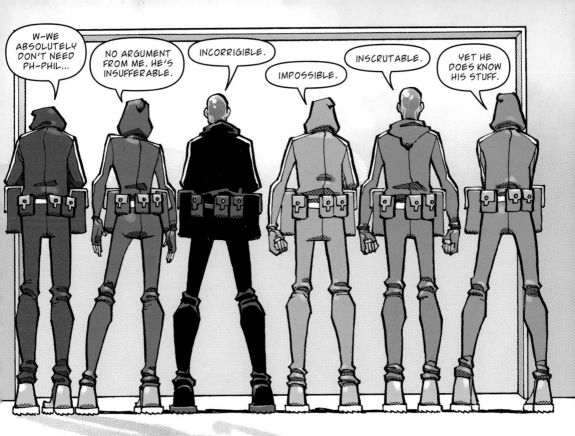

W-WE ABSOLUTELY DON'T NEED PH-PHIL...

NO ARGUMENT FROM ME. HE'S INSUFFERABLE.

INCORRIGIBLE.

IMPOSSIBLE.

INSCRUTABLE.

YET HE DOES KNOW HIS STUFF.

BIG WHOOP, THEY COULD'VE BUILT ANY OF US THE SAME WAY.

BUT THEY DIDN'T. AND HE KNOWS DARK MATTER.

IN LIGHT OF THE RECENT SITUATION, HE MIGHT BE MORE AMENABLE TO TEAMING UP—

WHAT UP, SHITBIRDS?

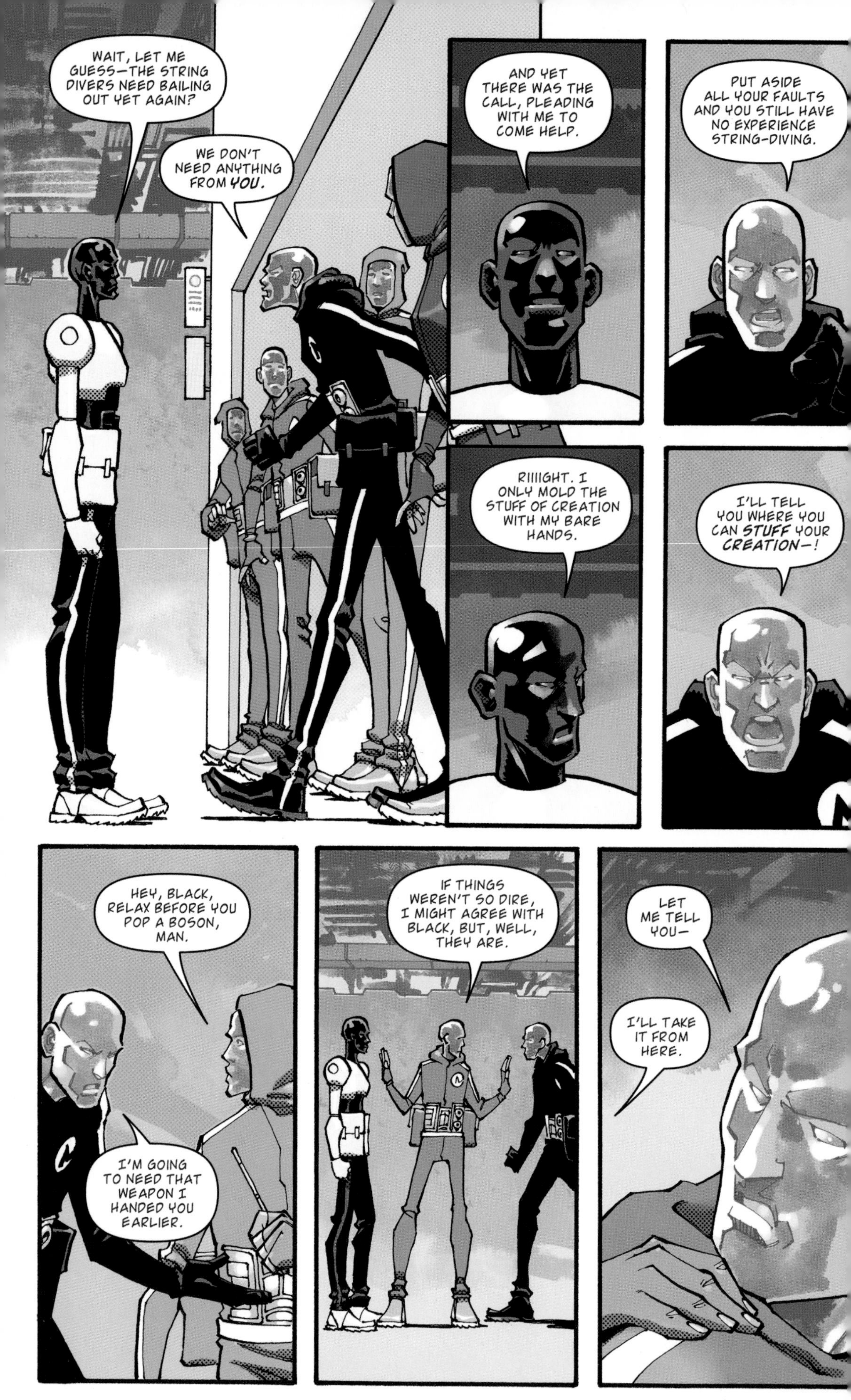
WAIT, LET ME GUESS—THE STRING DIVERS NEED BAILING OUT YET AGAIN?
WE DON'T NEED ANYTHING FROM *YOU.*
AND YET THERE WAS THE CALL, PLEADING WITH ME TO COME HELP.
PUT ASIDE ALL YOUR FAULTS AND YOU STILL HAVE NO EXPERIENCE STRING-DIVING.
RIIIIGHT. I ONLY MOLD THE STUFF OF CREATION WITH MY BARE HANDS.
I'LL TELL YOU WHERE YOU CAN *STUFF* YOUR *CREATION*—!
HEY, BLACK, RELAX BEFORE YOU POP A BOSON, MAN.
I'M GOING TO NEED THAT WEAPON I HANDED YOU EARLIER.
IF THINGS WEREN'T SO DIRE, I MIGHT AGREE WITH BLACK, BUT, WELL, THEY ARE.
LET ME TELL YOU—
I'LL TAKE IT FROM HERE.

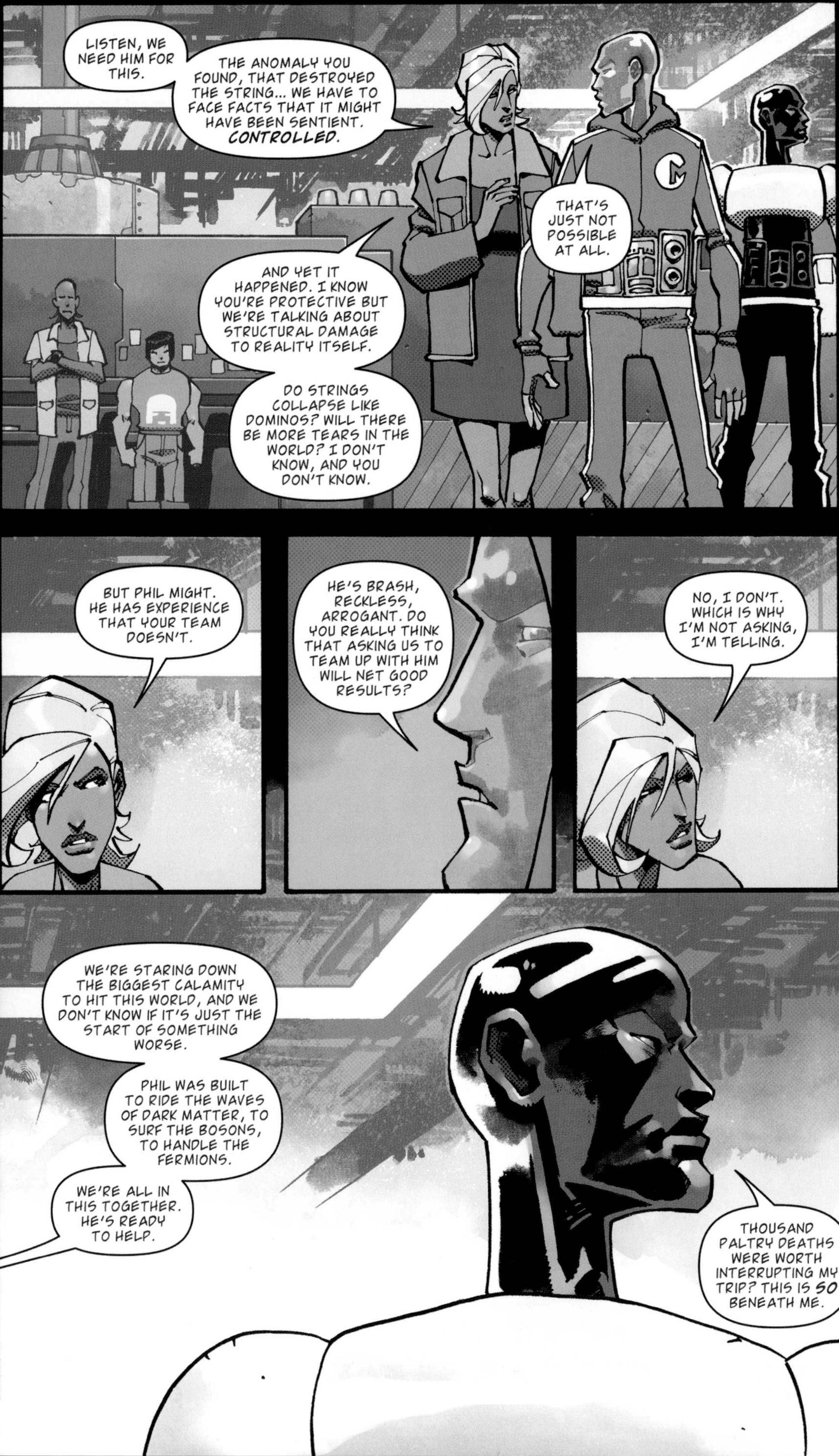
LISTEN, WE NEED HIM FOR THIS.
THE ANOMALY YOU FOUND, THAT DESTROYED THE STRING... WE HAVE TO FACE FACTS THAT IT MIGHT HAVE BEEN SENTIENT. CONTROLLED.
THAT'S JUST NOT POSSIBLE AT ALL.
AND YET IT HAPPENED. I KNOW YOU'RE PROTECTIVE BUT WE'RE TALKING ABOUT STRUCTURAL DAMAGE TO REALITY ITSELF.
DO STRINGS COLLAPSE LIKE DOMINOS? WILL THERE BE MORE TEARS IN THE WORLD? I DON'T KNOW, AND YOU DON'T KNOW.
BUT PHIL MIGHT. HE HAS EXPERIENCE THAT YOUR TEAM DOESN'T.
HE'S BRASH, RECKLESS, ARROGANT. DO YOU REALLY THINK THAT ASKING US TO TEAM UP WITH HIM WILL NET GOOD RESULTS?
NO, I DON'T. WHICH IS WHY I'M NOT ASKING, I'M TELLING.
WE'RE STARING DOWN THE BIGGEST CALAMITY TO HIT THIS WORLD, AND WE DON'T KNOW IF IT'S JUST THE START OF SOMETHING WORSE.
PHIL WAS BUILT TO RIDE THE WAVES OF DARK MATTER, TO SURF THE BOSONS, TO HANDLE THE FERMIONS.
WE'RE ALL IN THIS TOGETHER. HE'S READY TO HELP.
THOUSAND PALTRY DEATHS WERE WORTH INTERRUPTING MY TRIP? THIS IS SO BENEATH ME.

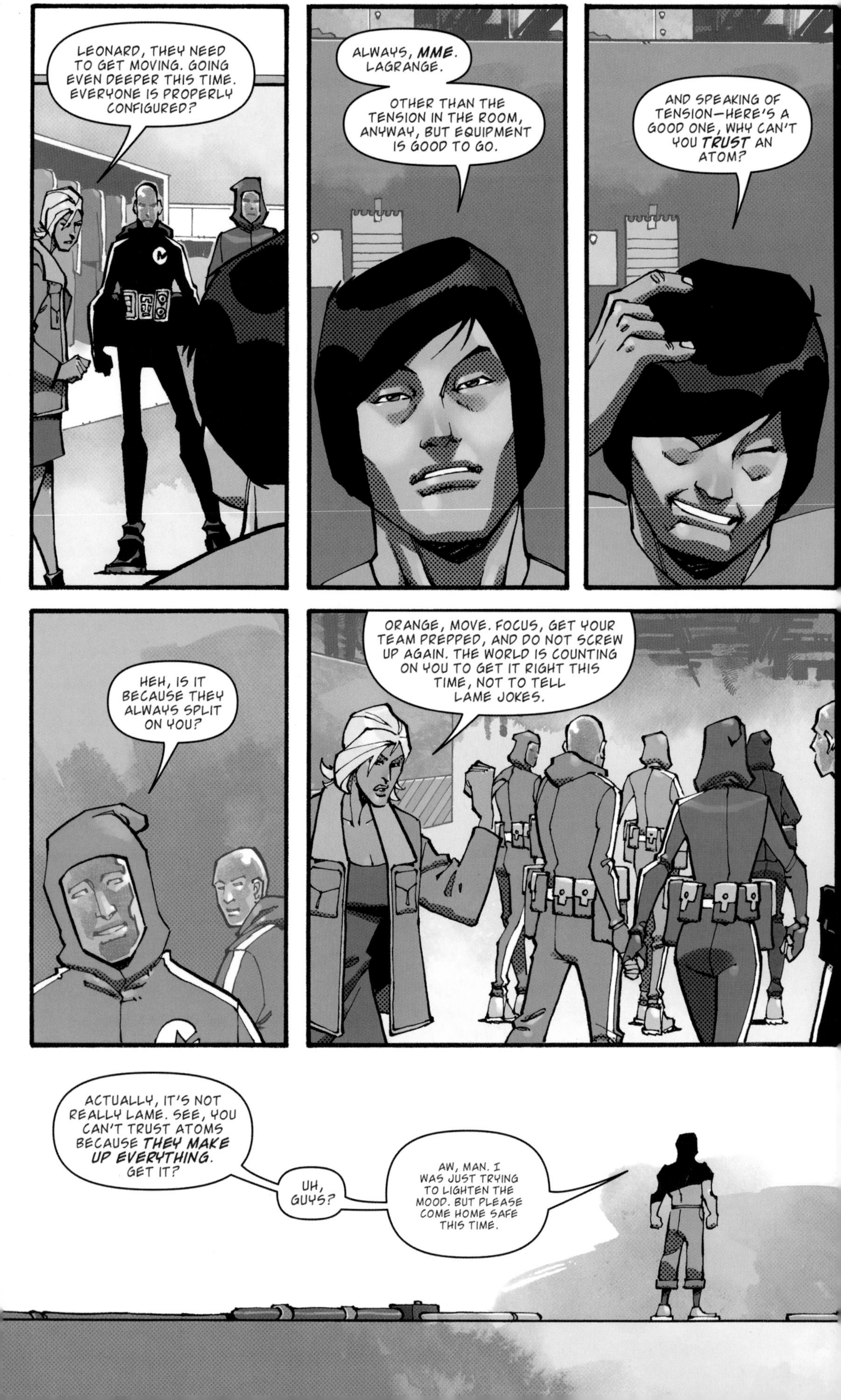
LEONARD, THEY NEED TO GET MOVING. GOING EVEN DEEPER THIS TIME. EVERYONE IS PROPERLY CONFIGURED?
ALWAYS, MME. LAGRANGE.
OTHER THAN THE TENSION IN THE ROOM, ANYWAY, BUT EQUIPMENT IS GOOD TO GO.
AND SPEAKING OF TENSION—HERE'S A GOOD ONE, WHY CAN'T YOU TRUST AN ATOM?
HEH, IS IT BECAUSE THEY ALWAYS SPLIT ON YOU?
ORANGE, MOVE. FOCUS, GET YOUR TEAM PREPPED, AND DO NOT SCREW UP AGAIN. THE WORLD IS COUNTING ON YOU TO GET IT RIGHT THIS TIME, NOT TO TELL LAME JOKES.
ACTUALLY, IT'S NOT REALLY LAME. SEE, YOU CAN'T TRUST ATOMS BECAUSE THEY MAKE UP EVERYTHING. GET IT?
UH, GUYS?
AW, MAN. I WAS JUST TRYING TO LIGHTEN THE MOOD. BUT PLEASE COME HOME SAFE THIS TIME.

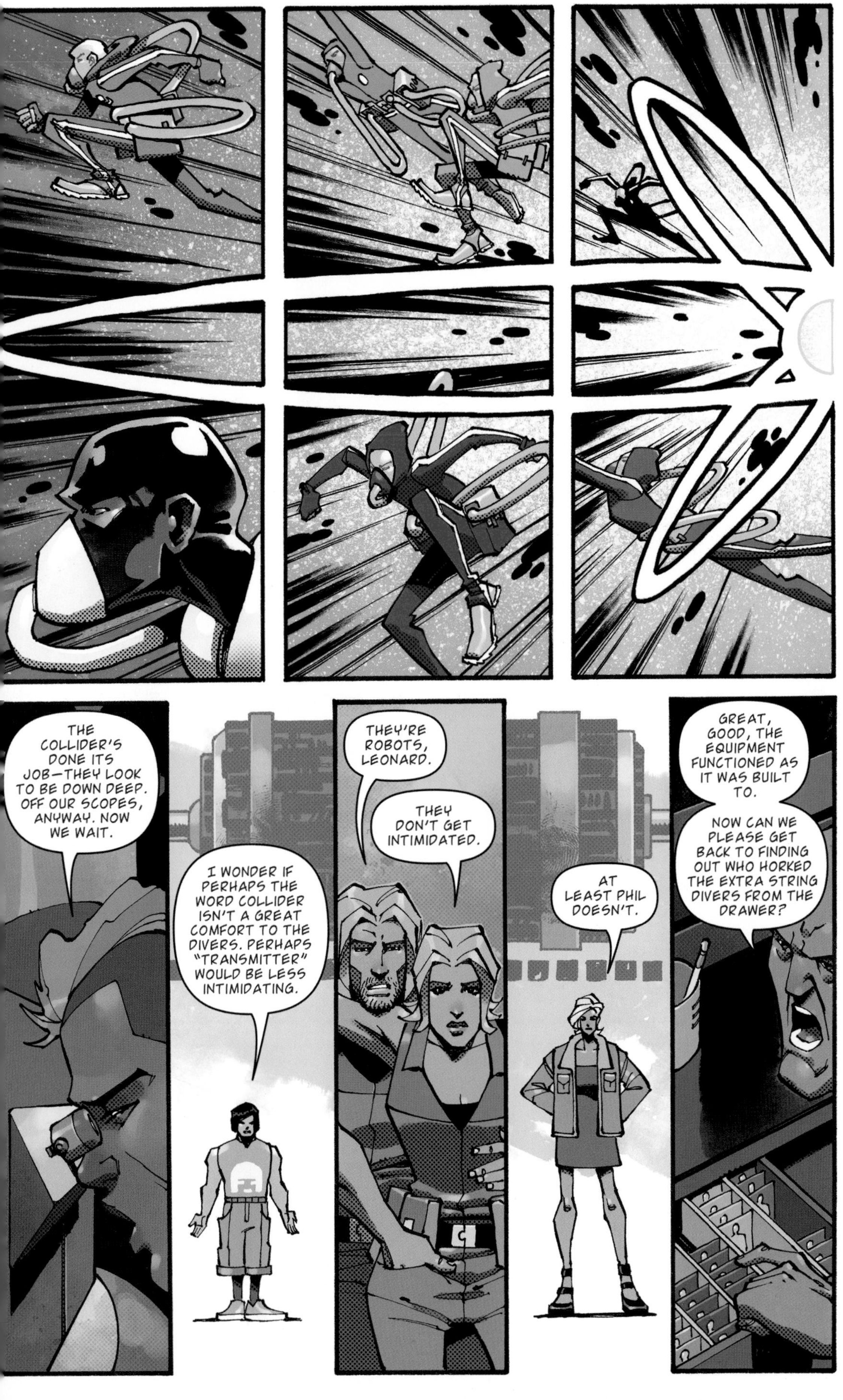
THE COLLIDER'S DONE ITS JOB—THEY LOOK TO BE DOWN DEEP. OFF OUR SCOPES, ANYWAY. NOW WE WAIT.
I WONDER IF PERHAPS THE WORD COLLIDER ISN'T A GREAT COMFORT TO THE DIVERS. PERHAPS "TRANSMITTER" WOULD BE LESS INTIMIDATING.
THEY'RE ROBOTS, LEONARD.
THEY DON'T GET INTIMIDATED.
AT LEAST PHIL DOESN'T.
GREAT, GOOD, THE EQUIPMENT FUNCTIONED AS IT WAS BUILT TO.
NOW CAN WE PLEASE GET BACK TO FINDING OUT WHO HORKED THE EXTRA STRING DIVERS FROM THE DRAWER?

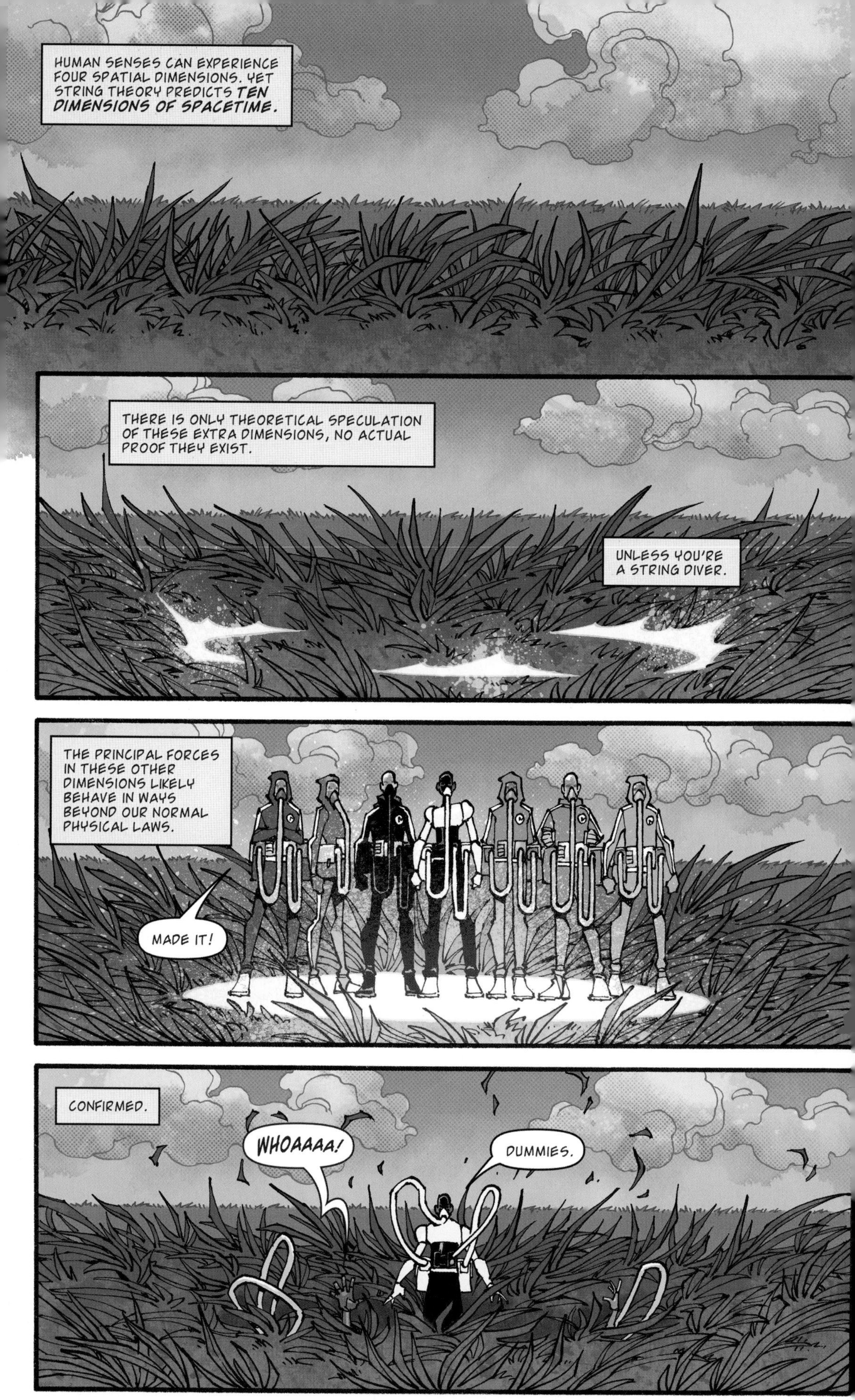
HUMAN SENSES CAN EXPERIENCE FOUR SPATIAL DIMENSIONS. YET STRING THEORY PREDICTS **TEN DIMENSIONS OF SPACETIME.**
THERE IS ONLY THEORETICAL SPECULATION OF THESE EXTRA DIMENSIONS, NO ACTUAL PROOF THEY EXIST.
UNLESS YOU'RE A STRING DIVER.
THE PRINCIPAL FORCES IN THESE OTHER DIMENSIONS LIKELY BEHAVE IN WAYS BEYOND OUR NORMAL PHYSICAL LAWS.
MADE IT!
CONFIRMED.
WHOAAAA!
DUMMIES.

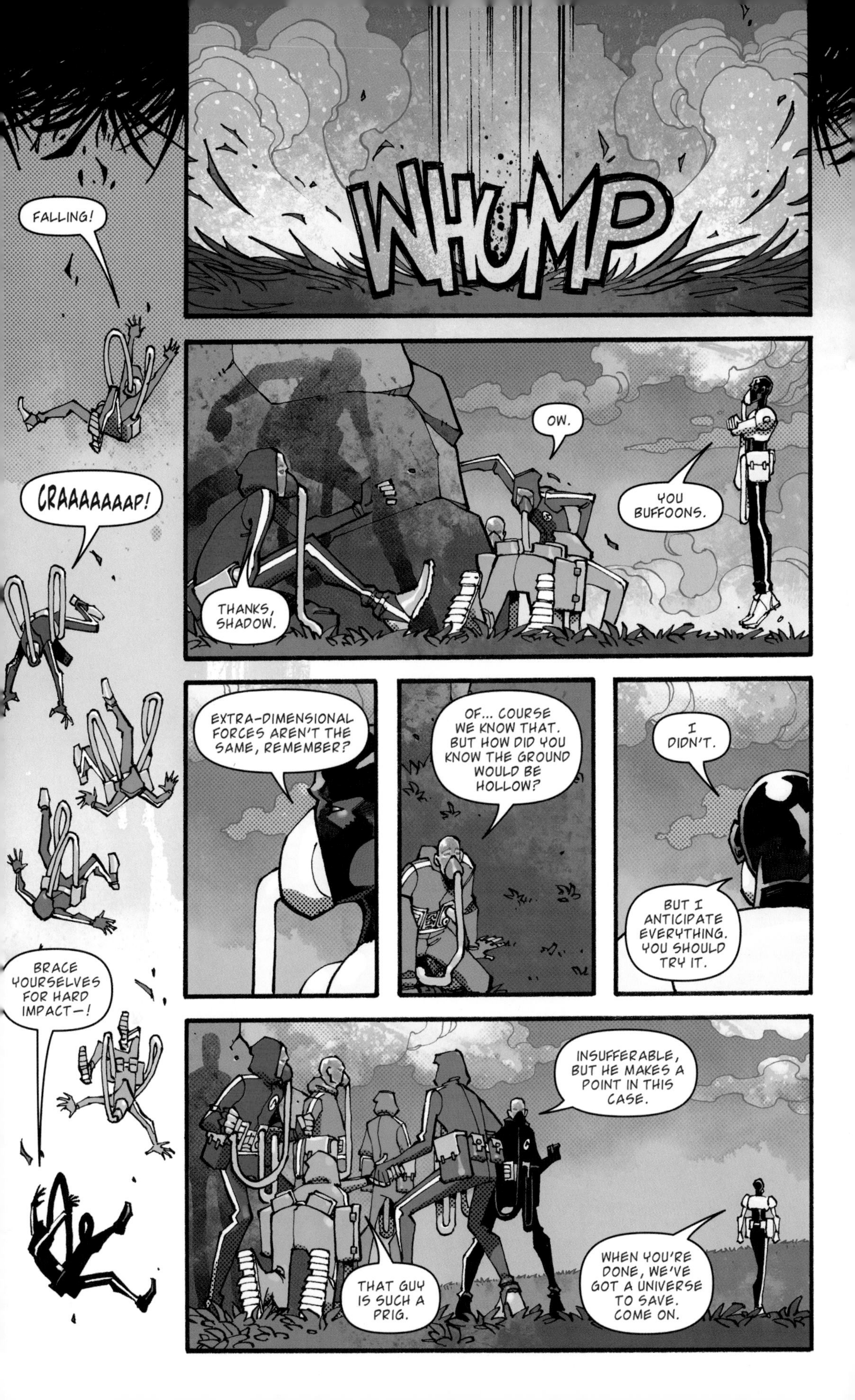
FALLING!
WHUMP
CRAAAAAAAP!
BRACE YOURSELVES FOR HARD IMPACT—!
OW.
YOU BUFFOONS.
THANKS, SHADOW.
EXTRA-DIMENSIONAL FORCES AREN'T THE SAME, REMEMBER?
OF... COURSE WE KNOW THAT. BUT HOW DID YOU KNOW THE GROUND WOULD BE HOLLOW?
I DIDN'T.
BUT I ANTICIPATE EVERYTHING. YOU SHOULD TRY IT.
INSUFFERABLE, BUT HE MAKES A POINT IN THIS CASE.
THAT GUY IS SUCH A PRIG.
WHEN YOU'RE DONE, WE'VE GOT A UNIVERSE TO SAVE. COME ON.

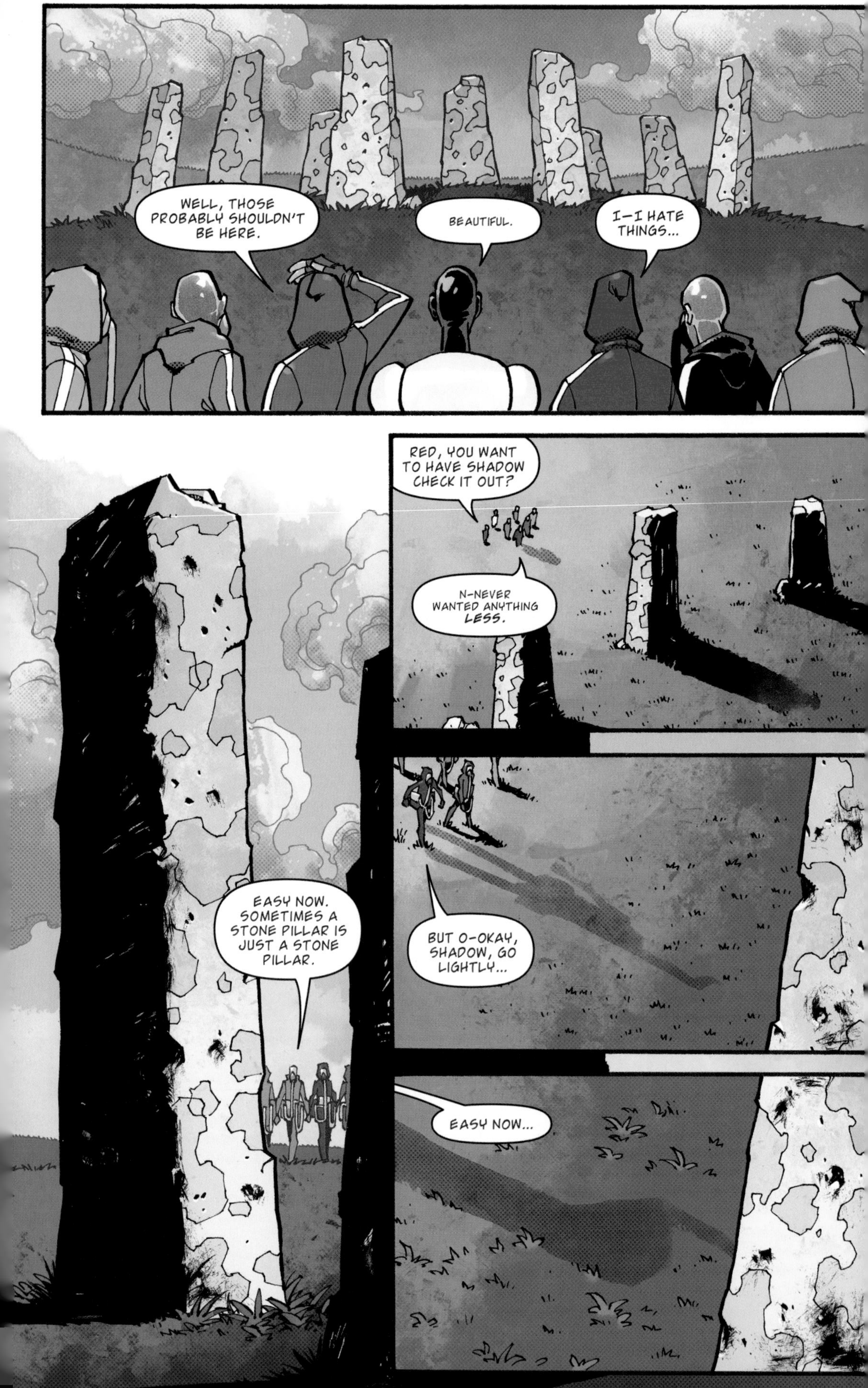
WELL, THOSE PROBABLY SHOULDN'T BE HERE.
BEAUTIFUL.
I—I HATE THINGS...
EASY NOW. SOMETIMES A STONE PILLAR IS JUST A STONE PILLAR.
RED, YOU WANT TO HAVE SHADOW CHECK IT OUT?
N-NEVER WANTED ANYTHING LESS.
BUT O-OKAY, SHADOW, GO LIGHTLY...
EASY NOW...

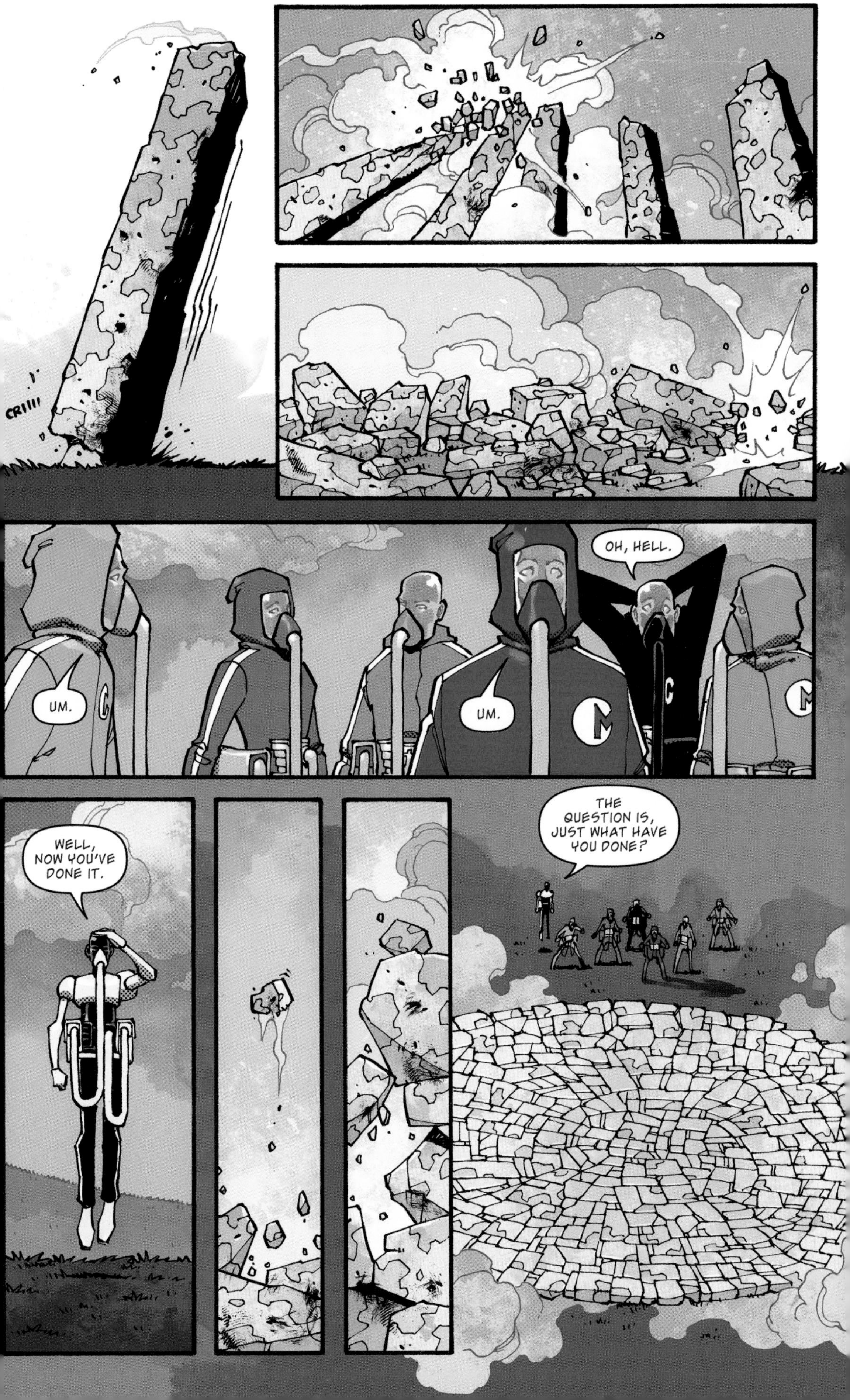
CRIIII
OH, HELL.
UM.
UM.
WELL, NOW YOU'VE DONE IT.
THE QUESTION IS, JUST WHAT HAVE YOU DONE?

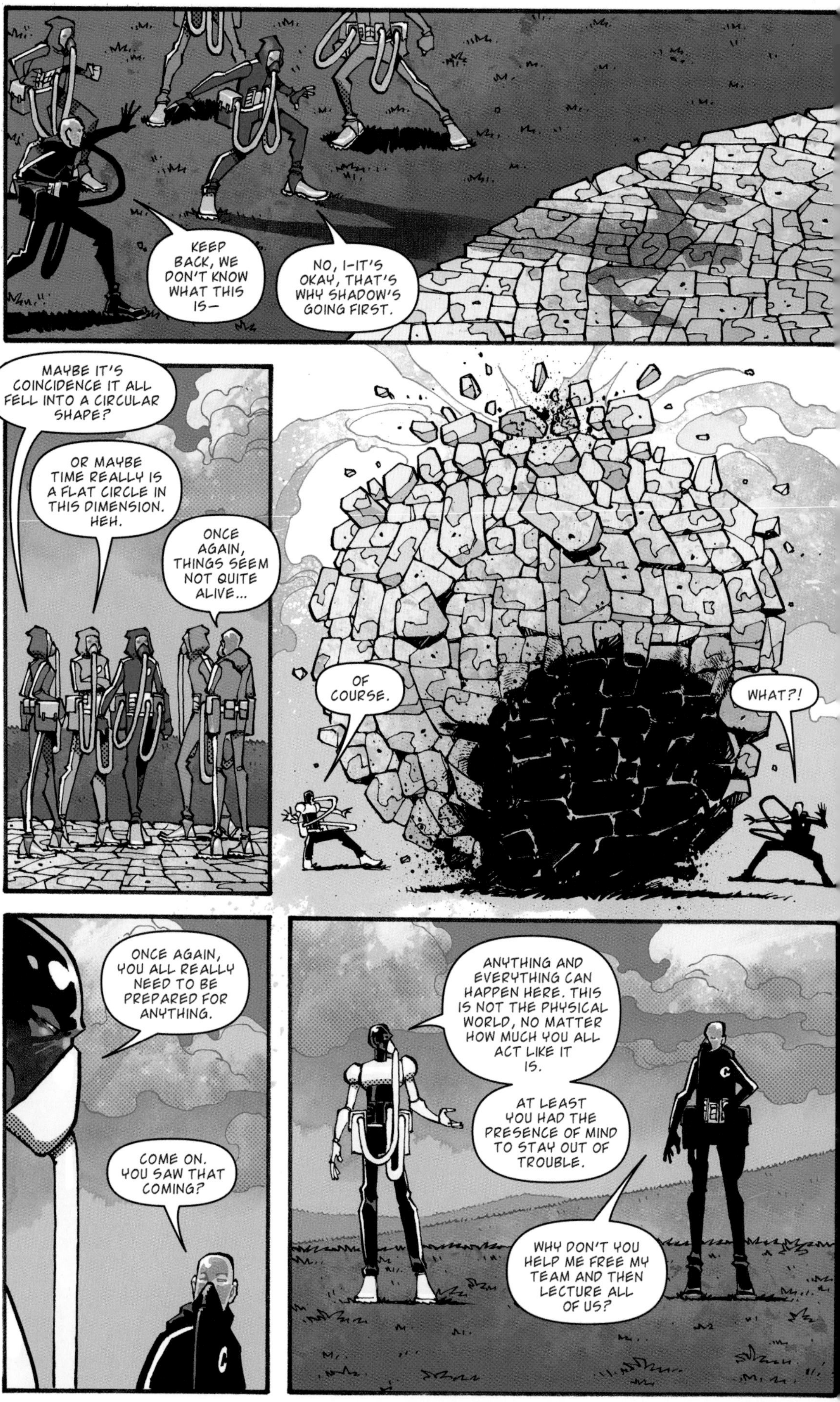
KEEP BACK, WE DON'T KNOW WHAT THIS IS—
NO, I-IT'S OKAY, THAT'S WHY SHADOW'S GOING FIRST.
MAYBE IT'S COINCIDENCE IT ALL FELL INTO A CIRCULAR SHAPE?
OR MAYBE TIME REALLY IS A FLAT CIRCLE IN THIS DIMENSION. HEH.
ONCE AGAIN, THINGS SEEM NOT QUITE ALIVE...
OF COURSE.
WHAT?!
ONCE AGAIN, YOU ALL REALLY NEED TO BE PREPARED FOR ANYTHING.
COME ON. YOU SAW THAT COMING?
ANYTHING AND EVERYTHING CAN HAPPEN HERE. THIS IS NOT THE PHYSICAL WORLD, NO MATTER HOW MUCH YOU ALL ACT LIKE IT IS.
AT LEAST YOU HAD THE PRESENCE OF MIND TO STAY OUT OF TROUBLE.
WHY DON'T YOU HELP ME FREE MY TEAM AND THEN LECTURE ALL OF US?

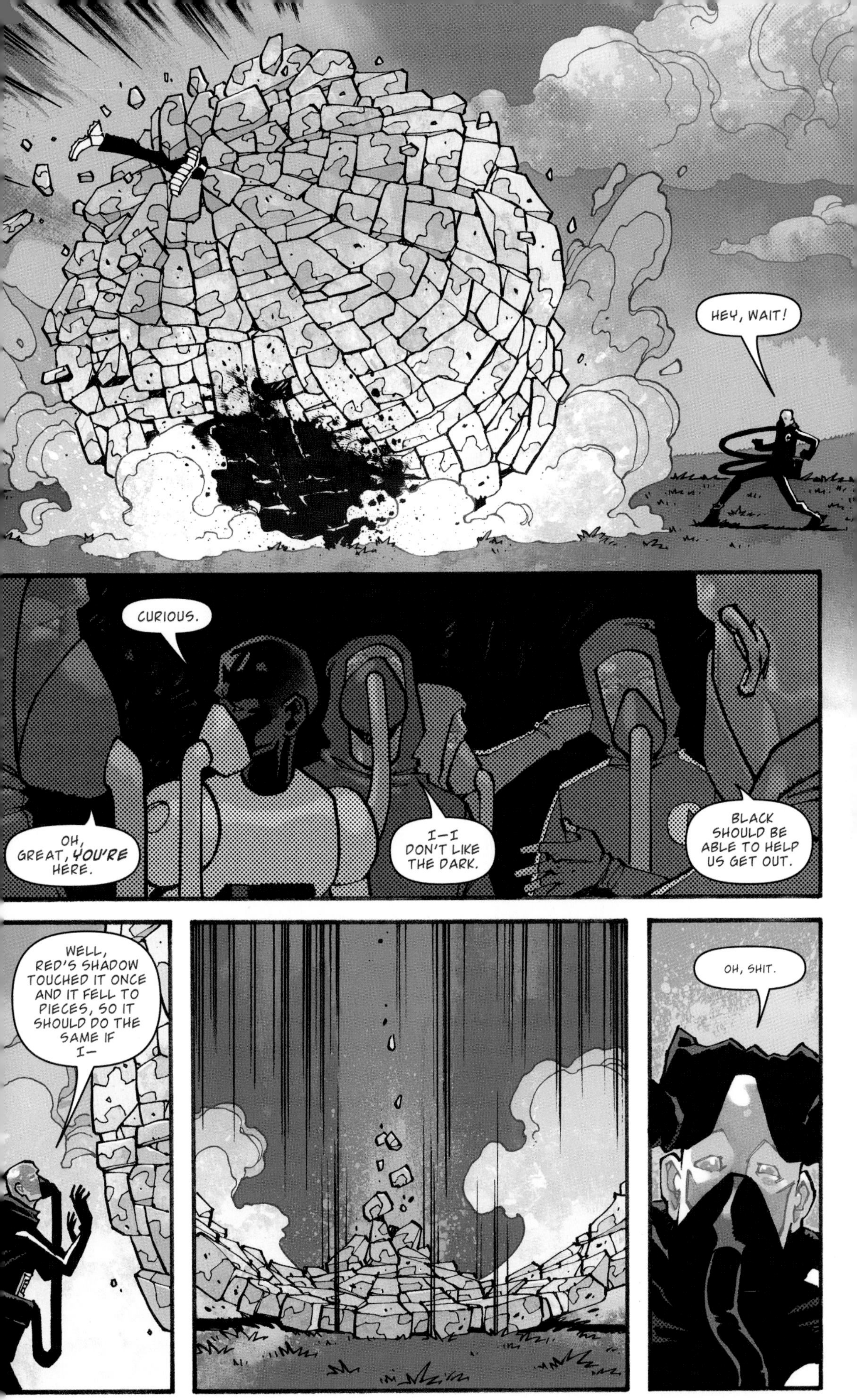
HEY, WAIT!
CURIOUS.
OH, GREAT, YOU'RE HERE.
I—I DON'T LIKE THE DARK.
BLACK SHOULD BE ABLE TO HELP US GET OUT.
WELL, RED'S SHADOW TOUCHED IT ONCE AND IT FELL TO PIECES, SO IT SHOULD DO THE SAME IF I—
OH, SHIT.

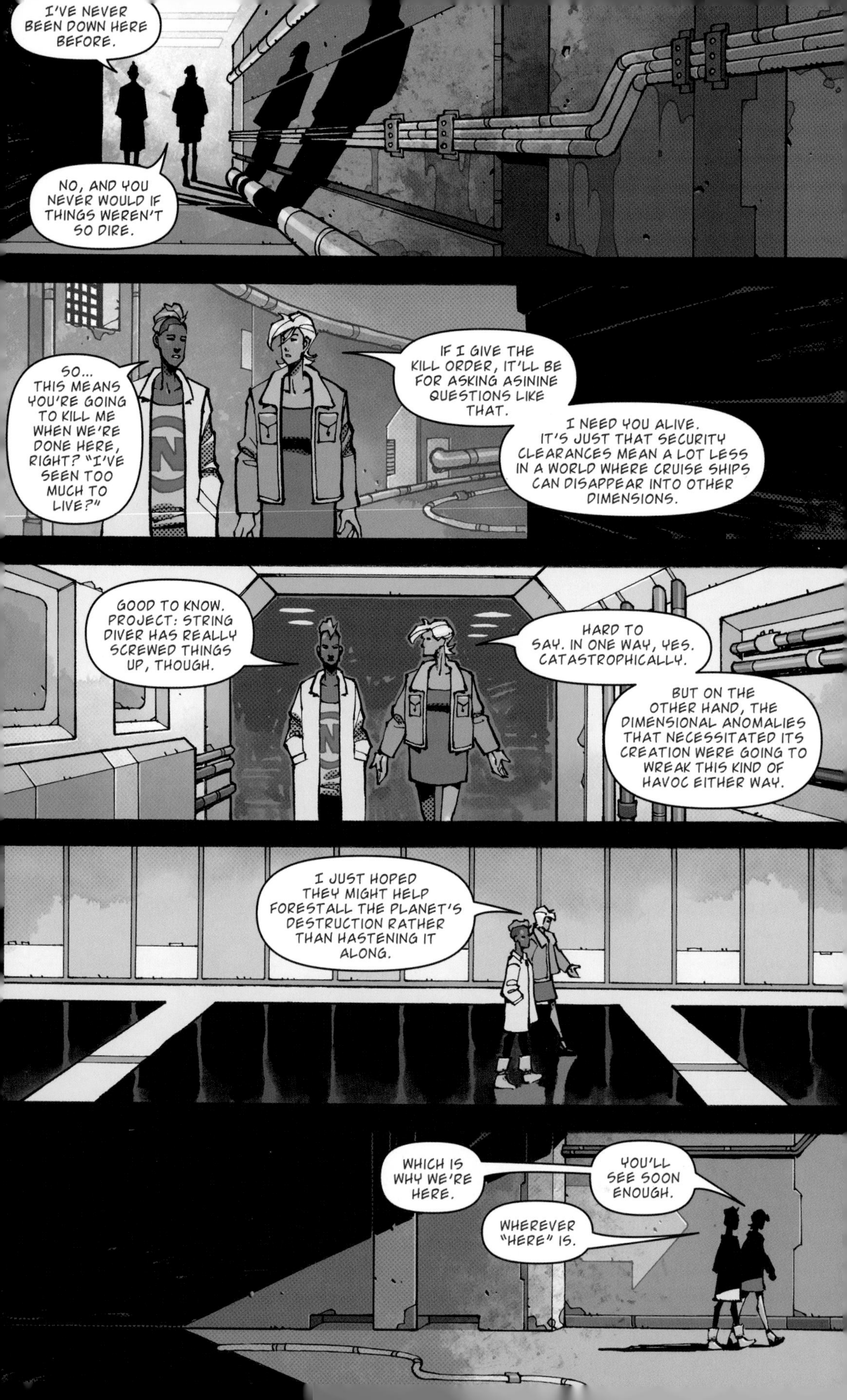
I'VE NEVER BEEN DOWN HERE BEFORE.
NO, AND YOU NEVER WOULD IF THINGS WEREN'T SO DIRE.
SO... THIS MEANS YOU'RE GOING TO KILL ME WHEN WE'RE DONE HERE, RIGHT? "I'VE SEEN TOO MUCH TO LIVE?"
IF I GIVE THE KILL ORDER, IT'LL BE FOR ASKING ASININE QUESTIONS LIKE THAT.
I NEED YOU ALIVE. IT'S JUST THAT SECURITY CLEARANCES MEAN A LOT LESS IN A WORLD WHERE CRUISE SHIPS CAN DISAPPEAR INTO OTHER DIMENSIONS.
GOOD TO KNOW. PROJECT: STRING DIVER HAS REALLY SCREWED THINGS UP, THOUGH.
HARD TO SAY. IN ONE WAY, YES. CATASTROPHICALLY.
BUT ON THE OTHER HAND, THE DIMENSIONAL ANOMALIES THAT NECESSITATED ITS CREATION WERE GOING TO WREAK THIS KIND OF HAVOC EITHER WAY.
I JUST HOPED THEY MIGHT HELP FORESTALL THE PLANET'S DESTRUCTION RATHER THAN HASTENING IT ALONG.
WHICH IS WHY WE'RE HERE.
YOU'LL SEE SOON ENOUGH.
WHEREVER "HERE" IS.

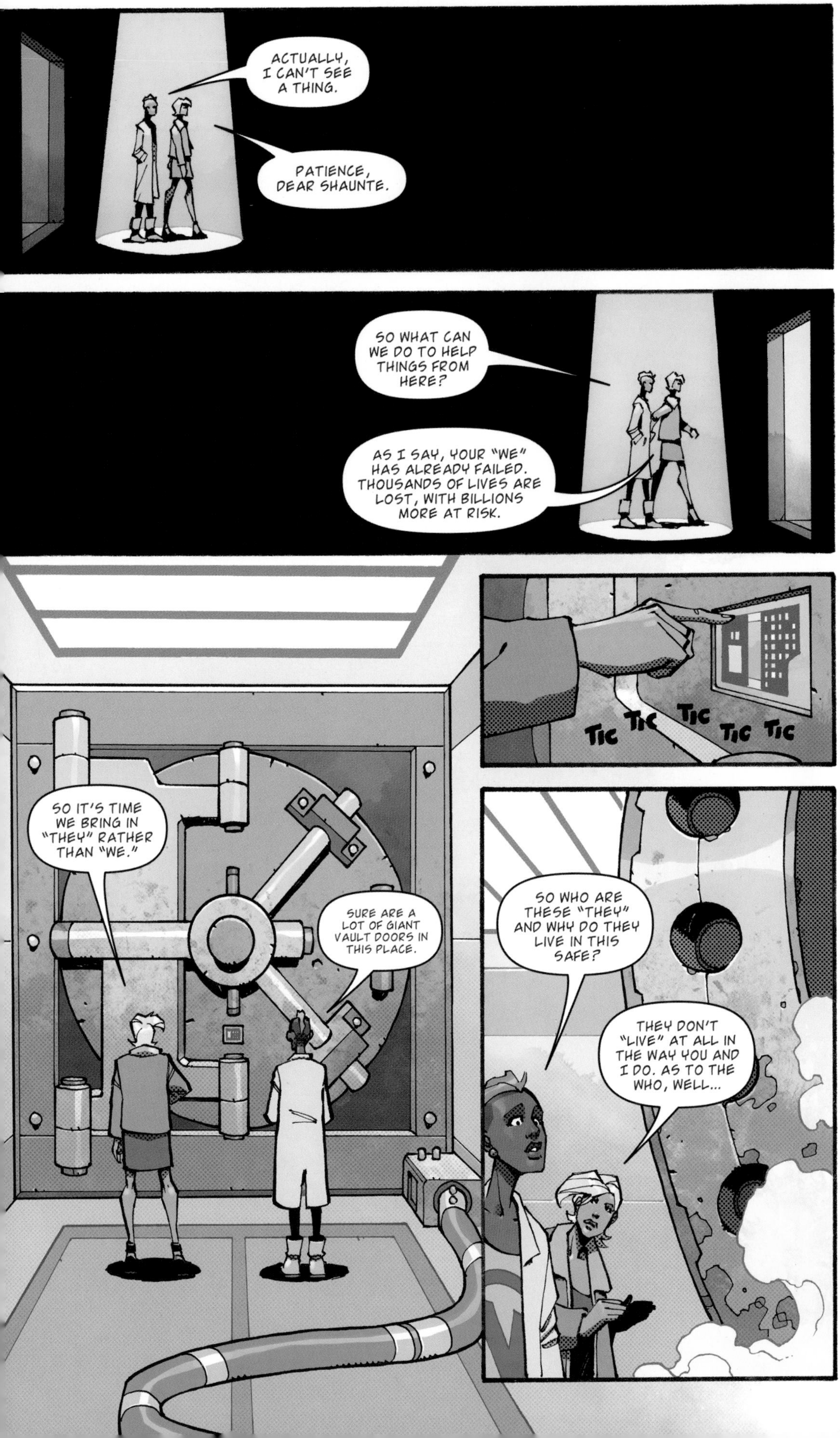
ACTUALLY, I CAN'T SEE A THING.
PATIENCE, DEAR SHAUNTE.
SO WHAT CAN WE DO TO HELP THINGS FROM HERE?
AS I SAY, YOUR "WE" HAS ALREADY FAILED. THOUSANDS OF LIVES ARE LOST, WITH BILLIONS MORE AT RISK.
SO IT'S TIME WE BRING IN "THEY" RATHER THAN "WE."
SURE ARE A LOT OF GIANT VAULT DOORS IN THIS PLACE.
TIC TIC TIC TIC TIC
SO WHO ARE THESE "THEY" AND WHY DO THEY LIVE IN THIS SAFE?
THEY DON'T "LIVE" AT ALL IN THE WAY YOU AND I DO. AS TO THE WHO, WELL...

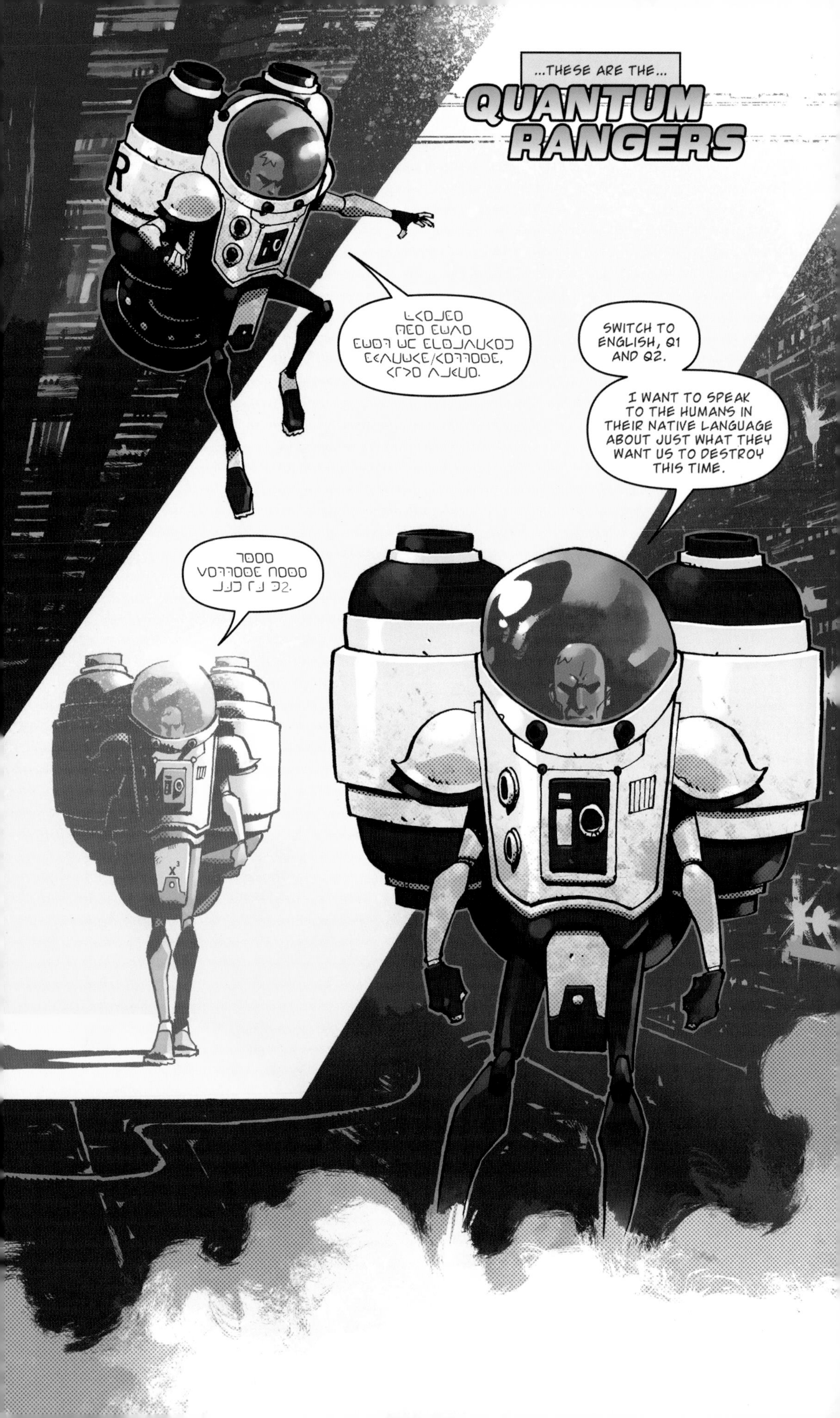
...THESE ARE THE...
QUANTUM RANGERS
SWITCH TO ENGLISH, Q1 AND Q2.
I WANT TO SPEAK TO THE HUMANS IN THEIR NATIVE LANGUAGE ABOUT JUST WHAT THEY WANT US TO DESTROY THIS TIME.

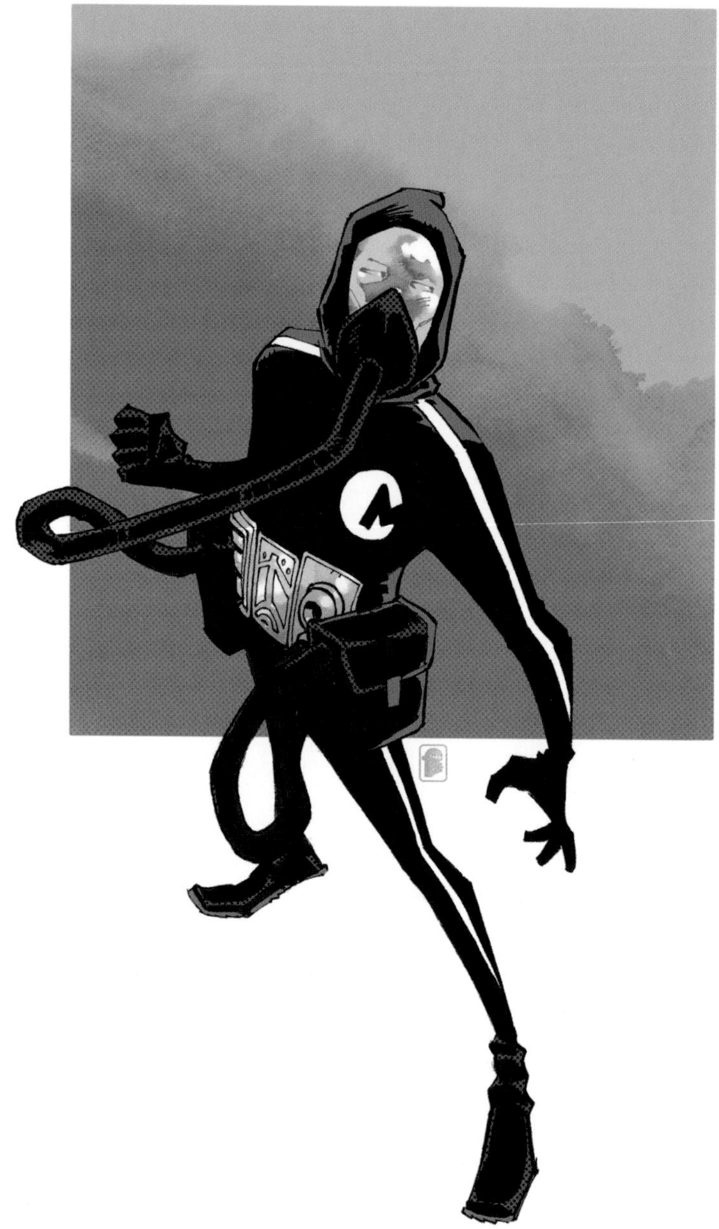

03 | ART BY NELSON DÁNIEL

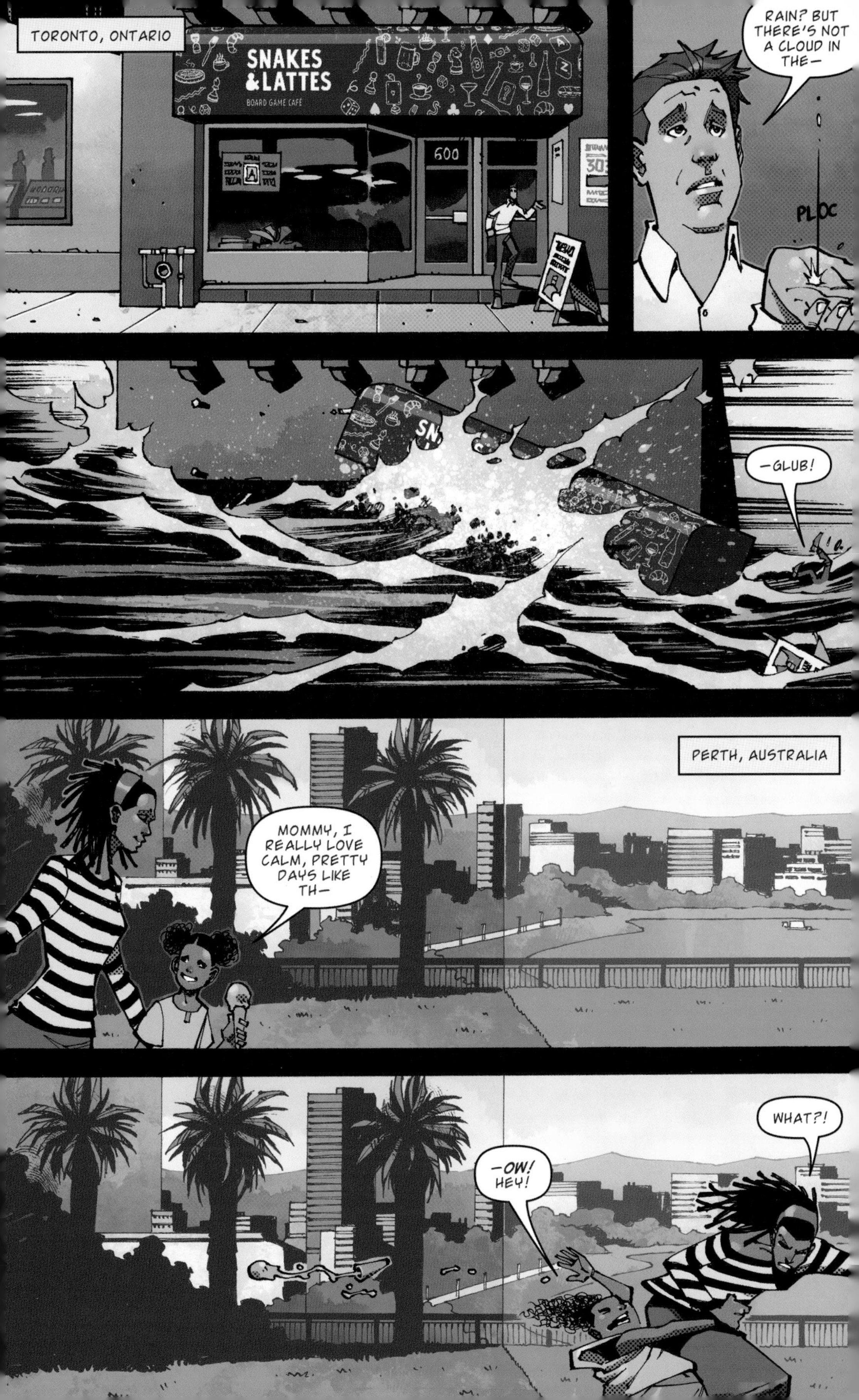
TORONTO, ONTARIO
SNAKES & LATTES
BOARD GAME CAFÉ
600
RAIN? BUT THERE'S NOT A CLOUD IN THE—
PLOC
SN
—GLUB!
PERTH, AUSTRALIA
MOMMY, I REALLY LOVE CALM, PRETTY DAYS LIKE TH—
—OW! HEY!
WHAT?!

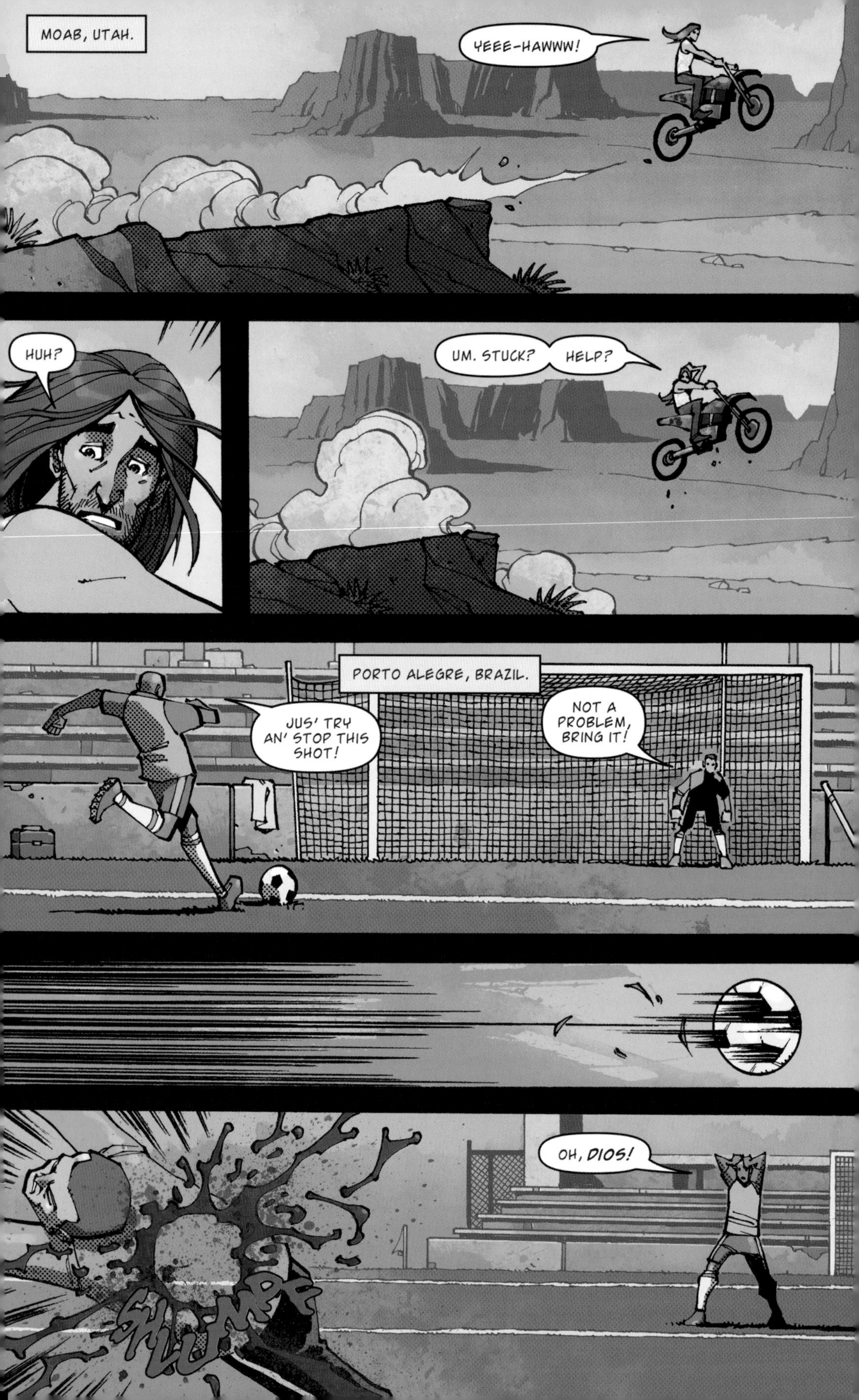
MOAB, UTAH.
YEEE-HAWWW!
HUH?
UM. STUCK?
HELP?
PORTO ALEGRE, BRAZIL.
JUS' TRY AN' STOP THIS SHOT!
NOT A PROBLEM, BRING IT!
OH, DIOS!
SHLUMPF

STRING DIVERS

UNIFIED CHAOS THEORY, part 3

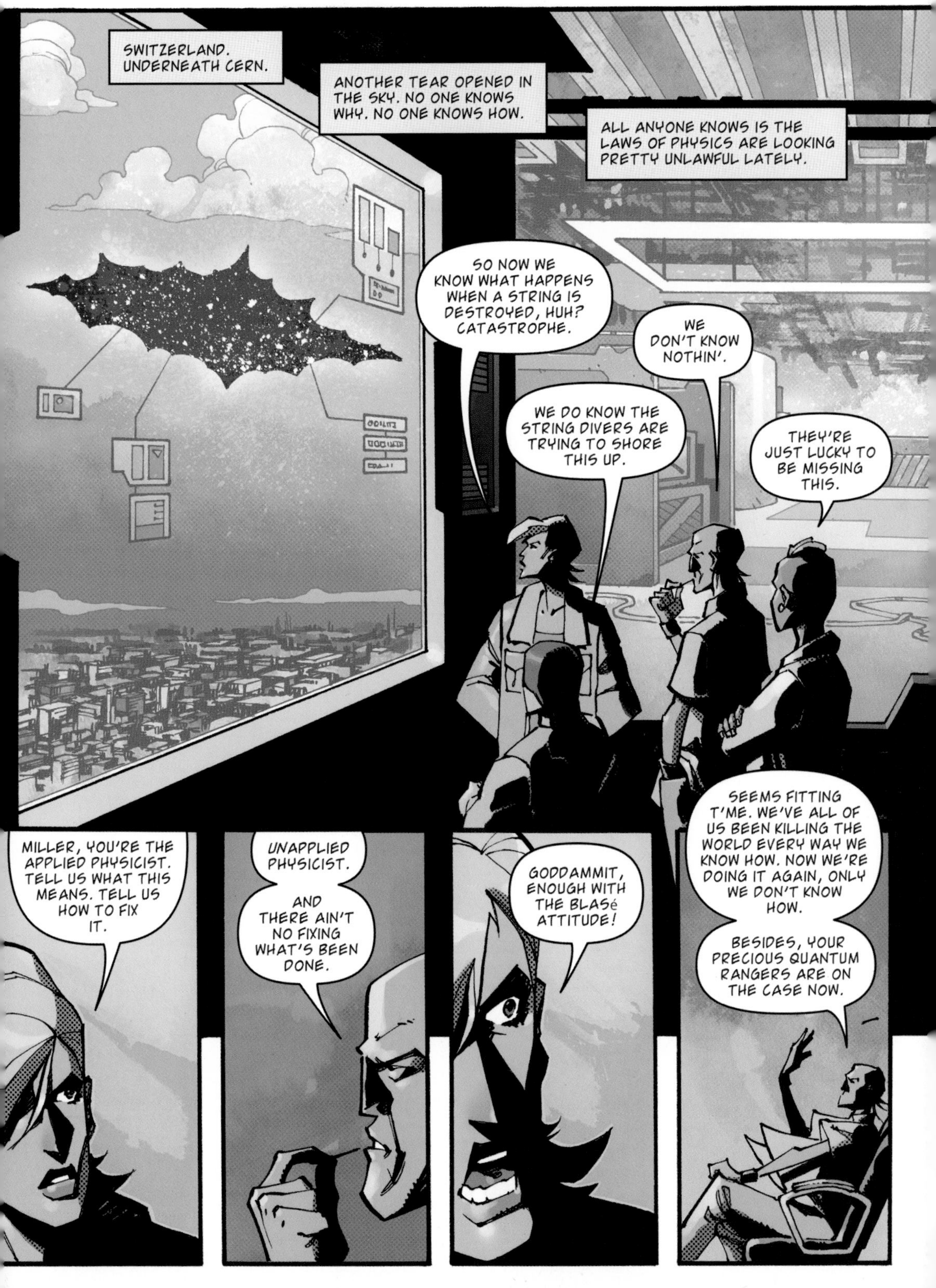
SWITZERLAND. UNDERNEATH CERN.
ANOTHER TEAR OPENED IN THE SKY. NO ONE KNOWS WHY. NO ONE KNOWS HOW.
ALL ANYONE KNOWS IS THE LAWS OF PHYSICS ARE LOOKING PRETTY UNLAWFUL LATELY.
SO NOW WE KNOW WHAT HAPPENS WHEN A STRING IS DESTROYED, HUH? CATASTROPHE.
WE DON'T KNOW NOTHIN'.
WE DO KNOW THE STRING DIVERS ARE TRYING TO SHORE THIS UP.
THEY'RE JUST LUCKY TO BE MISSING THIS.
MILLER, YOU'RE THE APPLIED PHYSICIST. TELL US WHAT THIS MEANS. TELL US HOW TO FIX IT.
UNAPPLIED PHYSICIST.
AND THERE AIN'T NO FIXING WHAT'S BEEN DONE.
GODDAMMIT, ENOUGH WITH THE BLASé ATTITUDE!
SEEMS FITTING T'ME. WE'VE ALL OF US BEEN KILLING THE WORLD EVERY WAY WE KNOW HOW. NOW WE'RE DOING IT AGAIN, ONLY WE DON'T KNOW HOW.
BESIDES, YOUR PRECIOUS QUANTUM RANGERS ARE ON THE CASE NOW.

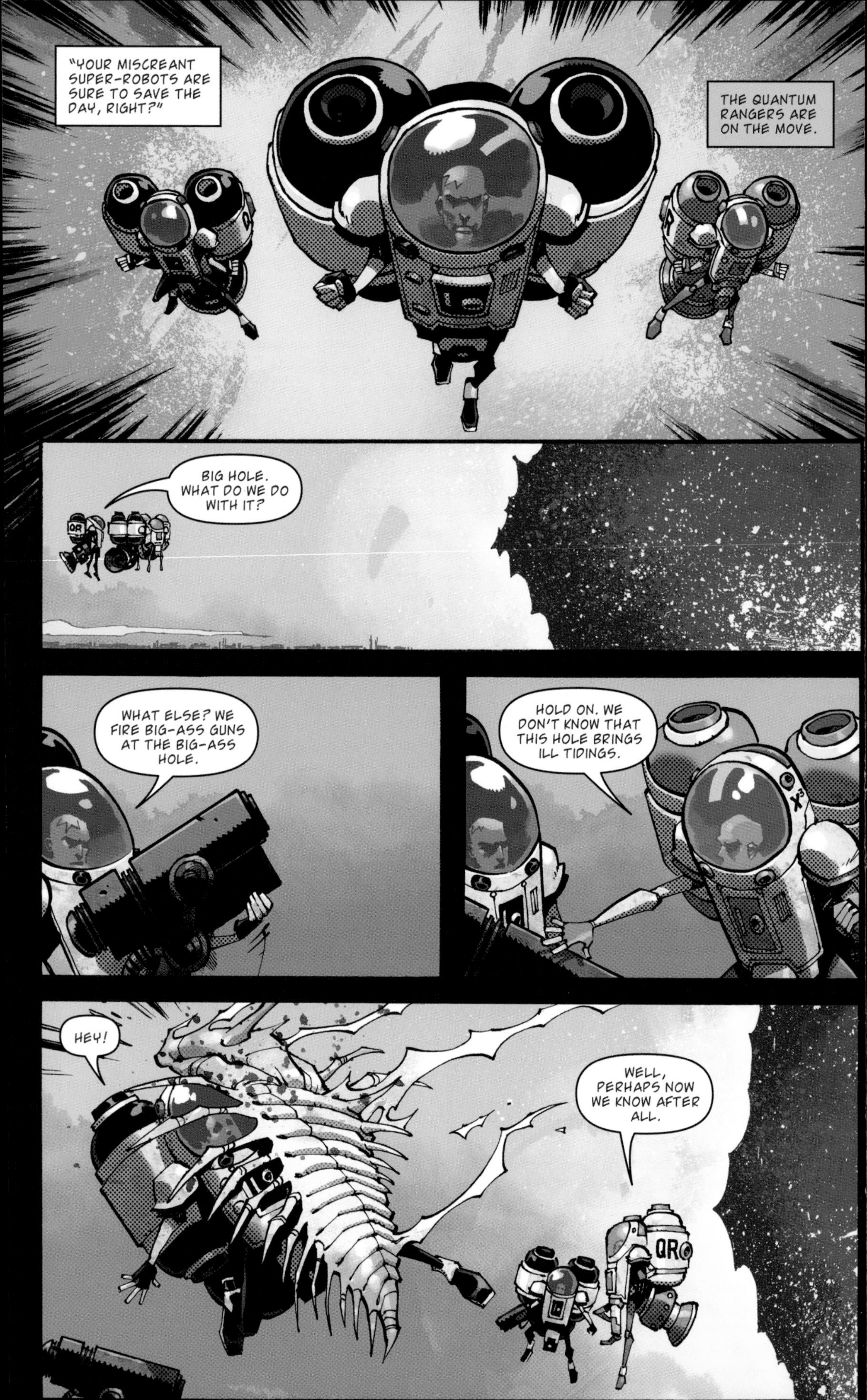
"YOUR MISCREANT SUPER-ROBOTS ARE SURE TO SAVE THE DAY, RIGHT?"
THE QUANTUM RANGERS ARE ON THE MOVE.
BIG HOLE. WHAT DO WE DO WITH IT?
WHAT ELSE? WE FIRE BIG-ASS GUNS AT THE BIG-ASS HOLE.
HOLD ON. WE DON'T KNOW THAT THIS HOLE BRINGS ILL TIDINGS.
HEY!
WELL, PERHAPS NOW WE KNOW AFTER ALL.

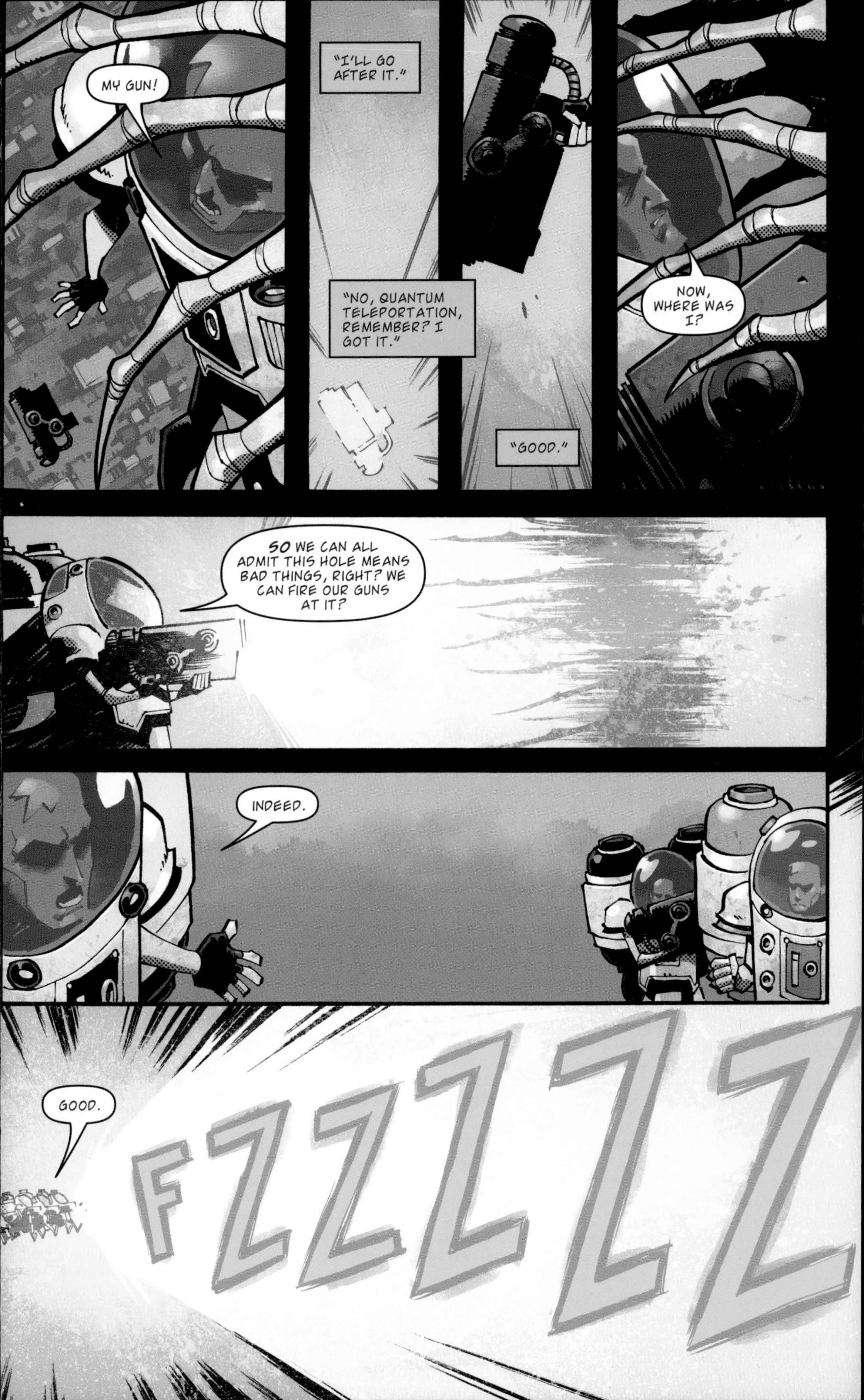
MY GUN!
"I'LL GO AFTER IT."
"NO, QUANTUM TELEPORTATION, REMEMBER? I GOT IT."
"GOOD."
NOW, WHERE WAS I?
SO WE CAN ALL ADMIT THIS HOLE MEANS BAD THINGS, RIGHT? WE CAN FIRE OUR GUNS AT IT?
INDEED.
GOOD.
FZZZZZ

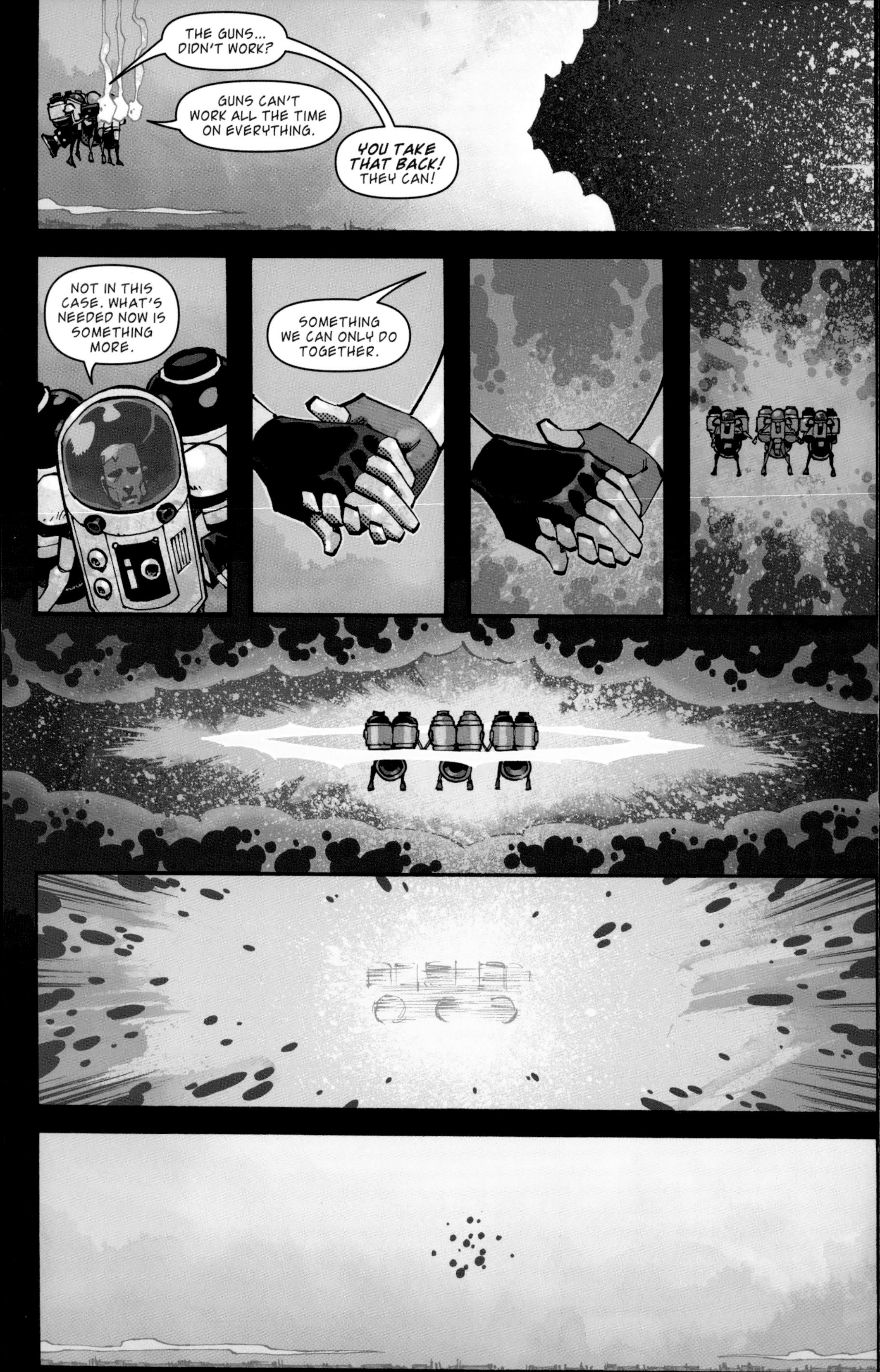
THE GUNS... DIDN'T WORK?
GUNS CAN'T WORK ALL THE TIME ON EVERYTHING.
YOU TAKE THAT BACK! THEY CAN!
NOT IN THIS CASE. WHAT'S NEEDED NOW IS SOMETHING MORE.
SOMETHING WE CAN ONLY DO TOGETHER.

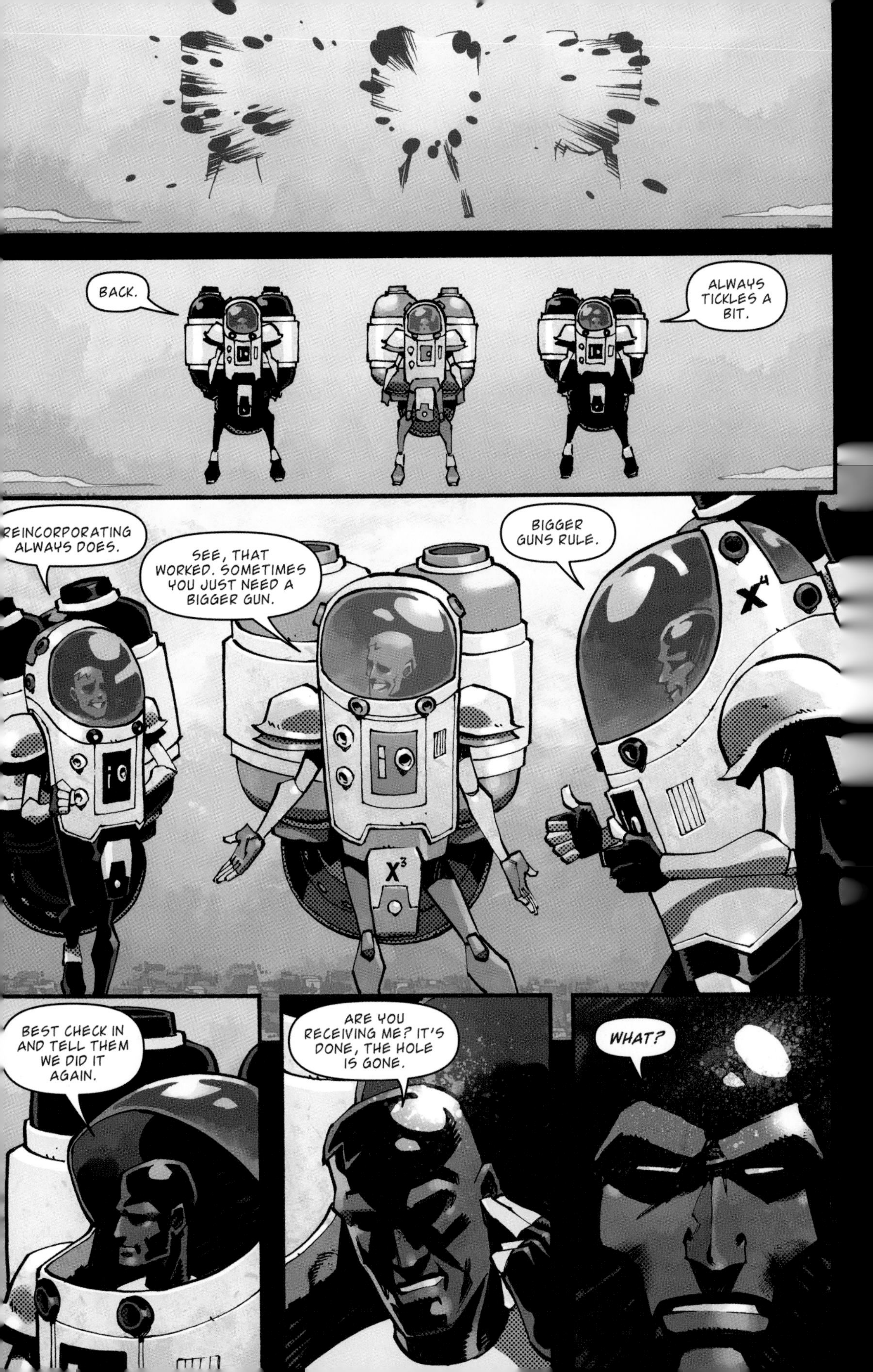

BACK.
ALWAYS TICKLES A BIT.
REINCORPORATING ALWAYS DOES.
SEE, THAT WORKED. SOMETIMES YOU JUST NEED A BIGGER GUN.
BIGGER GUNS RULE.
X4
X3
BEST CHECK IN AND TELL THEM WE DID IT AGAIN.
ARE YOU RECEIVING ME? IT'S DONE, THE HOLE IS GONE.
WHAT?

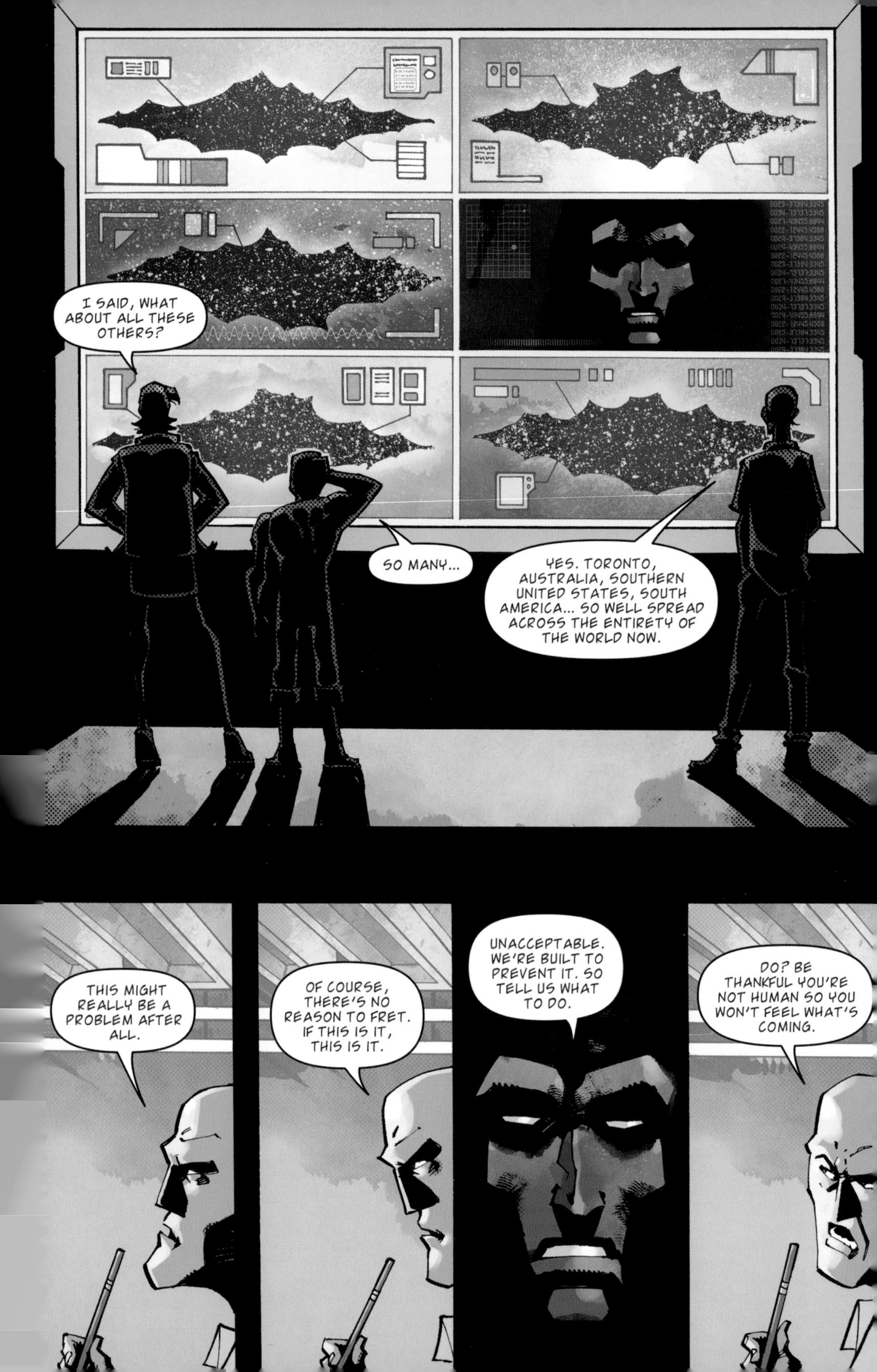
I SAID, WHAT ABOUT ALL THESE OTHERS?
SO MANY...
YES. TORONTO, AUSTRALIA, SOUTHERN UNITED STATES, SOUTH AMERICA... SO WELL SPREAD ACROSS THE ENTIRETY OF THE WORLD NOW.
THIS MIGHT REALLY BE A PROBLEM AFTER ALL.
OF COURSE, THERE'S NO REASON TO FRET. IF THIS IS IT, THIS IS IT.
UNACCEPTABLE. WE'RE BUILT TO PREVENT IT. SO TELL US WHAT TO DO.
DO? BE THANKFUL YOU'RE NOT HUMAN SO YOU WON'T FEEL WHAT'S COMING.

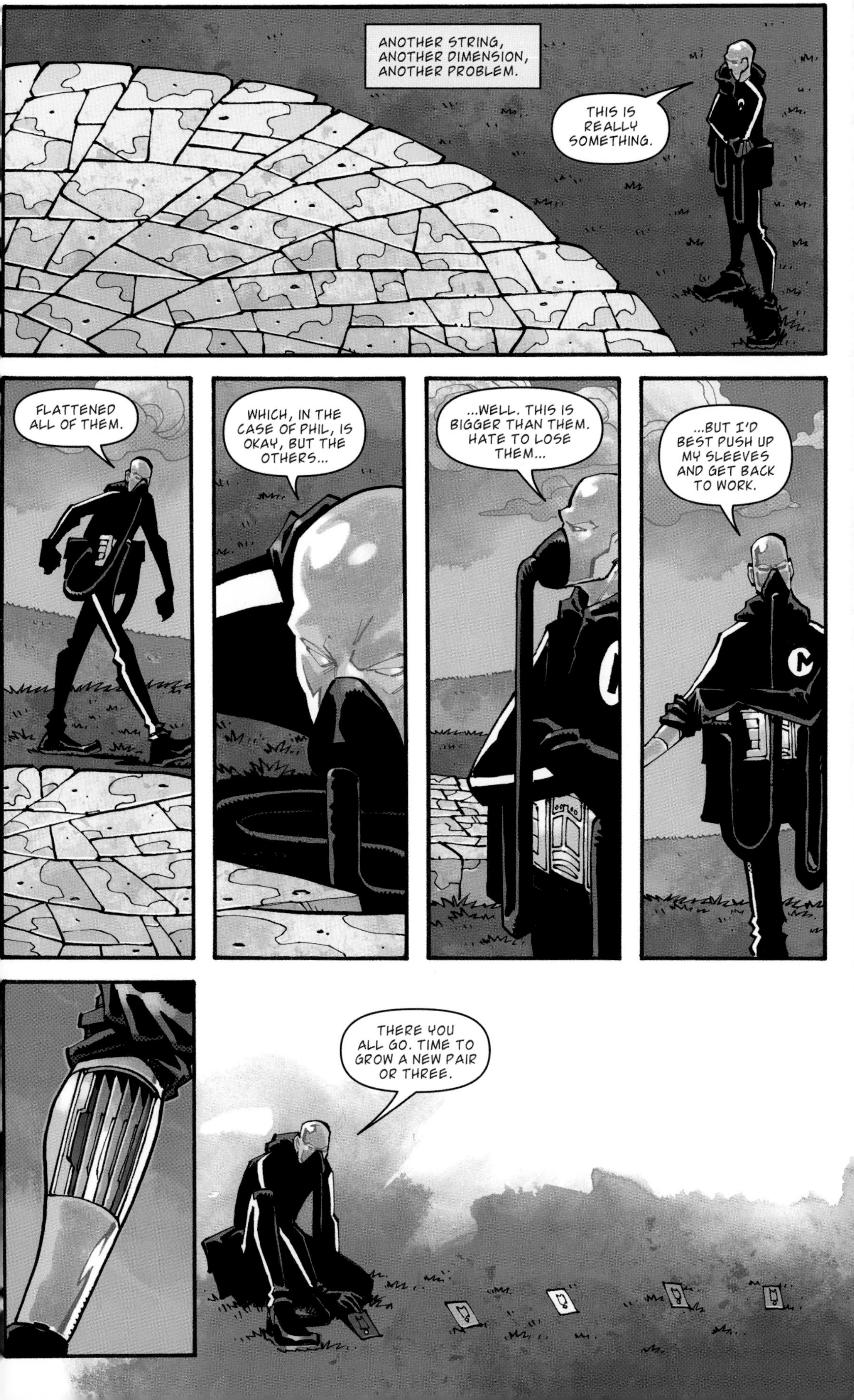
ANOTHER STRING, ANOTHER DIMENSION, ANOTHER PROBLEM.
THIS IS REALLY SOMETHING.
FLATTENED ALL OF THEM.
WHICH, IN THE CASE OF PHIL, IS OKAY, BUT THE OTHERS...
...WELL. THIS IS BIGGER THAN THEM. HATE TO LOSE THEM...
...BUT I'D BEST PUSH UP MY SLEEVES AND GET BACK TO WORK.
THERE YOU ALL GO. TIME TO GROW A NEW PAIR OR THREE.

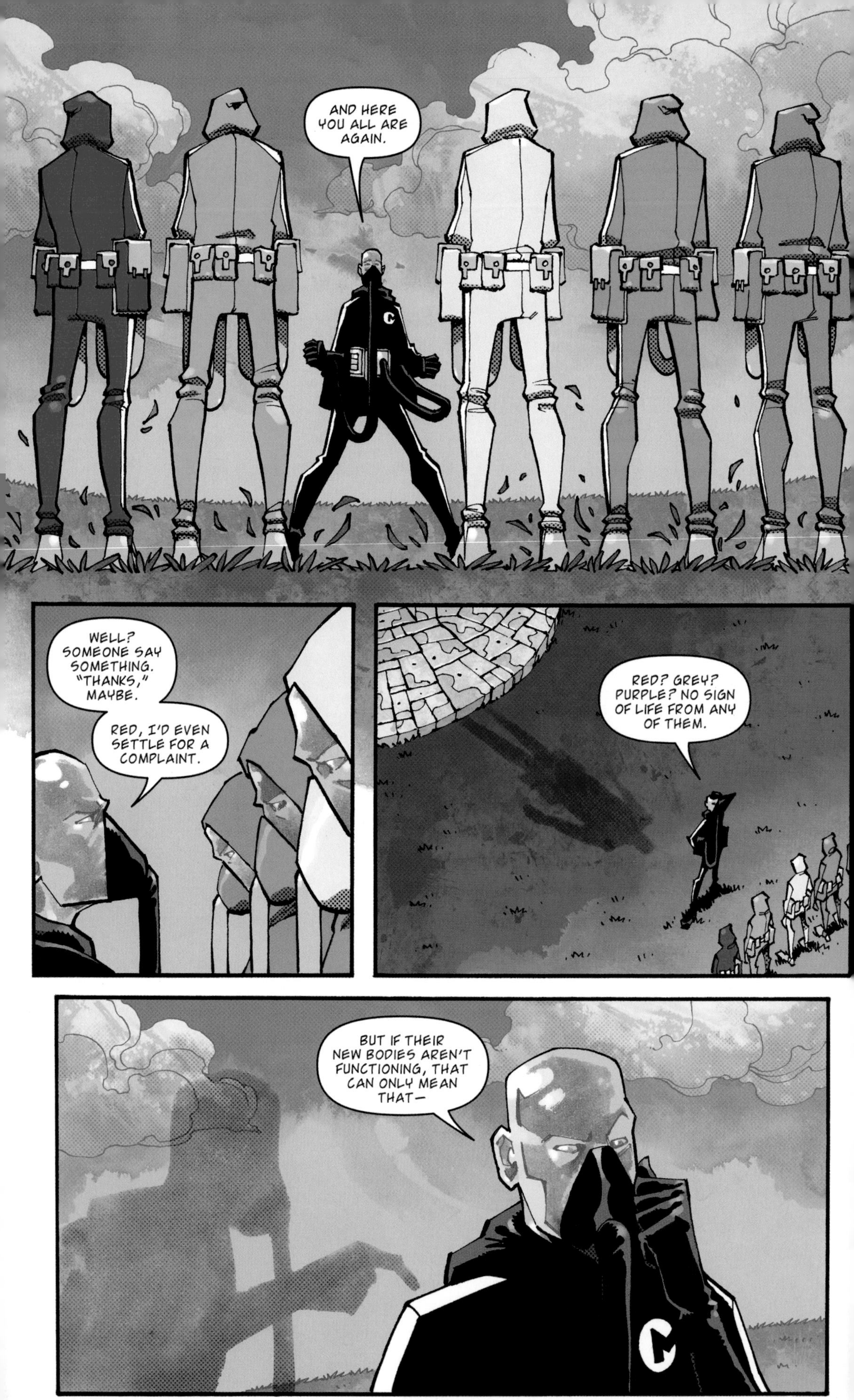
AND HERE YOU ALL ARE AGAIN.
WELL? SOMEONE SAY SOMETHING. "THANKS," MAYBE.
RED, I'D EVEN SETTLE FOR A COMPLAINT.
RED? GREY? PURPLE? NO SIGN OF LIFE FROM ANY OF THEM.
BUT IF THEIR NEW BODIES AREN'T FUNCTIONING, THAT CAN ONLY MEAN THAT—

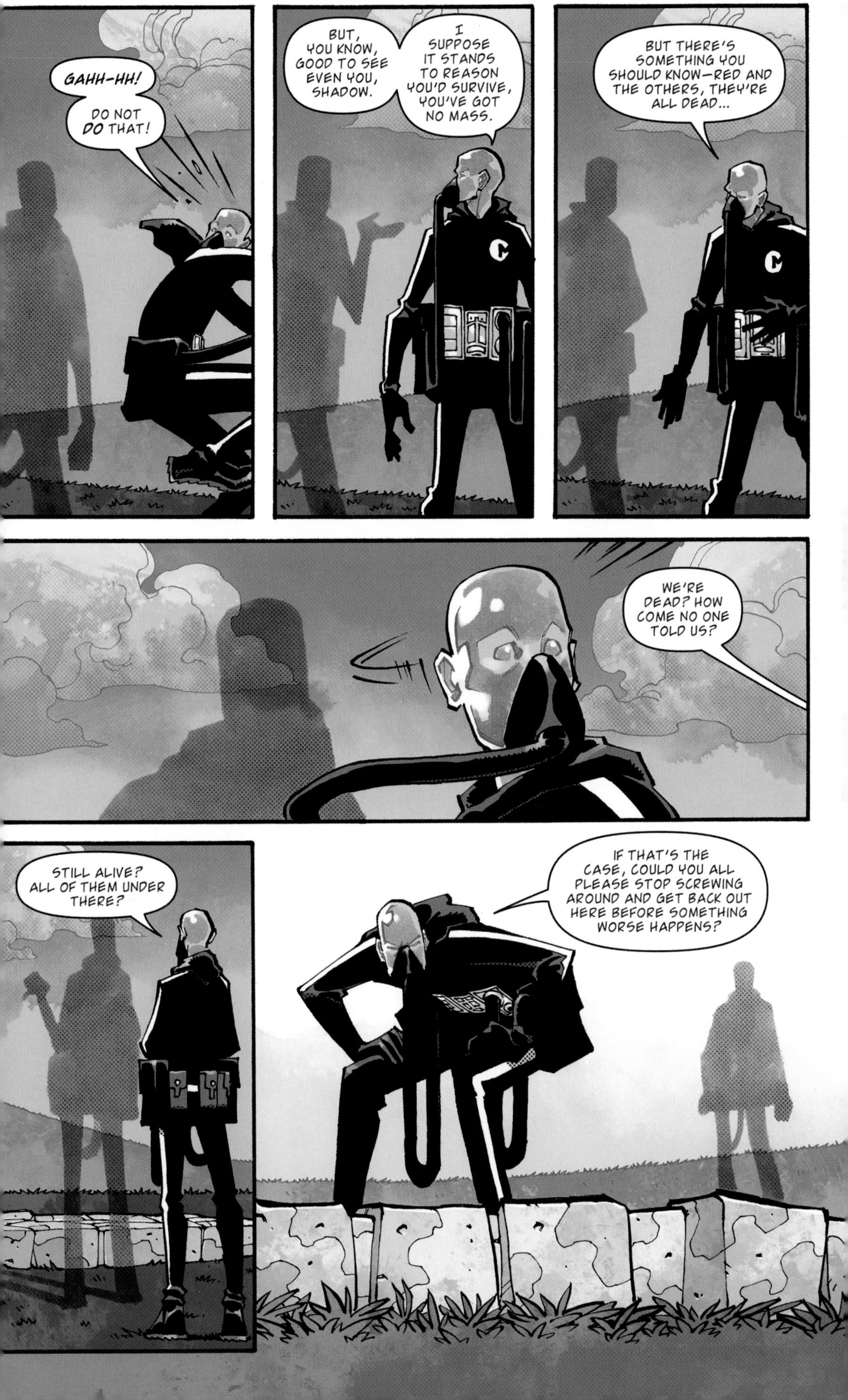
GAHH-HH!
DO NOT DO THAT!
BUT, YOU KNOW, GOOD TO SEE EVEN YOU, SHADOW.
I SUPPOSE IT STANDS TO REASON YOU'D SURVIVE, YOU'VE GOT NO MASS.
BUT THERE'S SOMETHING YOU SHOULD KNOW—RED AND THE OTHERS, THEY'RE ALL DEAD...
WE'RE DEAD? HOW COME NO ONE TOLD US?
STILL ALIVE? ALL OF THEM UNDER THERE?
IF THAT'S THE CASE, COULD YOU ALL PLEASE STOP SCREWING AROUND AND GET BACK OUT HERE BEFORE SOMETHING WORSE HAPPENS?

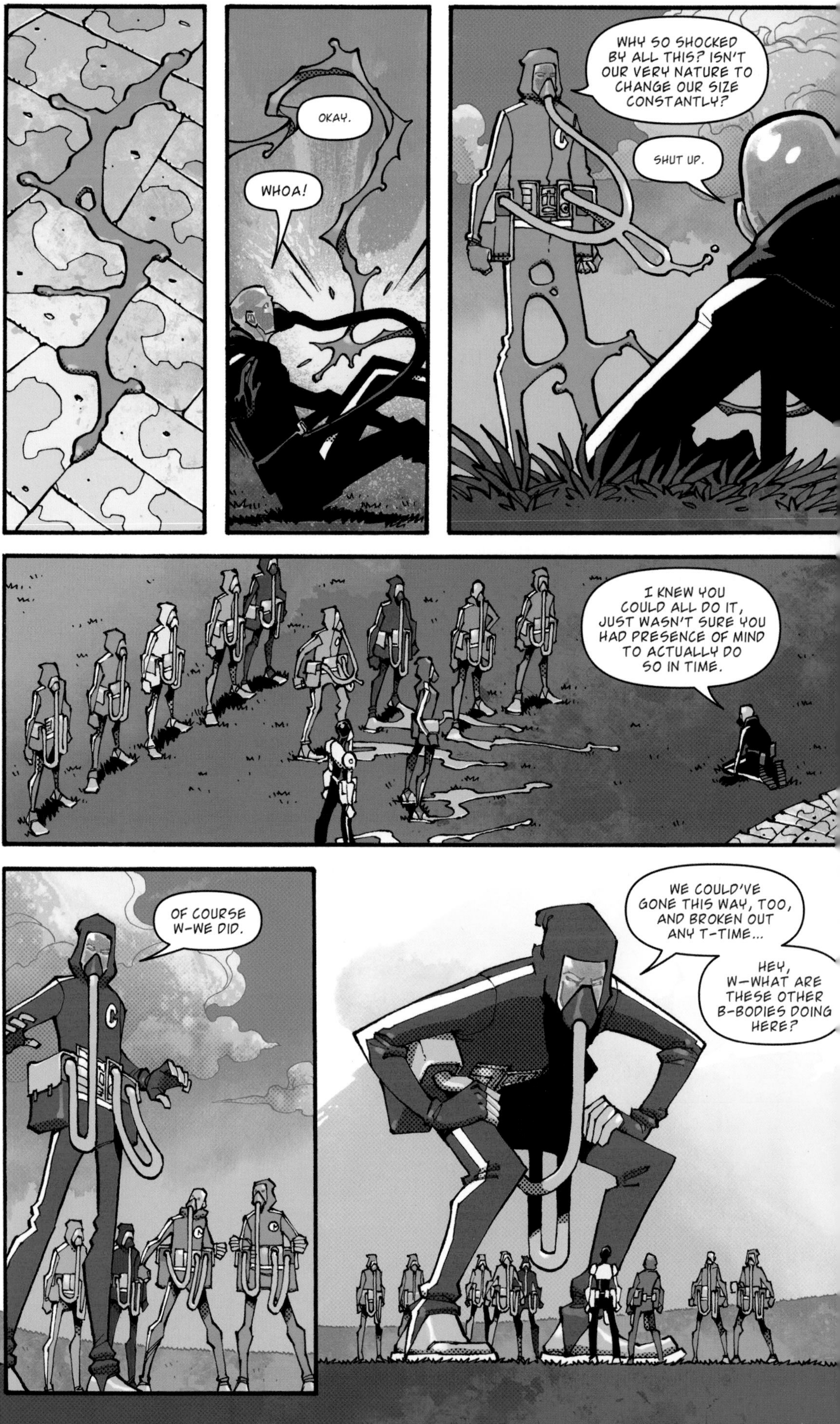
OKAY.
WHOA!
WHY SO SHOCKED BY ALL THIS? ISN'T OUR VERY NATURE TO CHANGE OUR SIZE CONSTANTLY?
SHUT UP.
I KNEW YOU COULD ALL DO IT, JUST WASN'T SURE YOU HAD PRESENCE OF MIND TO ACTUALLY DO SO IN TIME.
OF COURSE W-WE DID.
WE COULD'VE GONE THIS WAY, TOO, AND BROKEN OUT ANY T-TIME...
HEY, W-WHAT ARE THESE OTHER B-BODIES DOING HERE?

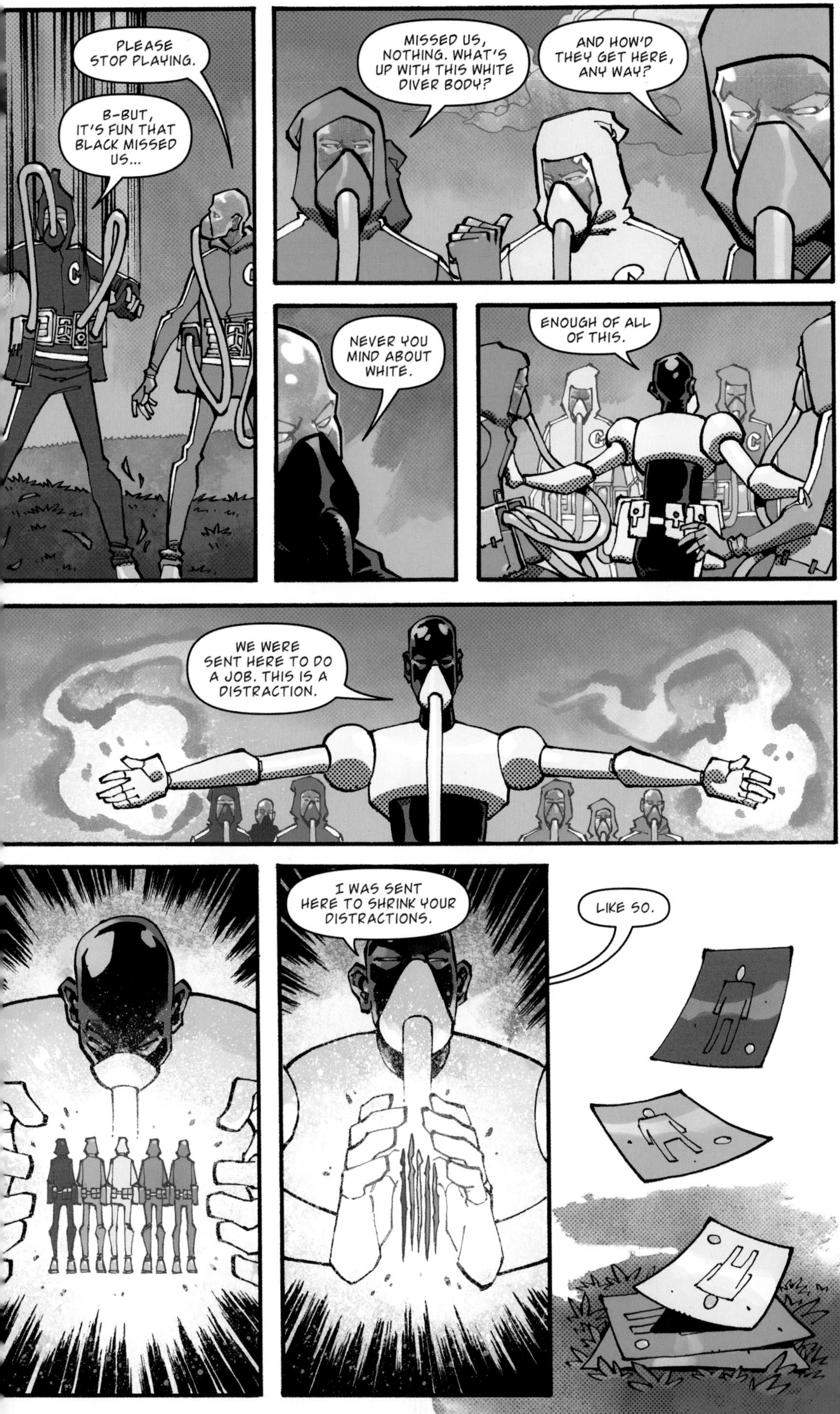
PLEASE STOP PLAYING.
B-BUT, IT'S FUN THAT BLACK MISSED US...
MISSED US, NOTHING. WHAT'S UP WITH THIS WHITE DIVER BODY?
AND HOW'D THEY GET HERE, ANY WAY?
NEVER YOU MIND ABOUT WHITE.
ENOUGH OF ALL OF THIS.
WE WERE SENT HERE TO DO A JOB. THIS IS A DISTRACTION.
I WAS SENT HERE TO SHRINK YOUR DISTRACTIONS.
LIKE SO.

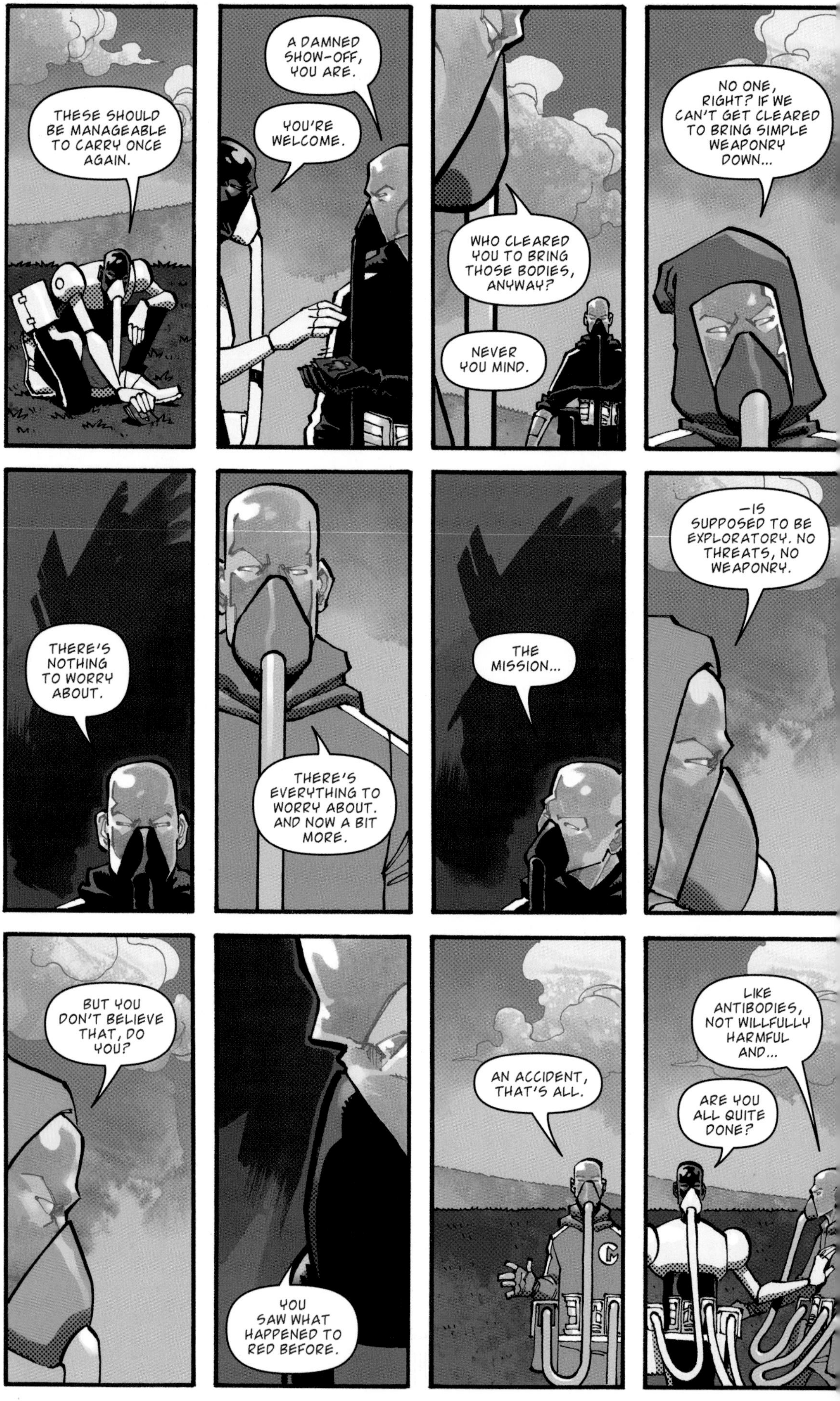
THESE SHOULD BE MANAGEABLE TO CARRY ONCE AGAIN.
A DAMNED SHOW-OFF, YOU ARE.
YOU'RE WELCOME.
WHO CLEARED YOU TO BRING THOSE BODIES, ANYWAY?
NEVER YOU MIND.
NO ONE, RIGHT? IF WE CAN'T GET CLEARED TO BRING SIMPLE WEAPONRY DOWN...
THERE'S NOTHING TO WORRY ABOUT.
THERE'S EVERYTHING TO WORRY ABOUT. AND NOW A BIT MORE.
THE MISSION...
—IS SUPPOSED TO BE EXPLORATORY. NO THREATS, NO WEAPONRY.
BUT YOU DON'T BELIEVE THAT, DO YOU?
YOU SAW WHAT HAPPENED TO RED BEFORE.
AN ACCIDENT, THAT'S ALL.
LIKE ANTIBODIES, NOT WILLFULLY HARMFUL AND...
ARE YOU ALL QUITE DONE?

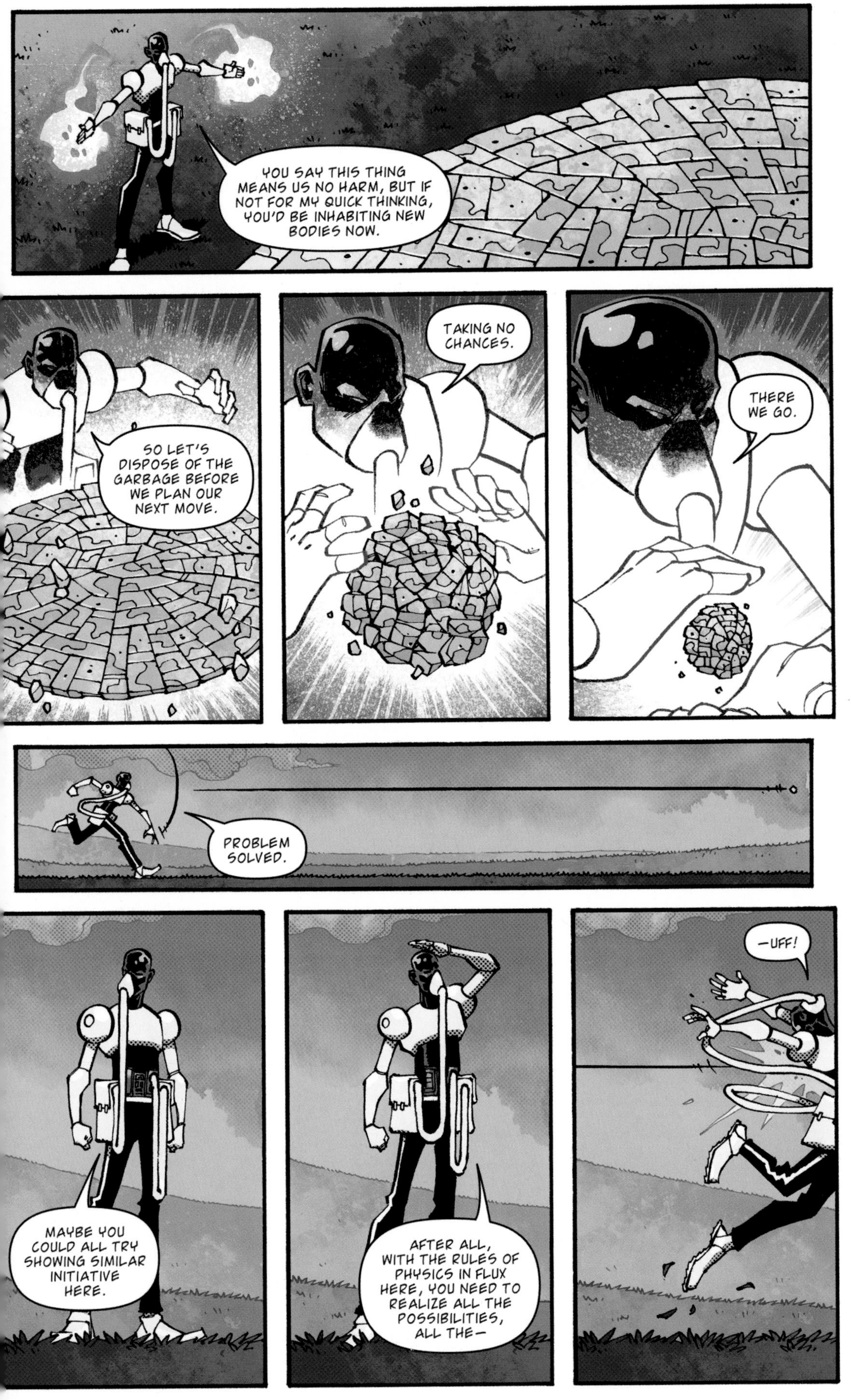
YOU SAY THIS THING MEANS US NO HARM, BUT IF NOT FOR MY QUICK THINKING, YOU'D BE INHABITING NEW BODIES NOW.
SO LET'S DISPOSE OF THE GARBAGE BEFORE WE PLAN OUR NEXT MOVE.
TAKING NO CHANCES.
THERE WE GO.
PROBLEM SOLVED.
MAYBE YOU COULD ALL TRY SHOWING SIMILAR INITIATIVE HERE.
AFTER ALL, WITH THE RULES OF PHYSICS IN FLUX HERE, YOU NEED TO REALIZE ALL THE POSSIBILITIES, ALL THE—
—UFF!

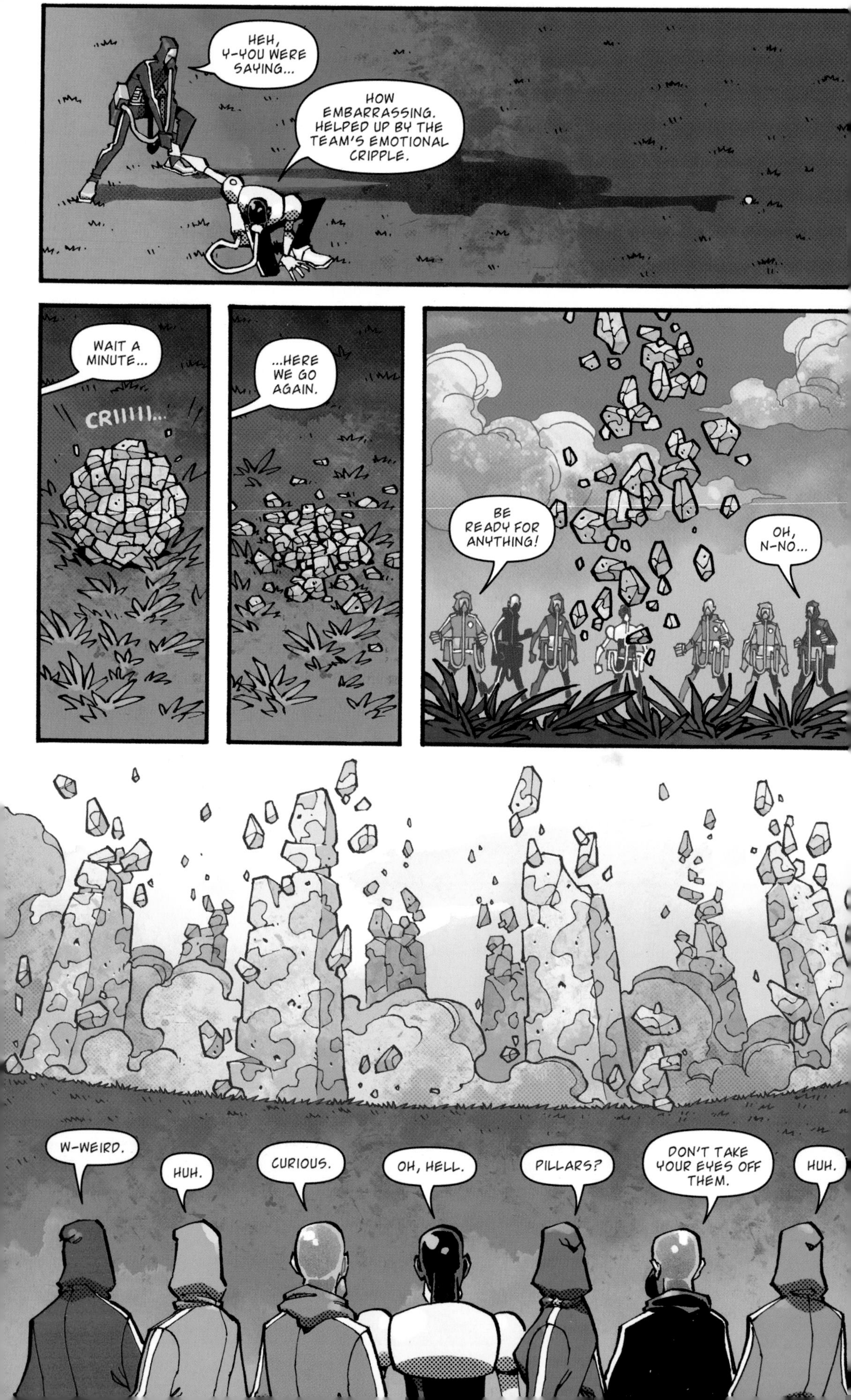
HEH, Y-YOU WERE SAYING...
HOW EMBARRASSING. HELPED UP BY THE TEAM'S EMOTIONAL CRIPPLE.
WAIT A MINUTE...
CRIIIII...
...HERE WE GO AGAIN.
BE READY FOR ANYTHING!
OH, N-NO...
W-WEIRD.
HUH.
CURIOUS.
OH, HELL.
PILLARS?
DON'T TAKE YOUR EYES OFF THEM.
HUH.

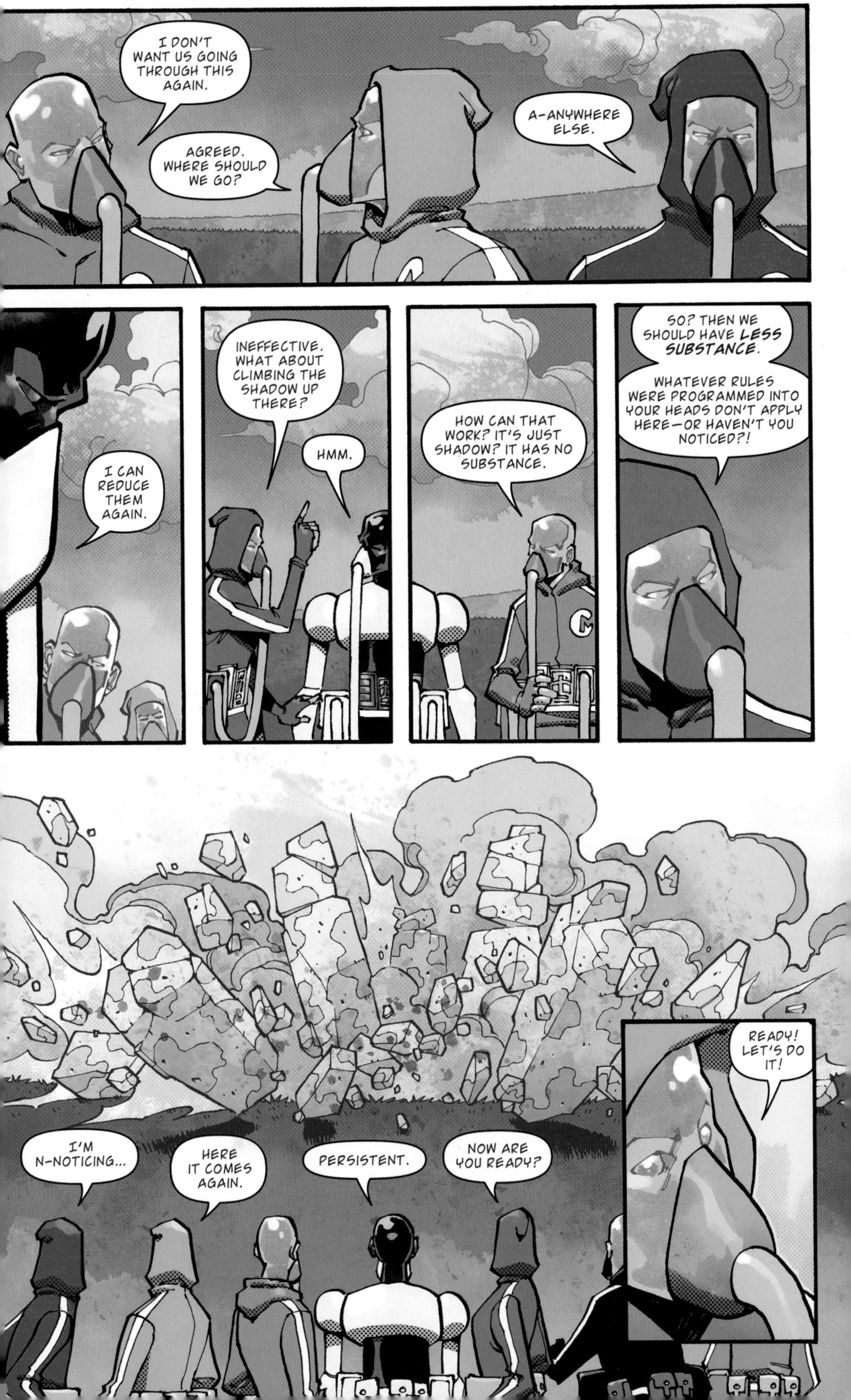
I DON'T WANT US GOING THROUGH THIS AGAIN.
AGREED. WHERE SHOULD WE GO?
A-ANYWHERE ELSE.
I CAN REDUCE THEM AGAIN.
INEFFECTIVE. WHAT ABOUT CLIMBING THE SHADOW UP THERE?
HMM.
HOW CAN THAT WORK? IT'S JUST SHADOW? IT HAS NO SUBSTANCE.
SO? THEN WE SHOULD HAVE *LESS SUBSTANCE*.
WHATEVER RULES WERE PROGRAMMED INTO YOUR HEADS DON'T APPLY HERE—OR HAVEN'T YOU NOTICED?!
I'M N-NOTICING...
HERE IT COMES AGAIN.
PERSISTENT.
NOW ARE YOU READY?
READY! LET'S DO IT!

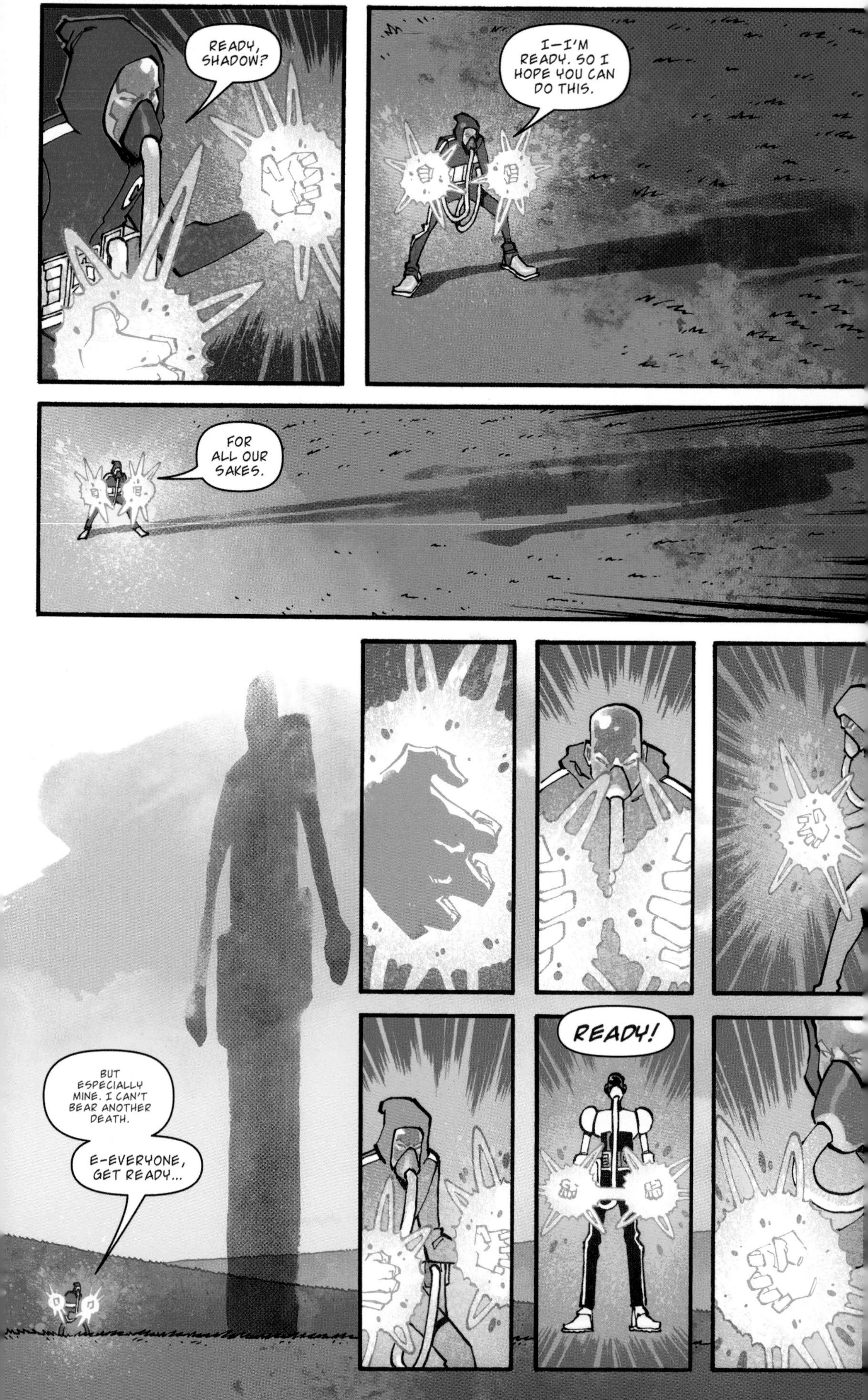
READY, SHADOW?
I—I'M READY. SO I HOPE YOU CAN DO THIS.
FOR ALL OUR SAKES.
BUT ESPECIALLY MINE. I CAN'T BEAR ANOTHER DEATH.
E-EVERYONE, GET READY...
READY!

CLIMB!

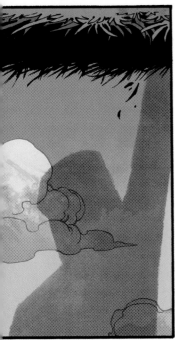

ALMOST THERE...

AT LEAST UP HERE, THERE'RE NO SENTIENT THREATS.

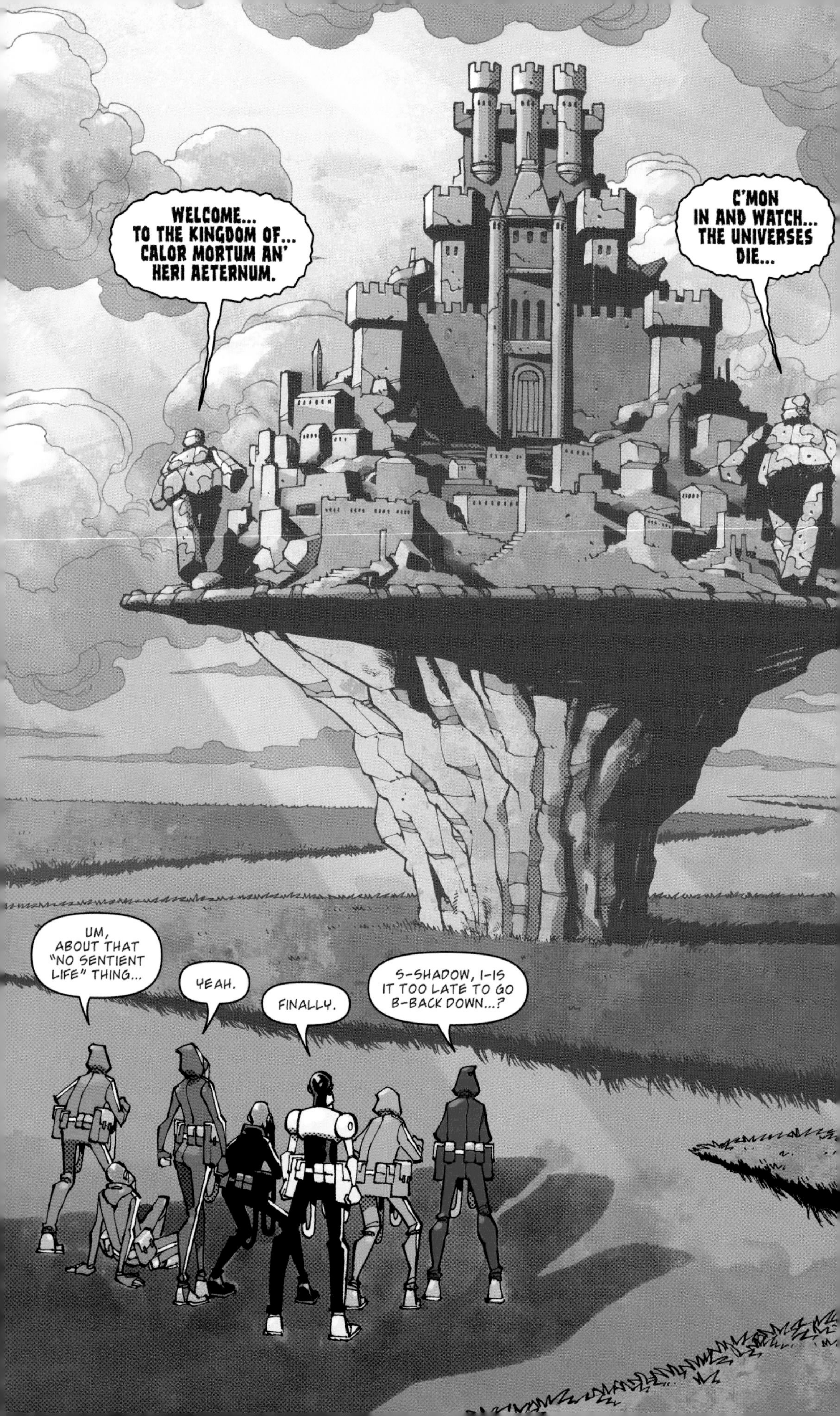
WELCOME... TO THE KINGDOM OF... CALOR MORTUM AN' HERI AETERNUM.
C'MON IN AND WATCH... THE UNIVERSES DIE...
UM, ABOUT THAT "NO SENTIENT LIFE" THING...
YEAH.
FINALLY.
S-SHADOW, I-IS IT TOO LATE TO GO B-BACK DOWN...?

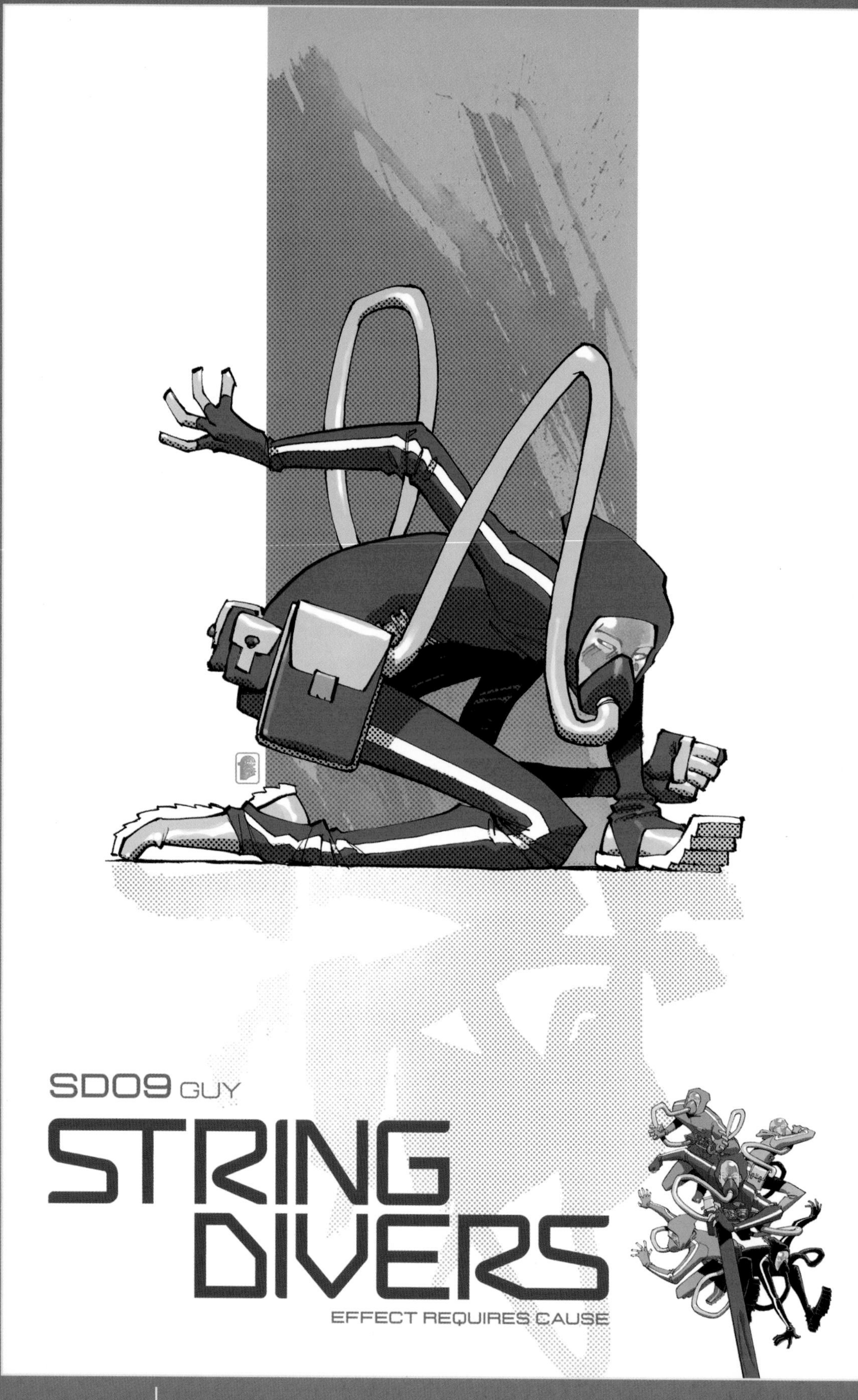
SD09 GUY
STRING DIVERS
EFFECT REQUIRES CAUSE

04 | ART BY NELSON DÁNIEL

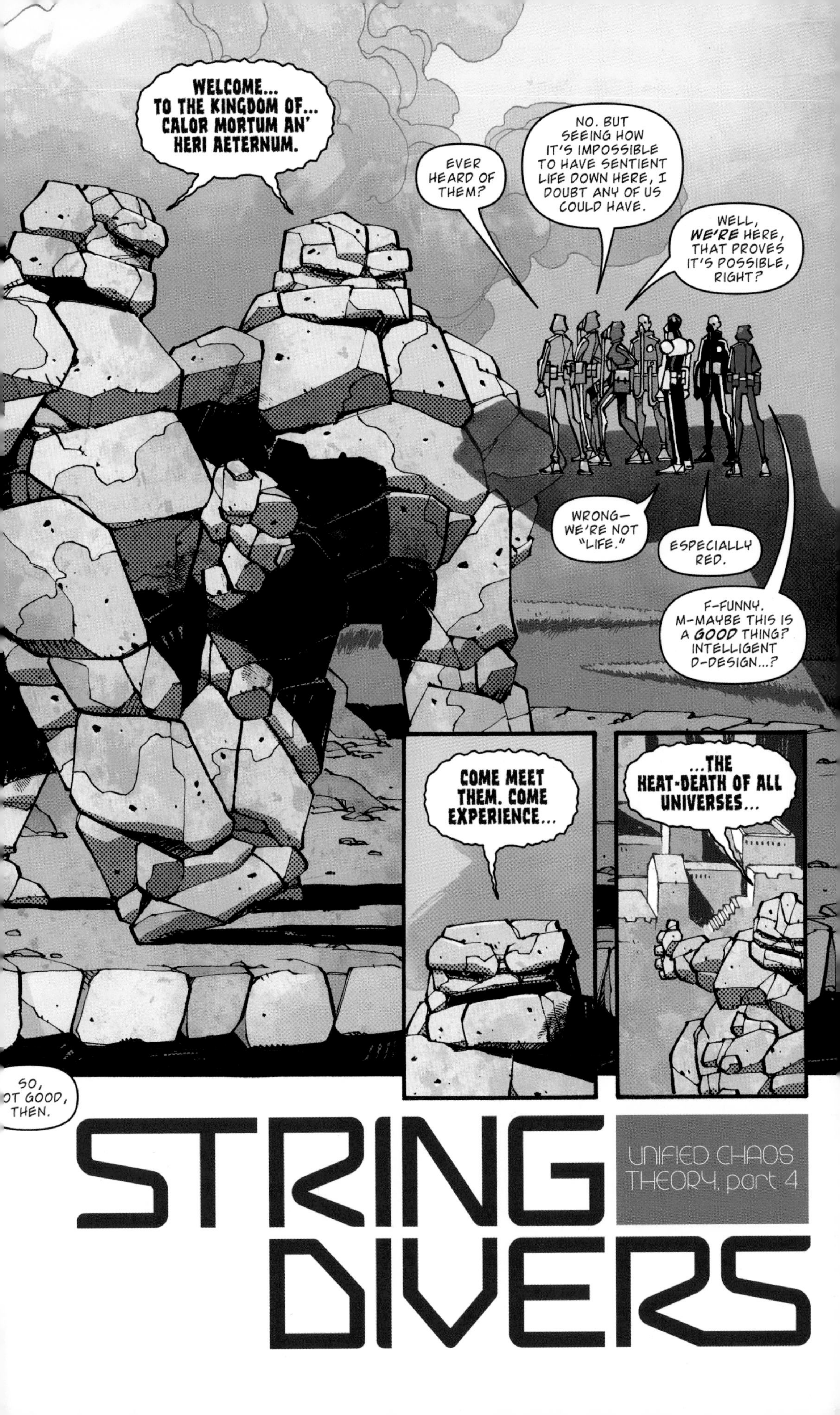
WELCOME... TO THE KINGDOM OF... CALOR MORTUM AN' HERI AETERNUM.
EVER HEARD OF THEM?
NO. BUT SEEING HOW IT'S IMPOSSIBLE TO HAVE SENTIENT LIFE DOWN HERE, I DOUBT ANY OF US COULD HAVE.
WELL, WE'RE HERE, THAT PROVES IT'S POSSIBLE, RIGHT?
WRONG— WE'RE NOT "LIFE."
ESPECIALLY RED.
F-FUNNY. M-MAYBE THIS IS A GOOD THING? INTELLIGENT D-DESIGN...?
COME MEET THEM. COME EXPERIENCE...
...THE HEAT-DEATH OF ALL UNIVERSES...
SO, OT GOOD, THEN.
STRING DIVERS
UNIFIED CHAOS THEORY, part 4

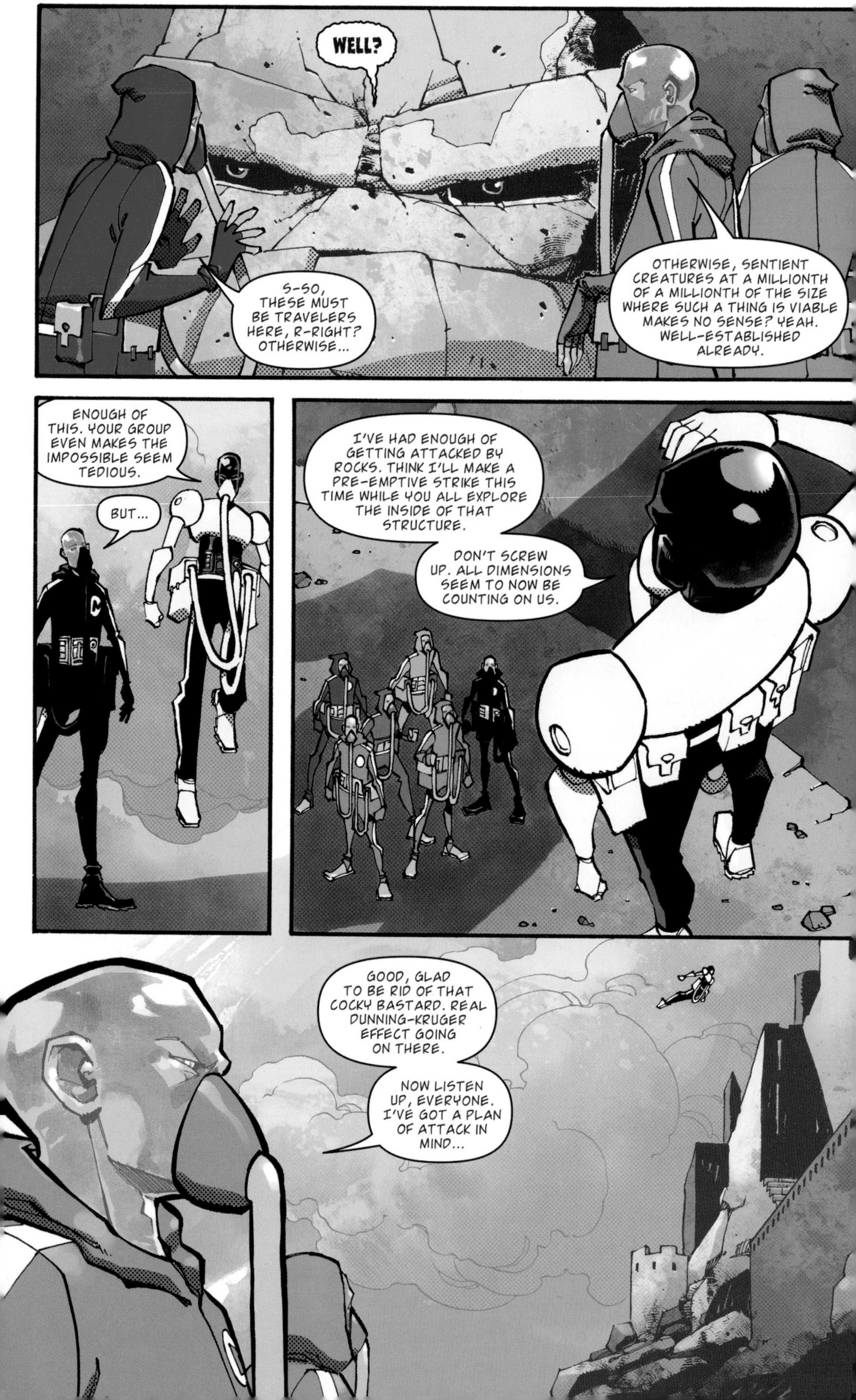
WELL?
S-SO, THESE MUST BE TRAVELERS HERE, R-RIGHT? OTHERWISE...
OTHERWISE, SENTIENT CREATURES AT A MILLIONTH OF A MILLIONTH OF THE SIZE WHERE SUCH A THING IS VIABLE MAKES NO SENSE? YEAH. WELL-ESTABLISHED ALREADY.
ENOUGH OF THIS. YOUR GROUP EVEN MAKES THE IMPOSSIBLE SEEM TEDIOUS.
BUT...
I'VE HAD ENOUGH OF GETTING ATTACKED BY ROCKS. THINK I'LL MAKE A PRE-EMPTIVE STRIKE THIS TIME WHILE YOU ALL EXPLORE THE INSIDE OF THAT STRUCTURE.
DON'T SCREW UP. ALL DIMENSIONS SEEM TO NOW BE COUNTING ON US.
GOOD, GLAD TO BE RID OF THAT COCKY BASTARD. REAL DUNNING-KRUGER EFFECT GOING ON THERE.
NOW LISTEN UP, EVERYONE. I'VE GOT A PLAN OF ATTACK IN MIND...

PHIL'S THE MOST OBNOXIOUS CONTRAPTION EVER BUILT BUT HE'S RIGHT ABOUT ONE THING—WE NEED INSIDE THAT CASTLE.

AND ONCE INSIDE, WE HAVE TO SHUT DOWN THIS *CALOR MORTUM* AND WHATEVER ELSE WE'RE UP AGAINST. IMPOSSIBLE OR NOT, WE CAN'T LET IT DO MORE DAMAGE TO THIS STRING OR ANY OTHER.

TO THAT END, I SUGGEST TEAMS. LET'S HIT THIS THING FROM ALL SIDES.

"RED, YOU AND BLACK PARTNER UP."

I W-WAS HOPING I COULD WAIT OUT HERE...

THANKS FOR THE STRONG BACK-UP, GREY.

"BLUE, MEET PURPLE."

HULLO.

YEAH, CHARMED. CAN WE GO NOW?

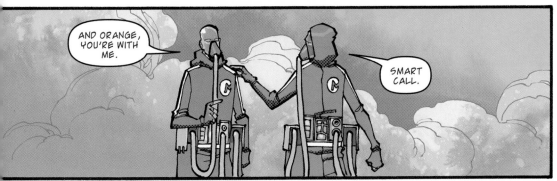

AND ORANGE, YOU'RE WITH ME.

SMART CALL.

OKAY, EVERYONE—WE KNOW LITERALLY NOTHING ABOUT WHAT WE'LL FIND INSIDE THIS STRUCTURE. BUT I'D EXPECT THE EXTRAORDINARY.

USE DIFFERENT ENTRANCES, EACH TEAM. LET'S PLAY IT SAFE, NOT RISK ANY MORE THAN TWO OF US AT EACH ENTRY POINT.

NOW—AGAINST HOPELESS ODDS, AT A NEAR-CREATION-LEVEL WHERE WE ARE COMPLETELY AND TOTALLY ON OUR OWN WITH NO POSSIBLE HELP FROM BACK HOME, LET'S GO SAVE THE UNIVERSE.

ALL THE UNIVERSES.

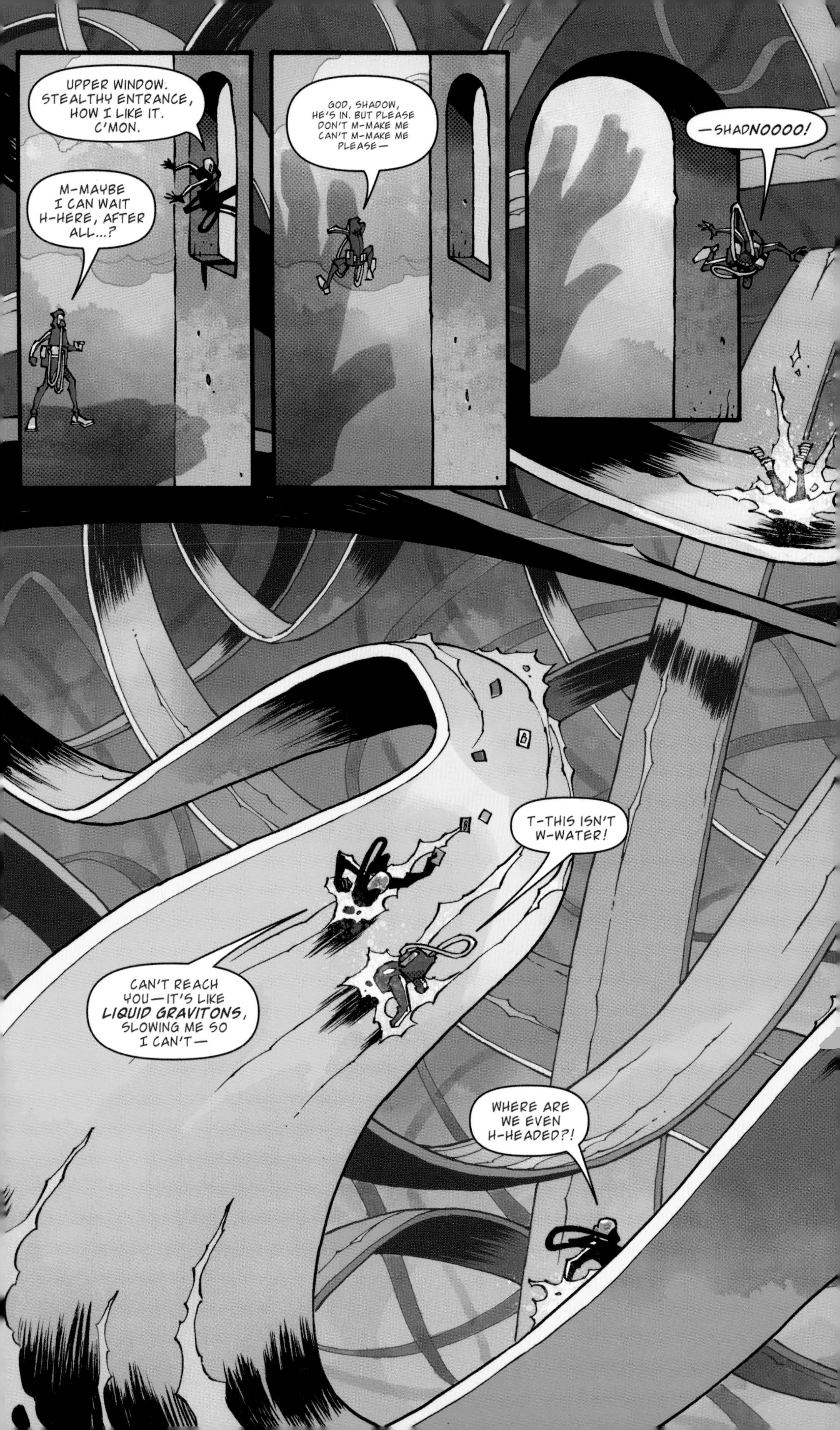
UPPER WINDOW. STEALTHY ENTRANCE, HOW I LIKE IT. C'MON.
M-MAYBE I CAN WAIT H-HERE, AFTER ALL...?
GOD, SHADOW, HE'S IN. BUT PLEASE DON'T M-MAKE ME CAN'T M-MAKE ME PLEASE—
—SHADNOOOO!
T-THIS ISN'T W-WATER!
CAN'T REACH YOU—IT'S LIKE LIQUID GRAVITONS, SLOWING ME SO I CAN'T—
WHERE ARE WE EVEN H-HEADED?!

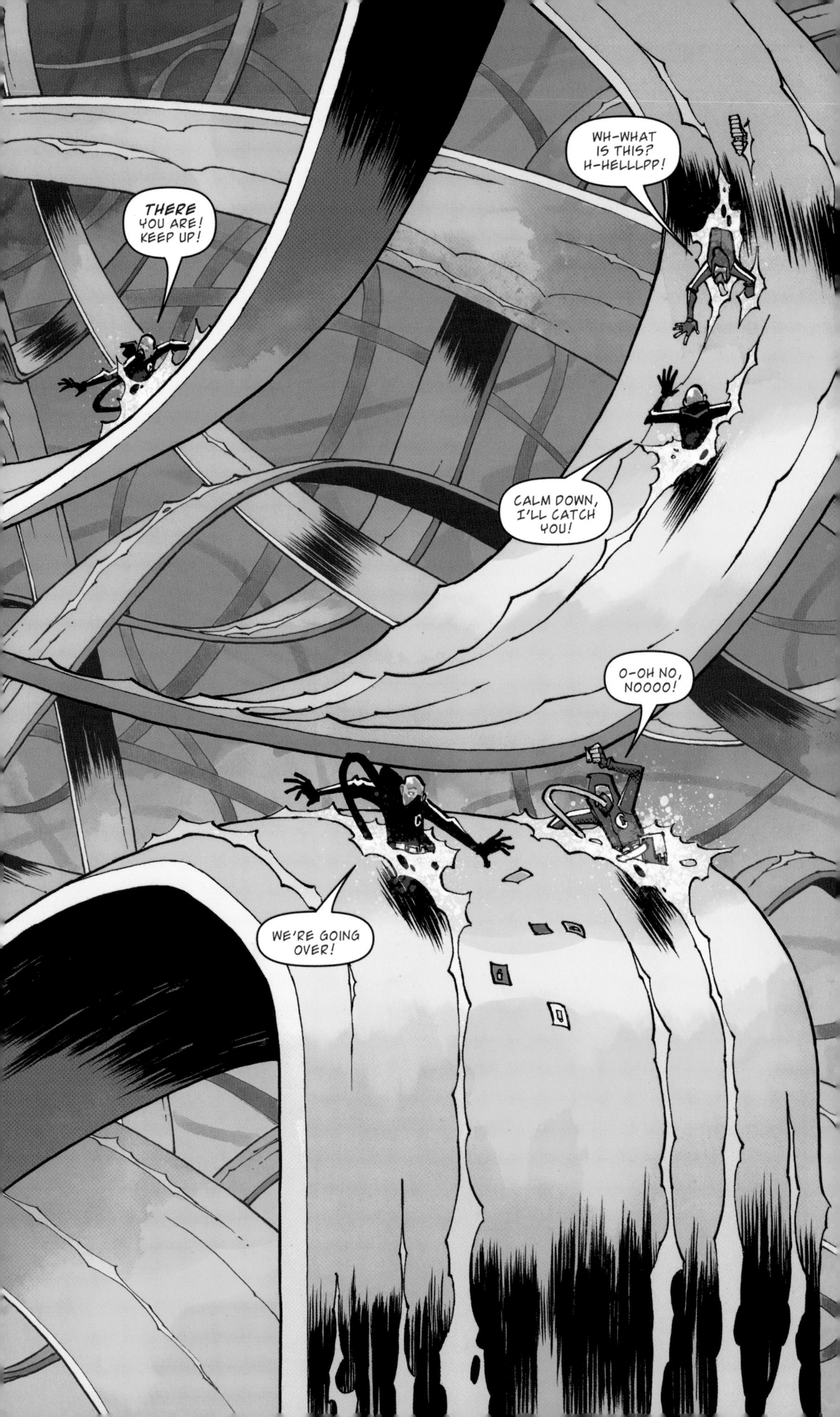
WH-WHAT IS THIS? H-HELLLPP!
THERE YOU ARE! KEEP UP!
CALM DOWN, I'LL CATCH YOU!
O-OH NO, NOOOO!
WE'RE GOING OVER!

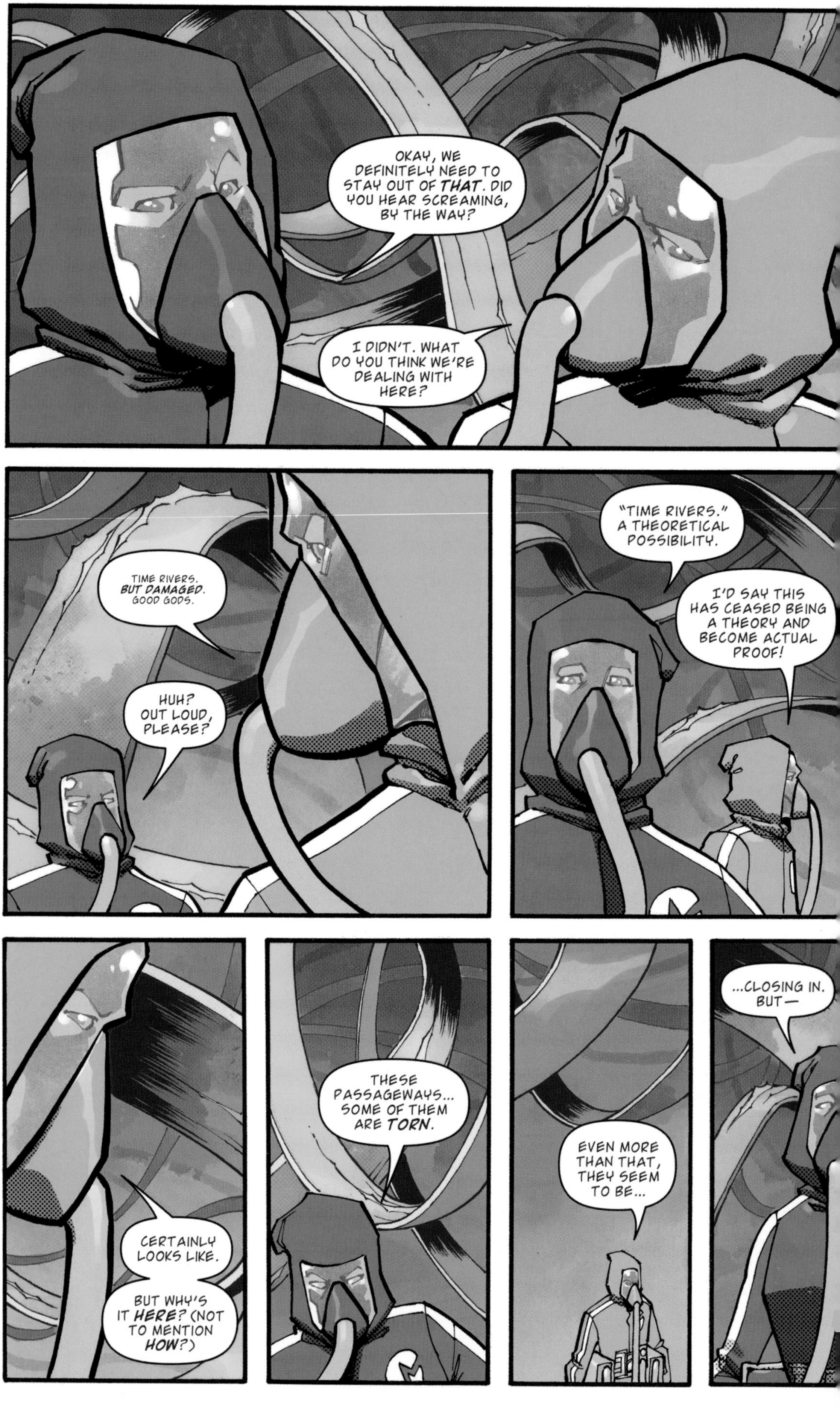
OKAY, WE DEFINITELY NEED TO STAY OUT OF THAT. DID YOU HEAR SCREAMING, BY THE WAY?
I DIDN'T. WHAT DO YOU THINK WE'RE DEALING WITH HERE?
TIME RIVERS. BUT DAMAGED. GOOD GODS.
HUH? OUT LOUD, PLEASE?
"TIME RIVERS." A THEORETICAL POSSIBILITY.
I'D SAY THIS HAS CEASED BEING A THEORY AND BECOME ACTUAL PROOF!
CERTAINLY LOOKS LIKE.
BUT WHY'S IT HERE? (NOT TO MENTION HOW?)
THESE PASSAGEWAYS... SOME OF THEM ARE TORN.
EVEN MORE THAN THAT, THEY SEEM TO BE...
...CLOSING IN. BUT—

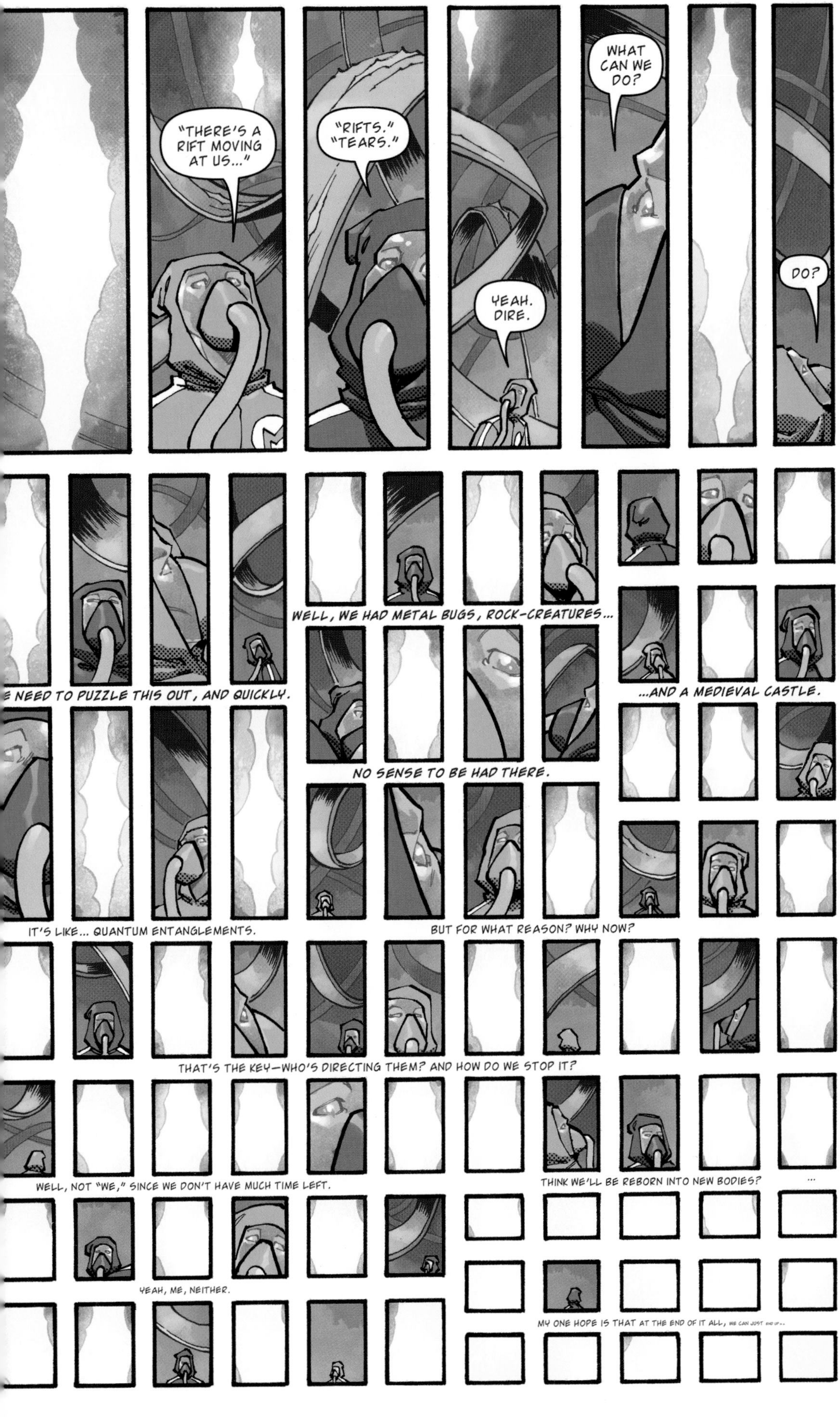

"THERE'S A RIFT MOVING AT US..."
"RIFTS." "TEARS."
YEAH. DIRE.
WHAT CAN WE DO?
DO?
E NEED TO PUZZLE THIS OUT, AND QUICKLY.
WELL, WE HAD METAL BUGS, ROCK-CREATURES...
...AND A MEDIEVAL CASTLE.
NO SENSE TO BE HAD THERE.
IT'S LIKE... QUANTUM ENTANGLEMENTS.
BUT FOR WHAT REASON? WHY NOW?
THAT'S THE KEY—WHO'S DIRECTING THEM? AND HOW DO WE STOP IT?
WELL, NOT "WE," SINCE WE DON'T HAVE MUCH TIME LEFT.
THINK WE'LL BE REBORN INTO NEW BODIES?
...
YEAH, ME, NEITHER.
MY ONE HOPE IS THAT AT THE END OF IT ALL, WE CAN JUST END UP...

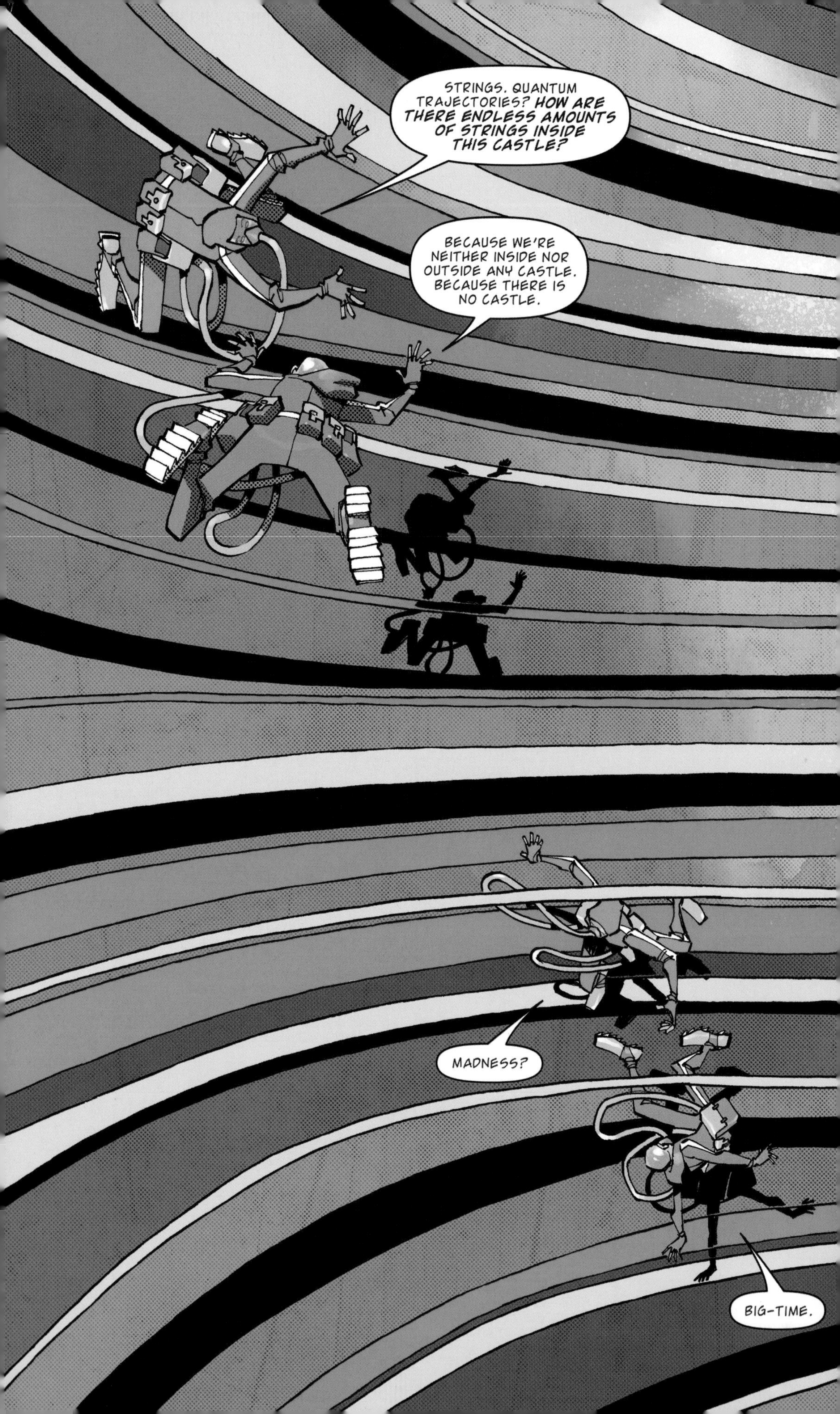
STRINGS. QUANTUM TRAJECTORIES? **HOW ARE THERE ENDLESS AMOUNTS OF STRINGS INSIDE THIS CASTLE?**
BECAUSE WE'RE NEITHER INSIDE NOR OUTSIDE ANY CASTLE. BECAUSE THERE IS NO CASTLE.
MADNESS?
BIG-TIME.

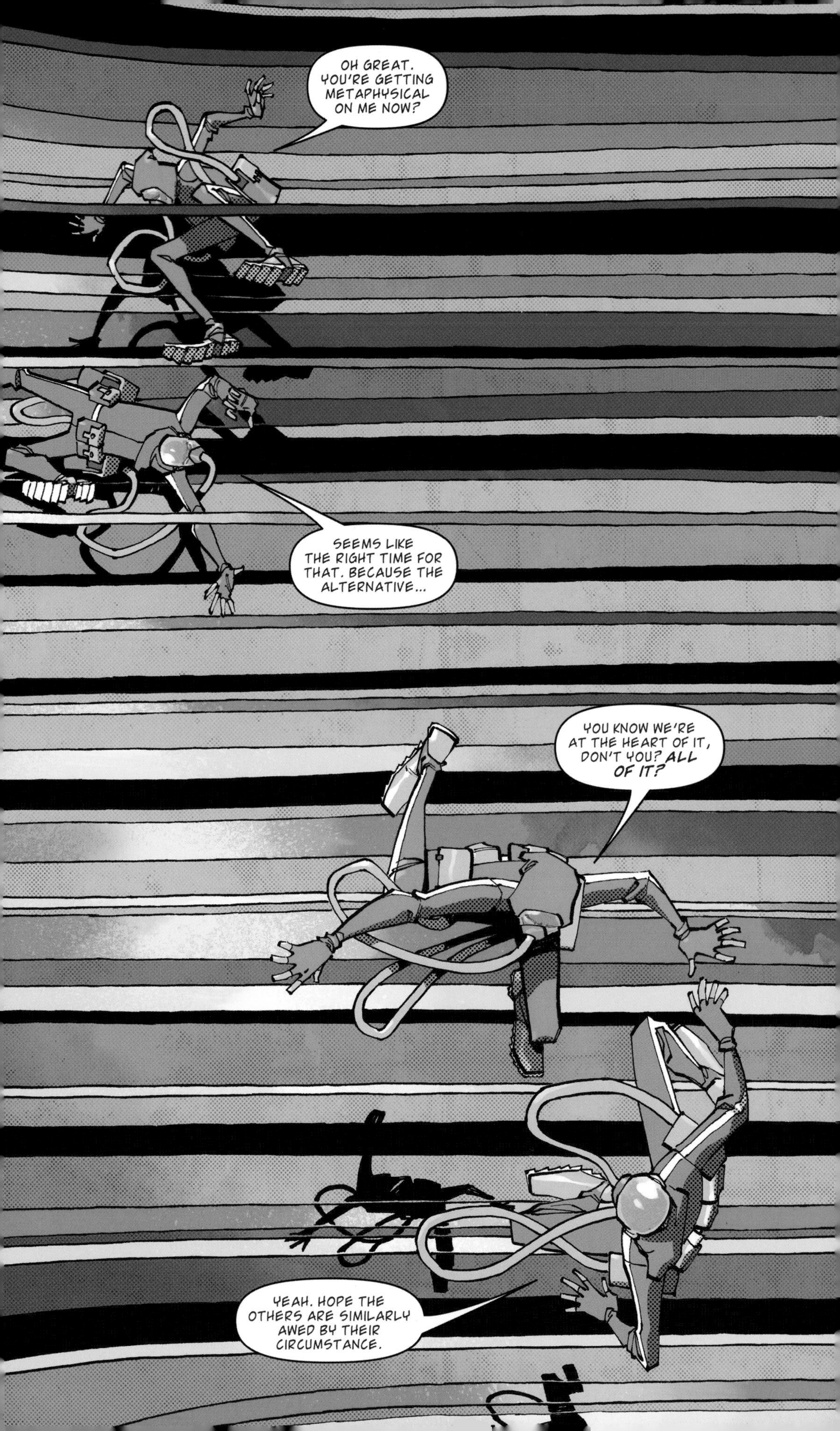
OH GREAT. YOU'RE GETTING METAPHYSICAL ON ME NOW?
SEEMS LIKE THE RIGHT TIME FOR THAT. BECAUSE THE ALTERNATIVE...
YOU KNOW WE'RE AT THE HEART OF IT, DON'T YOU? ***ALL OF IT?***
YEAH. HOPE THE OTHERS ARE SIMILARLY AWED BY THEIR CIRCUMSTANCE.

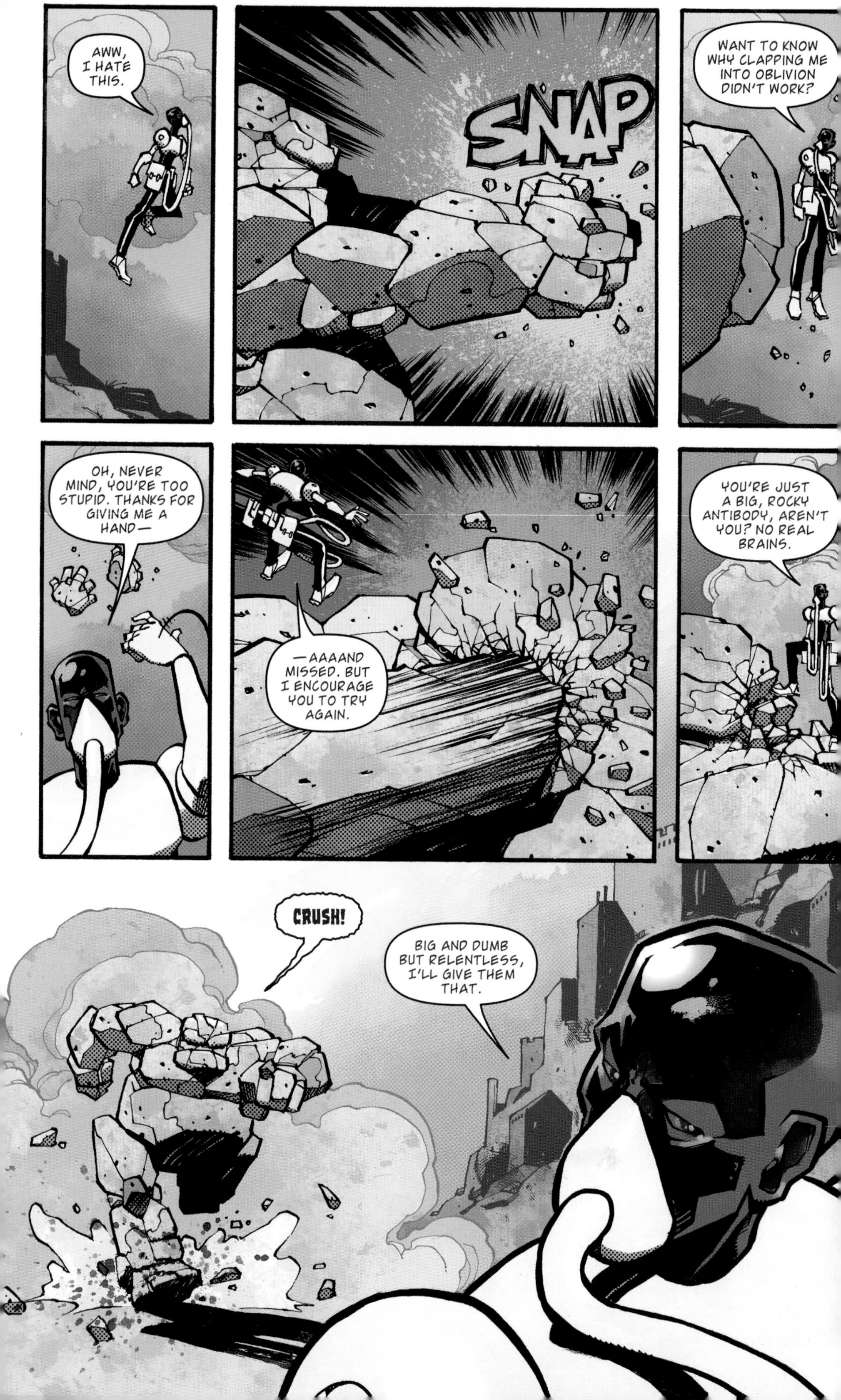
AWW, I HATE THIS.
SNAP
WANT TO KNOW WHY CLAPPING ME INTO OBLIVION DIDN'T WORK?
OH, NEVER MIND, YOU'RE TOO STUPID. THANKS FOR GIVING ME A HAND—
—AAAAND MISSED. BUT I ENCOURAGE YOU TO TRY AGAIN.
YOU'RE JUST A BIG, ROCKY ANTIBODY, AREN'T YOU? NO REAL BRAINS.
CRUSH!
BIG AND DUMB BUT RELENTLESS, I'LL GIVE THEM THAT.

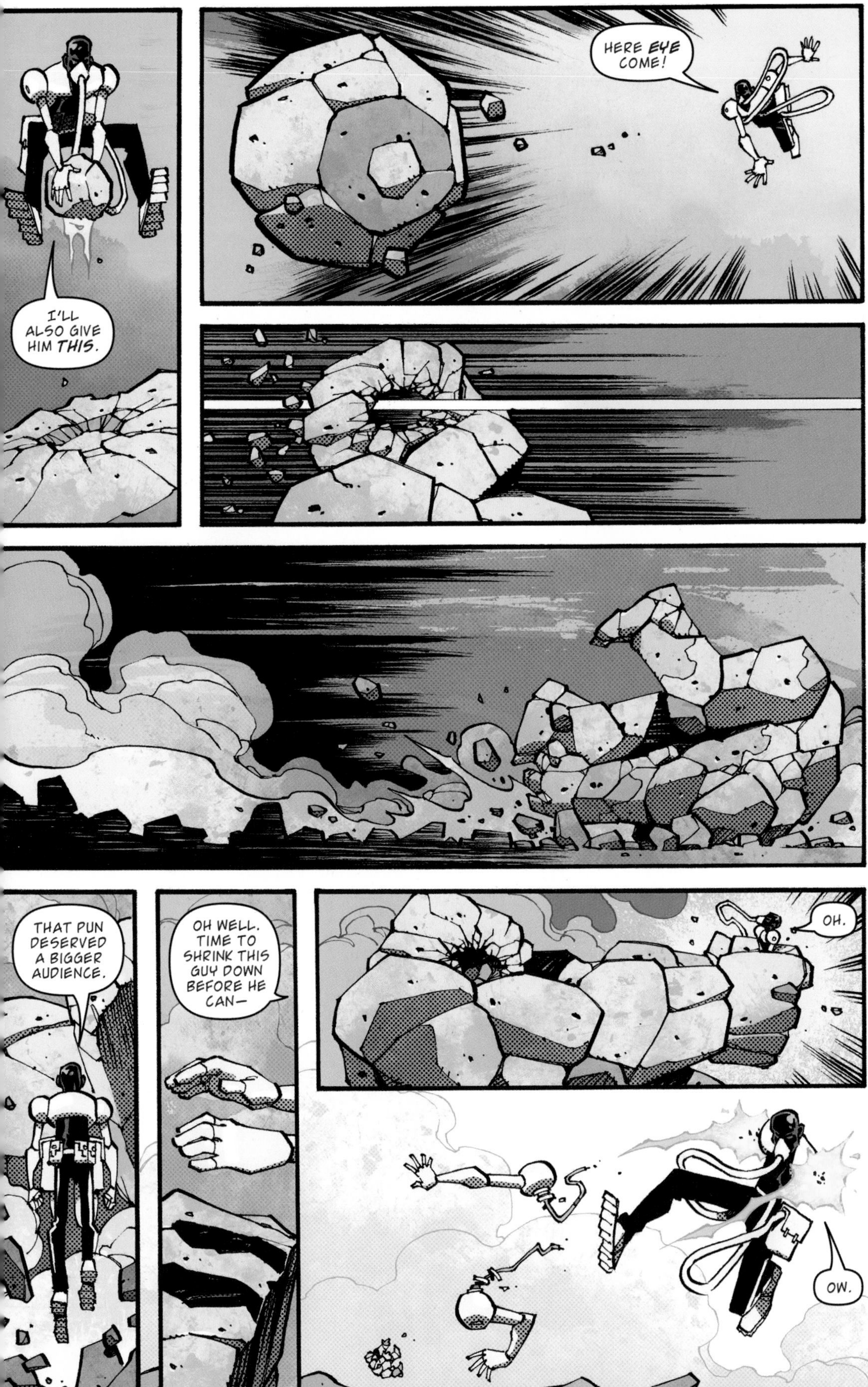
I'LL ALSO GIVE HIM *THIS*.
HERE *EYE* COME!
THAT PUN DESERVED A BIGGER AUDIENCE.
OH WELL. TIME TO SHRINK THIS GUY DOWN BEFORE HE CAN—
OH.
OW.

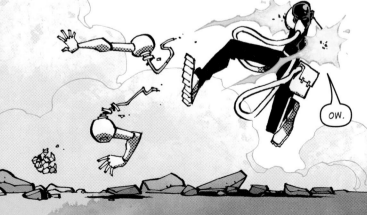

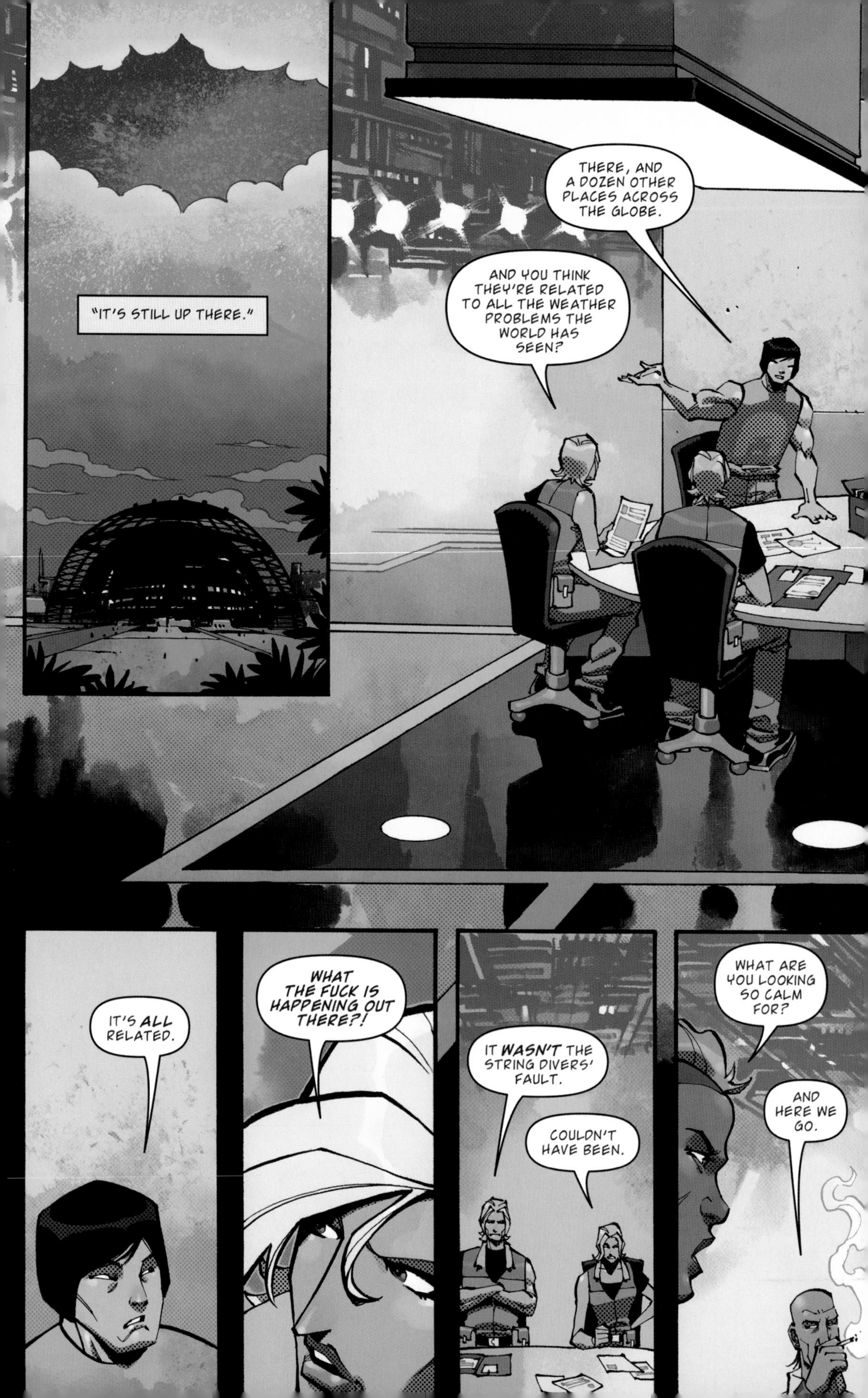
"IT'S STILL UP THERE."
THERE, AND A DOZEN OTHER PLACES ACROSS THE GLOBE.
AND YOU THINK THEY'RE RELATED TO ALL THE WEATHER PROBLEMS THE WORLD HAS SEEN?
IT'S ALL RELATED.
WHAT THE FUCK IS HAPPENING OUT THERE?!
IT WASN'T THE STRING DIVERS' FAULT.
COULDN'T HAVE BEEN.
WHAT ARE YOU LOOKING SO CALM FOR?
AND HERE WE GO.

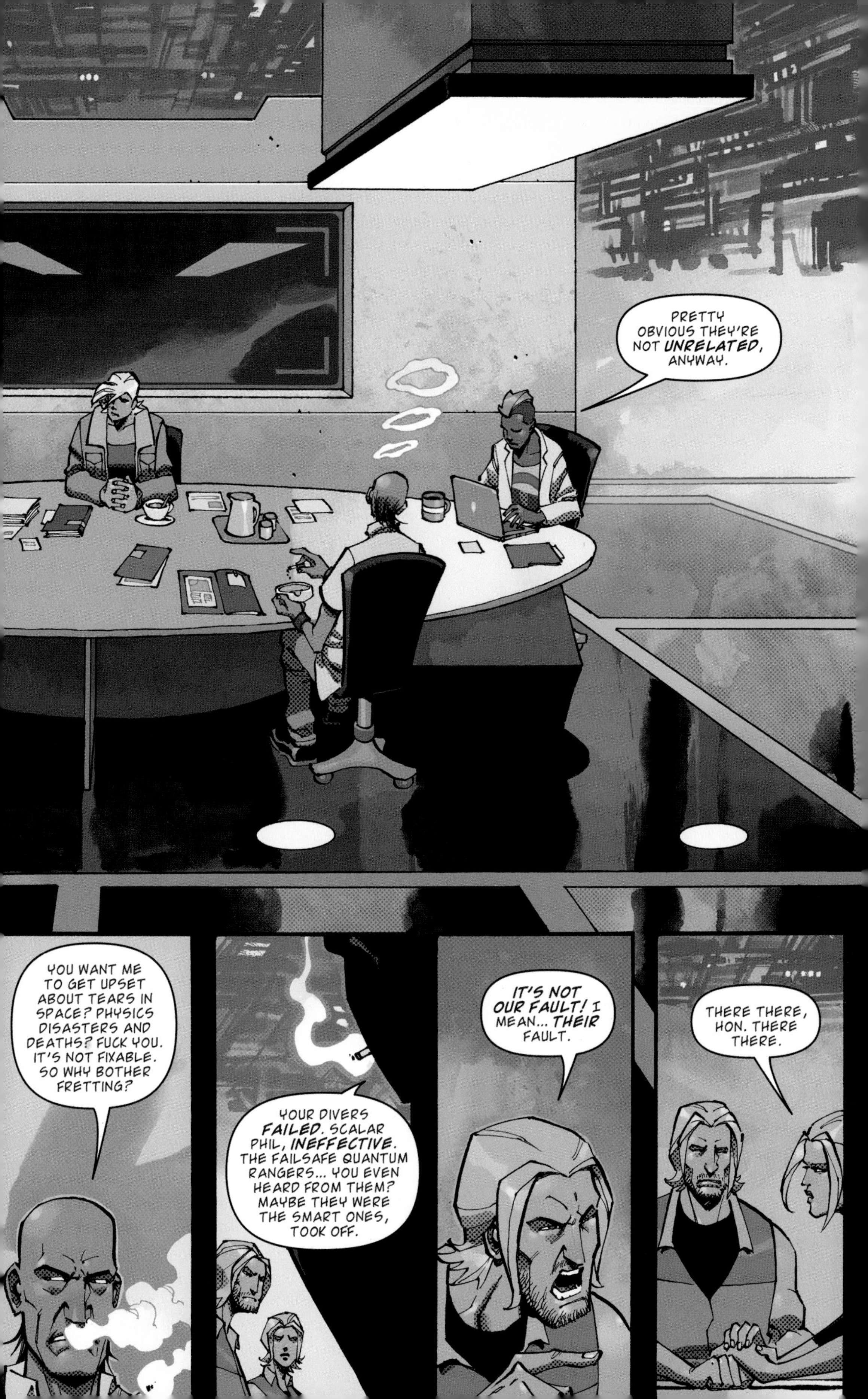
PRETTY OBVIOUS THEY'RE NOT UNRELATED, ANYWAY.
YOU WANT ME TO GET UPSET ABOUT TEARS IN SPACE? PHYSICS DISASTERS AND DEATHS? FUCK YOU. IT'S NOT FIXABLE. SO WHY BOTHER FRETTING?
YOUR DIVERS FAILED. SCALAR PHIL, INEFFECTIVE. THE FAILSAFE QUANTUM RANGERS... YOU EVEN HEARD FROM THEM? MAYBE THEY WERE THE SMART ONES, TOOK OFF.
IT'S NOT OUR FAULT! I MEAN... THEIR FAULT.
THERE THERE, HON. THERE THERE.

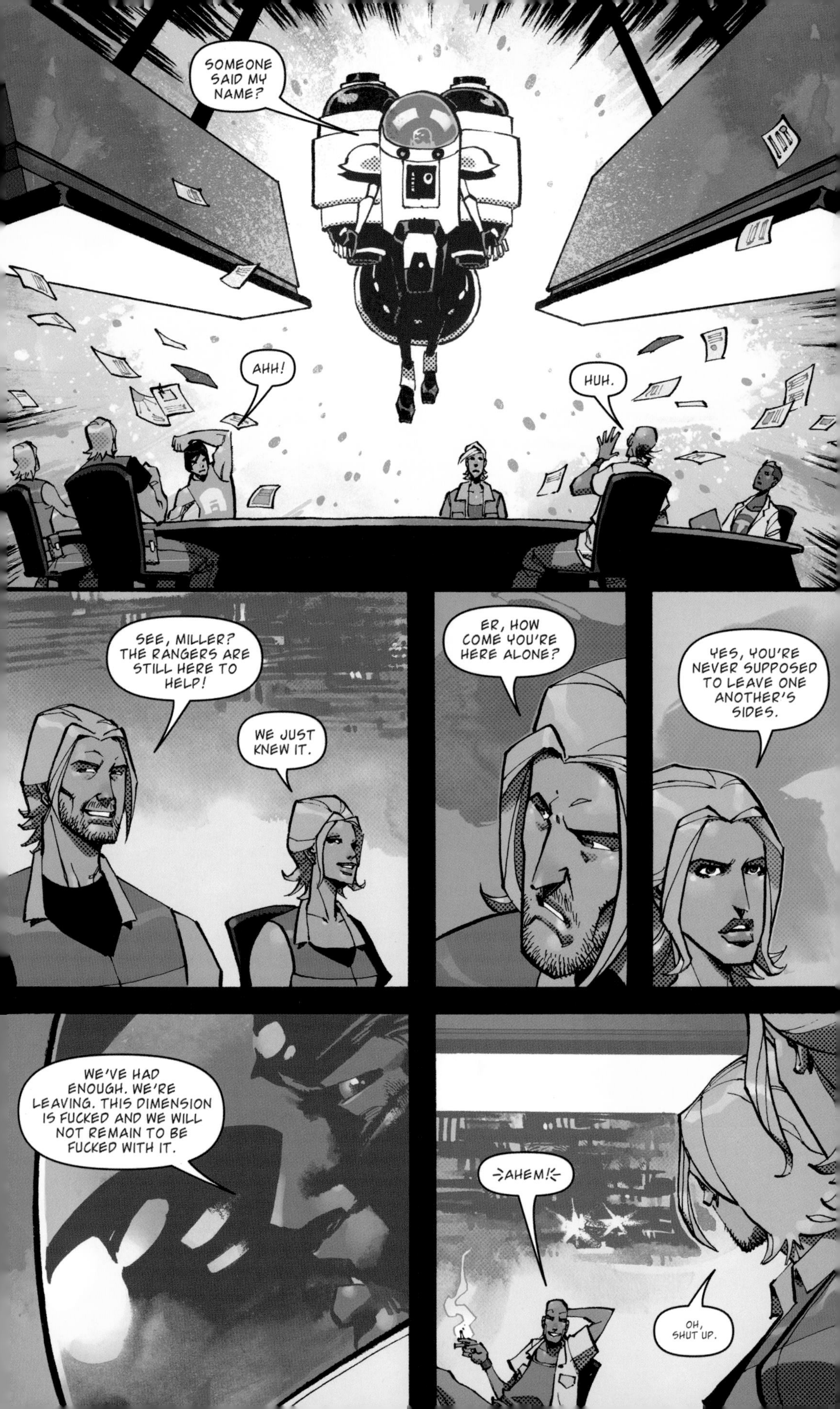
SOMEONE SAID MY NAME?
AHH!
HUH.
SEE, MILLER? THE RANGERS ARE STILL HERE TO HELP!
WE JUST KNEW IT.
ER, HOW COME YOU'RE HERE ALONE?
YES, YOU'RE NEVER SUPPOSED TO LEAVE ONE ANOTHER'S SIDES.
WE'VE HAD ENOUGH. WE'RE LEAVING. THIS DIMENSION IS FUCKED AND WE WILL NOT REMAIN TO BE FUCKED WITH IT.
AHEM!
OH, SHUT UP.

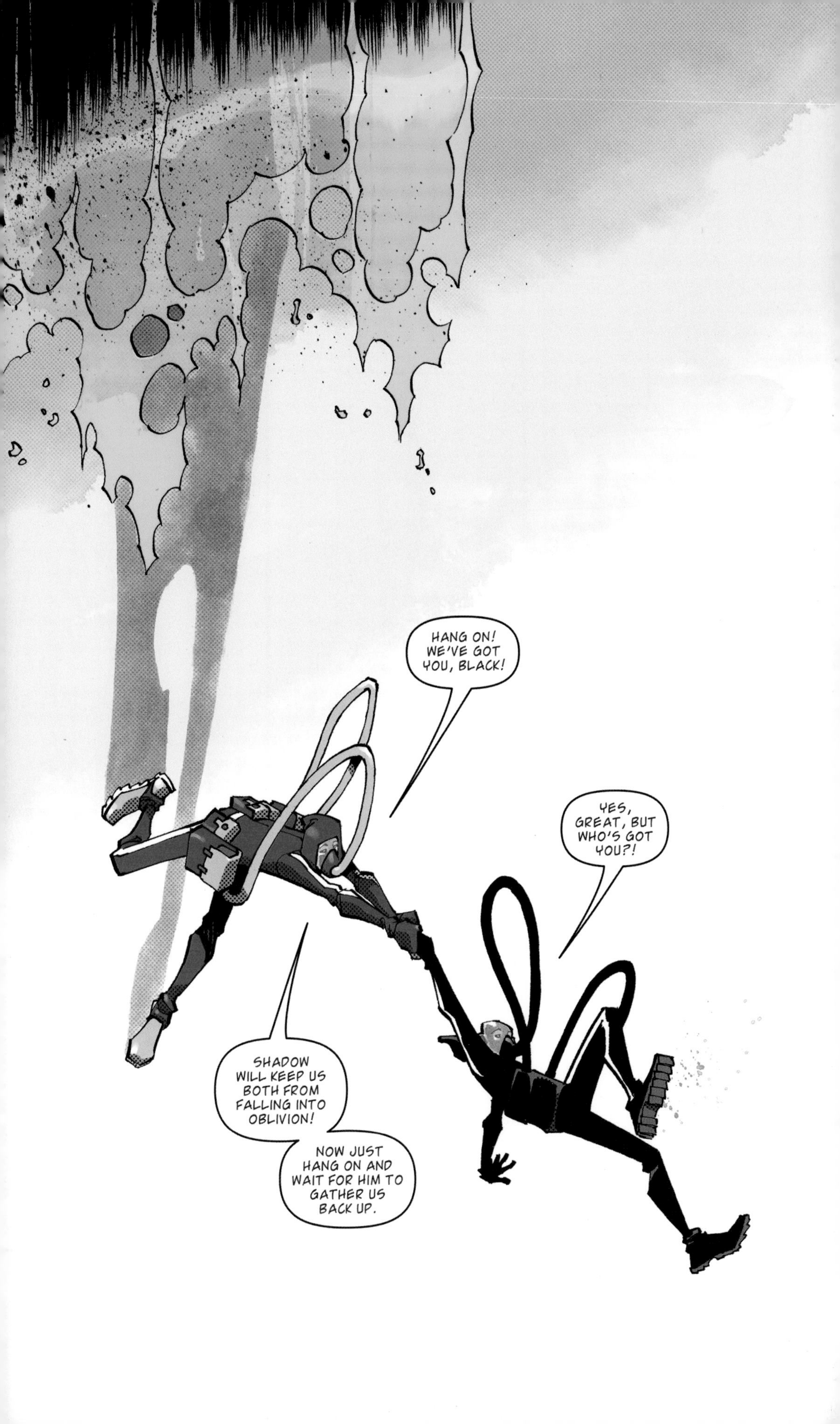
HANG ON! WE'VE GOT YOU, BLACK!
YES, GREAT, BUT WHO'S GOT YOU?!
SHADOW WILL KEEP US BOTH FROM FALLING INTO OBLIVION!
NOW JUST HANG ON AND WAIT FOR HIM TO GATHER US BACK UP.

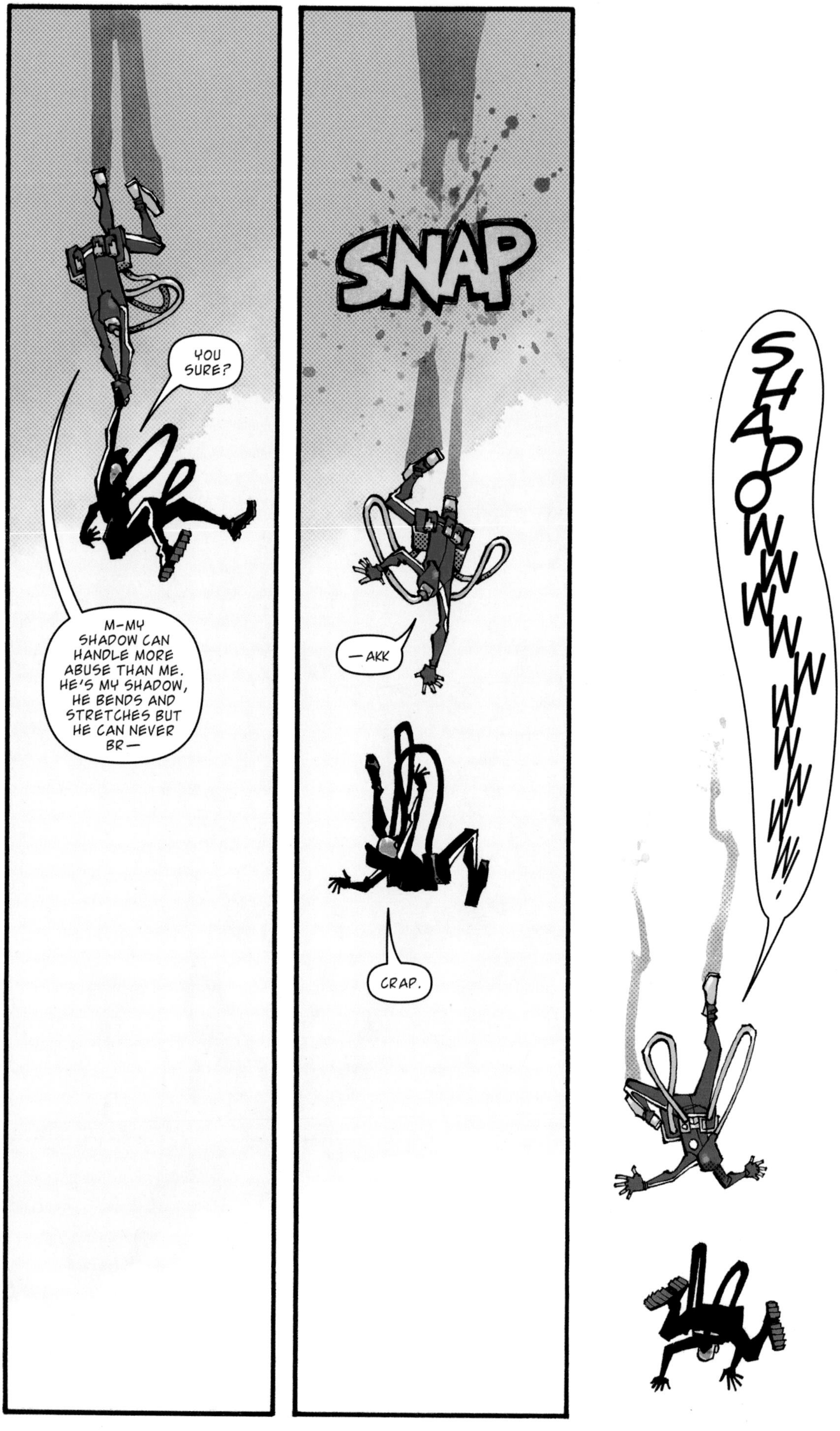
YOU SURE?
M-MY SHADOW CAN HANDLE MORE ABUSE THAN ME. HE'S MY SHADOW, HE BENDS AND STRETCHES BUT HE CAN NEVER BR—
SNAP
—AKK
CRAP.
SHADOWWWWWWWWW!

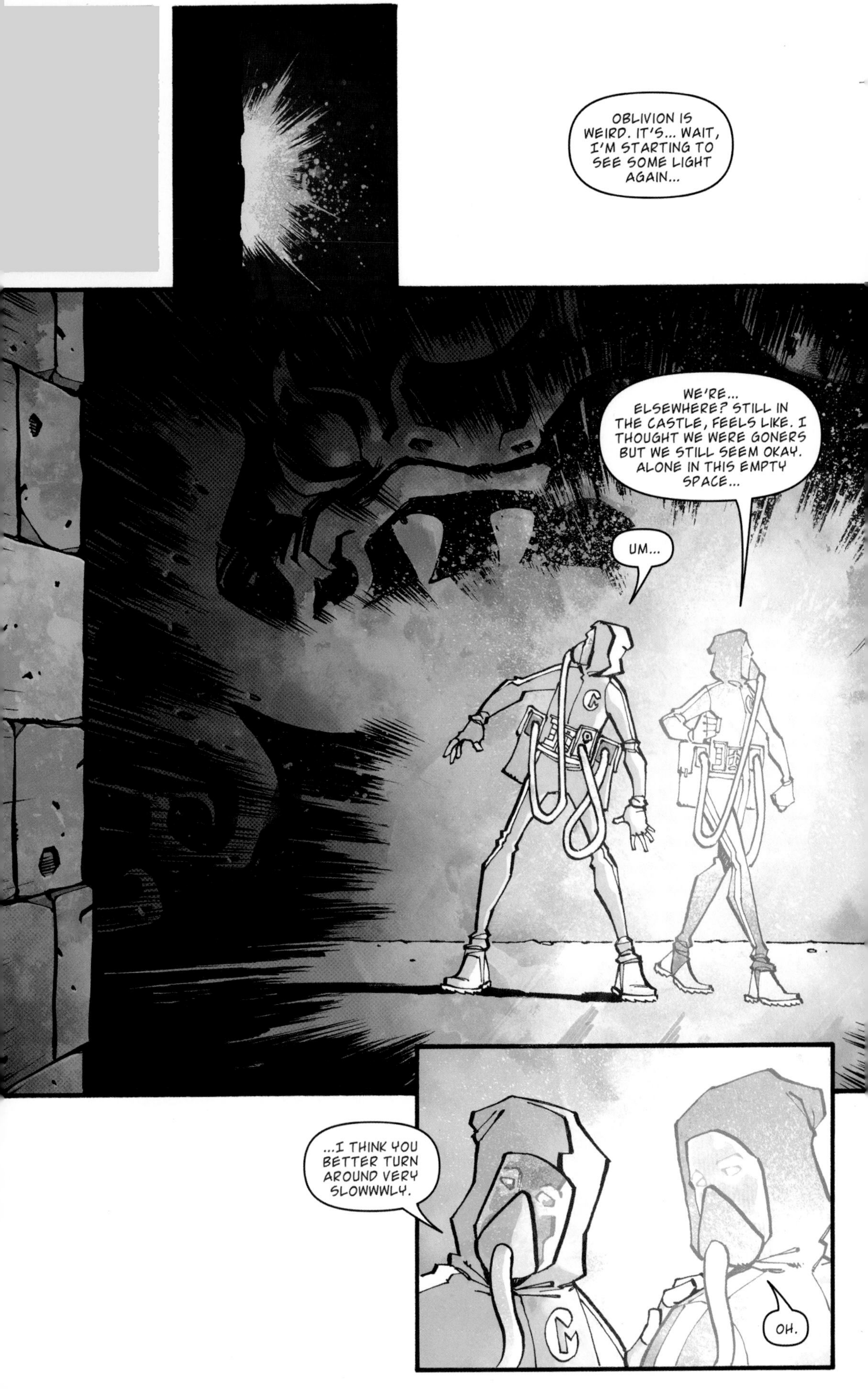
OBLIVION IS WEIRD. IT'S... WAIT, I'M STARTING TO SEE SOME LIGHT AGAIN...
WE'RE... ELSEWHERE? STILL IN THE CASTLE, FEELS LIKE. I THOUGHT WE WERE GONERS BUT WE STILL SEEM OKAY. ALONE IN THIS EMPTY SPACE...
UM...
...I THINK YOU BETTER TURN AROUND VERY SLOWWWLY.
OH.

THESE STRINGS ARE LOVELY.
I FEEL SO SERENE HERE AMONGST THEM. I THINK ALL THAT "CALOR MORTEM" TALK WAS JUST PARROTED BABBLE FROM THOSE BARELY SENTIENT ROCK-THINGS.

IT'S NOT AS THOUGH THERE COULD REALLY BE SOME MALEVOLENT PRESENCE HERE AT THE HEART OF CREATION.
UH...

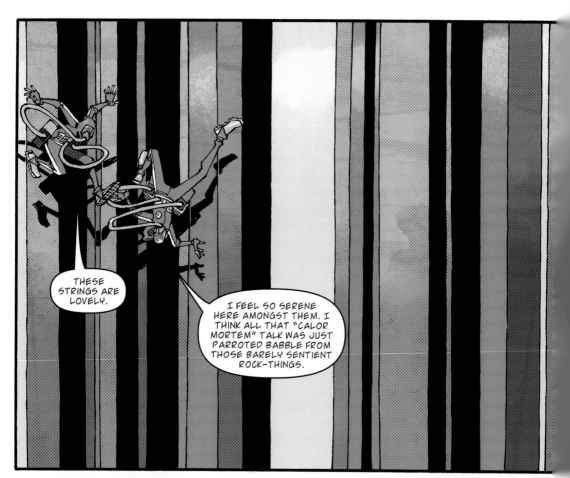

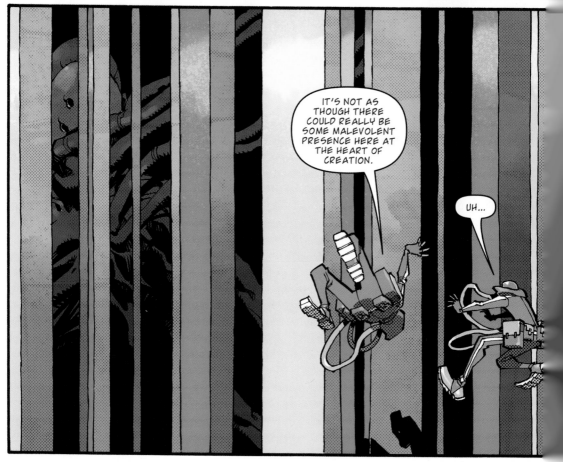

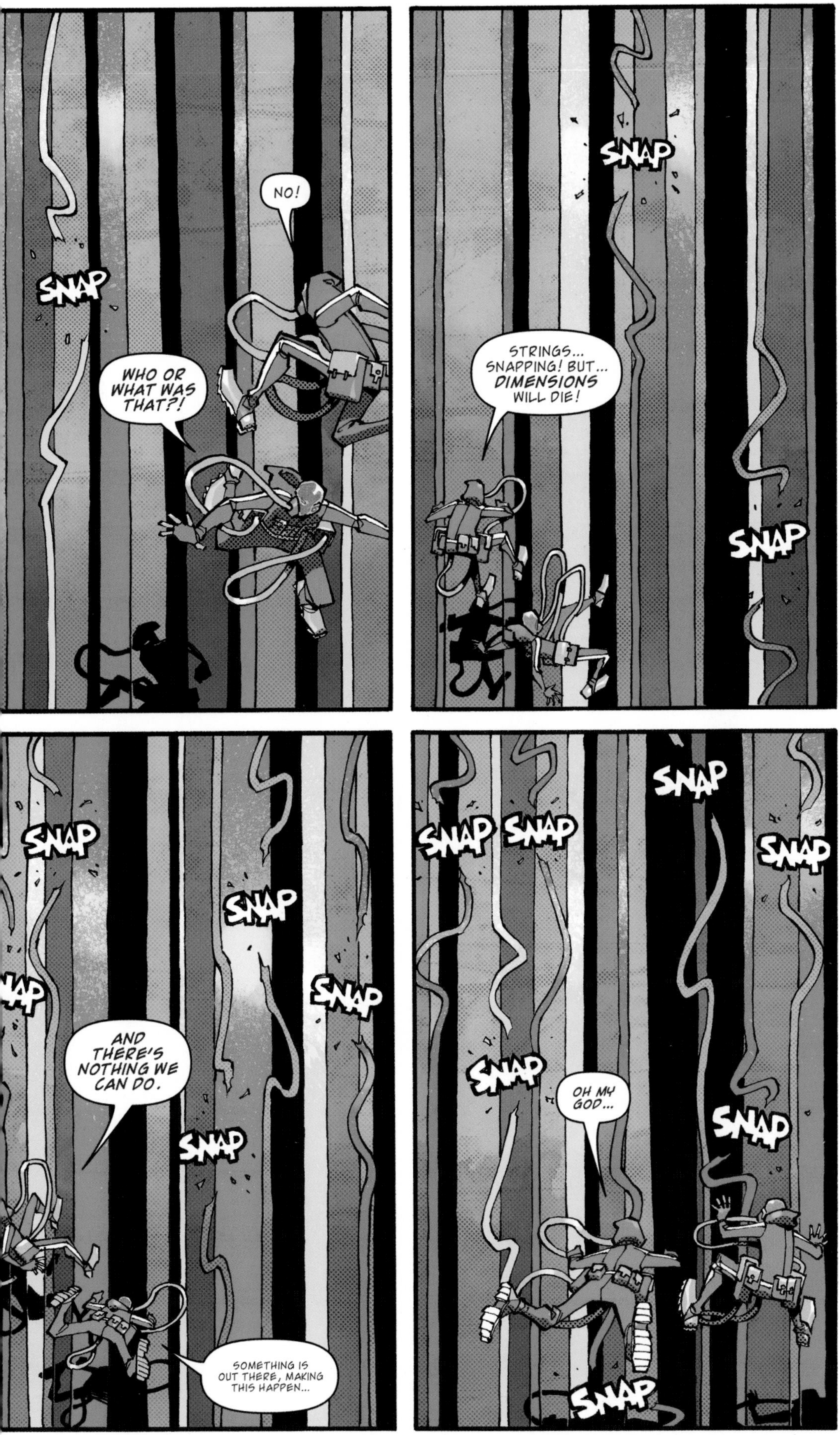
NO!
SNAP
WHO OR WHAT WAS THAT?!
SNAP
STRINGS... SNAPPING! BUT... DIMENSIONS WILL DIE!
SNAP
SNAP
SNAP
SNAP
AND THERE'S NOTHING WE CAN DO.
SNAP
SOMETHING IS OUT THERE, MAKING THIS HAPPEN...
SNAP
SNAP
SNAP
SNAP
SNAP
OH MY GOD...
SNAP
SNAP

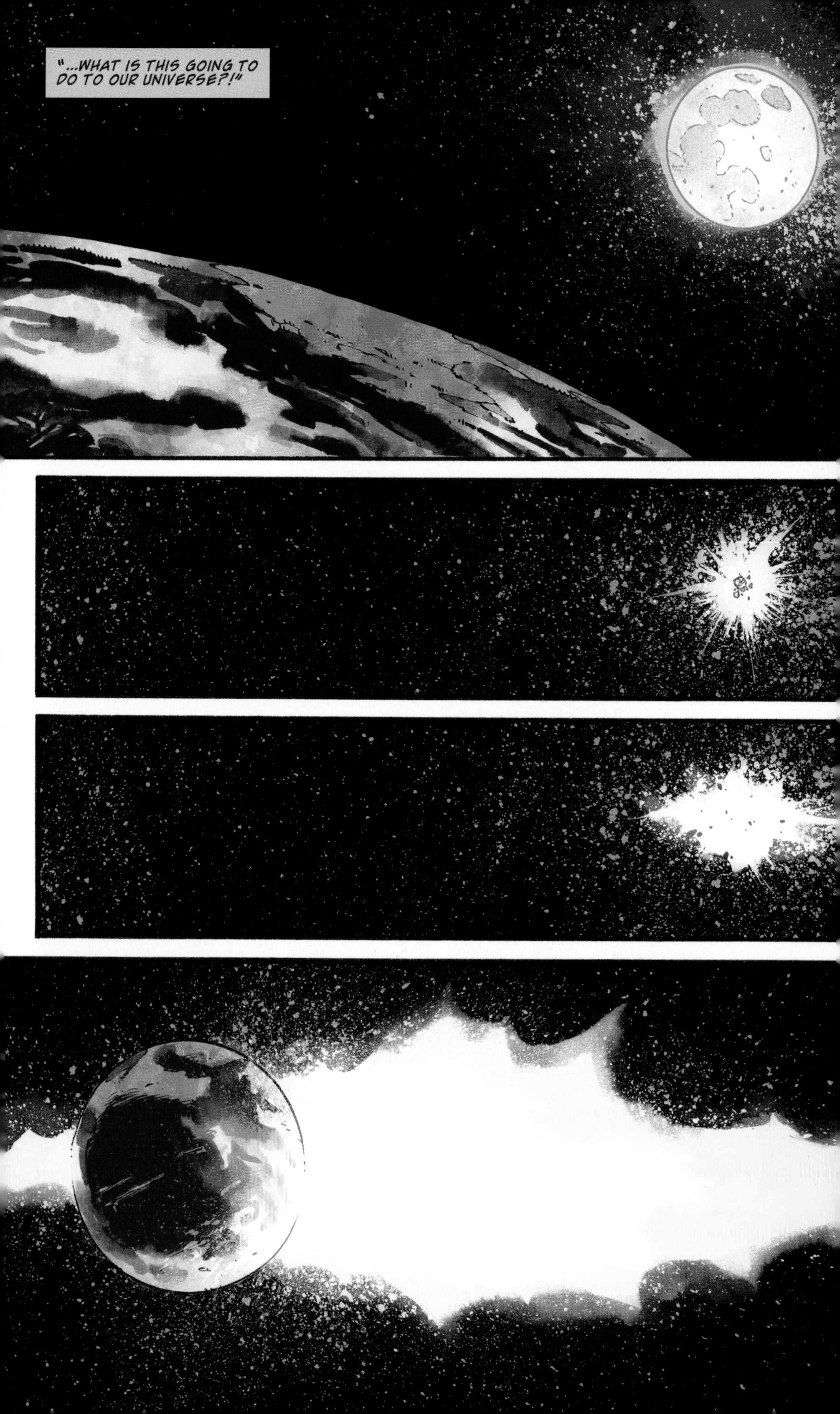
"...WHAT IS THIS GOING TO DO TO OUR UNIVERSE?!"

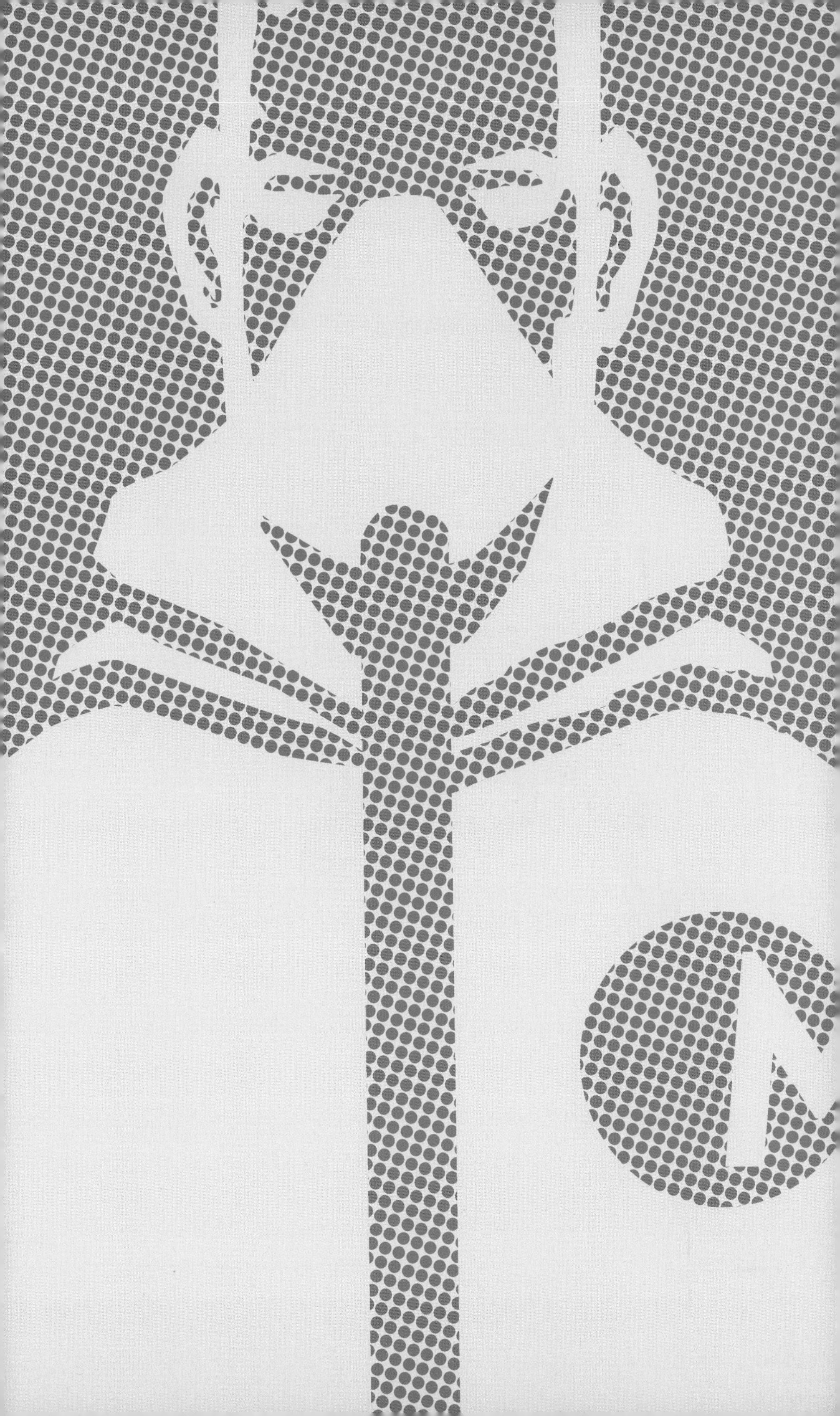

05 | ART BY NELSON DÁNIEL

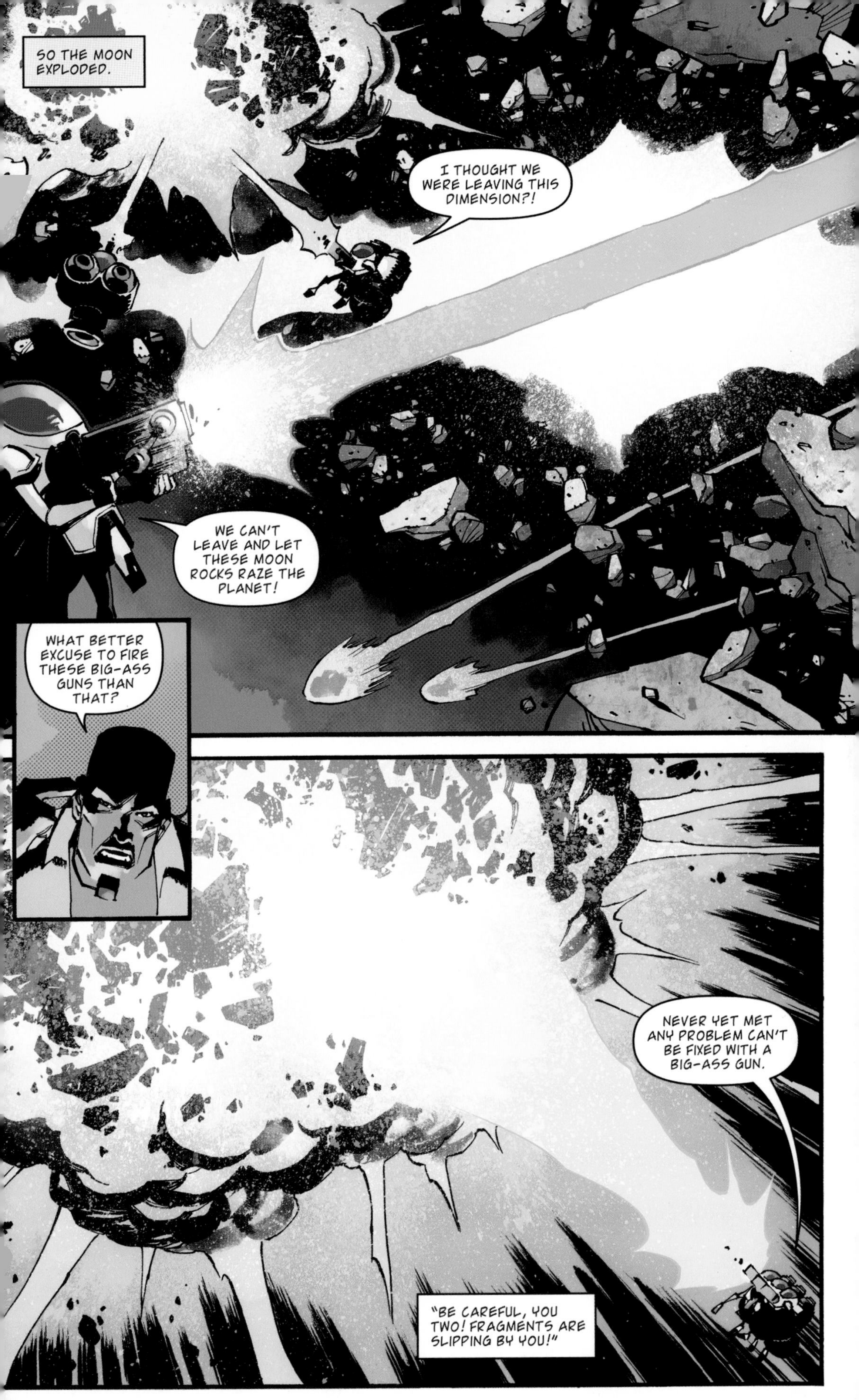

SO THE MOON EXPLODED.
I THOUGHT WE WERE LEAVING THIS DIMENSION?!
WE CAN'T LEAVE AND LET THESE MOON ROCKS RAZE THE PLANET!
WHAT BETTER EXCUSE TO FIRE THESE BIG-ASS GUNS THAN THAT?
NEVER YET MET ANY PROBLEM CAN'T BE FIXED WITH A BIG-ASS GUN.
"BE CAREFUL, YOU TWO! FRAGMENTS ARE SLIPPING BY YOU!"

STRING DIVERS

UNIFIED CHAOS THEORY, part 5

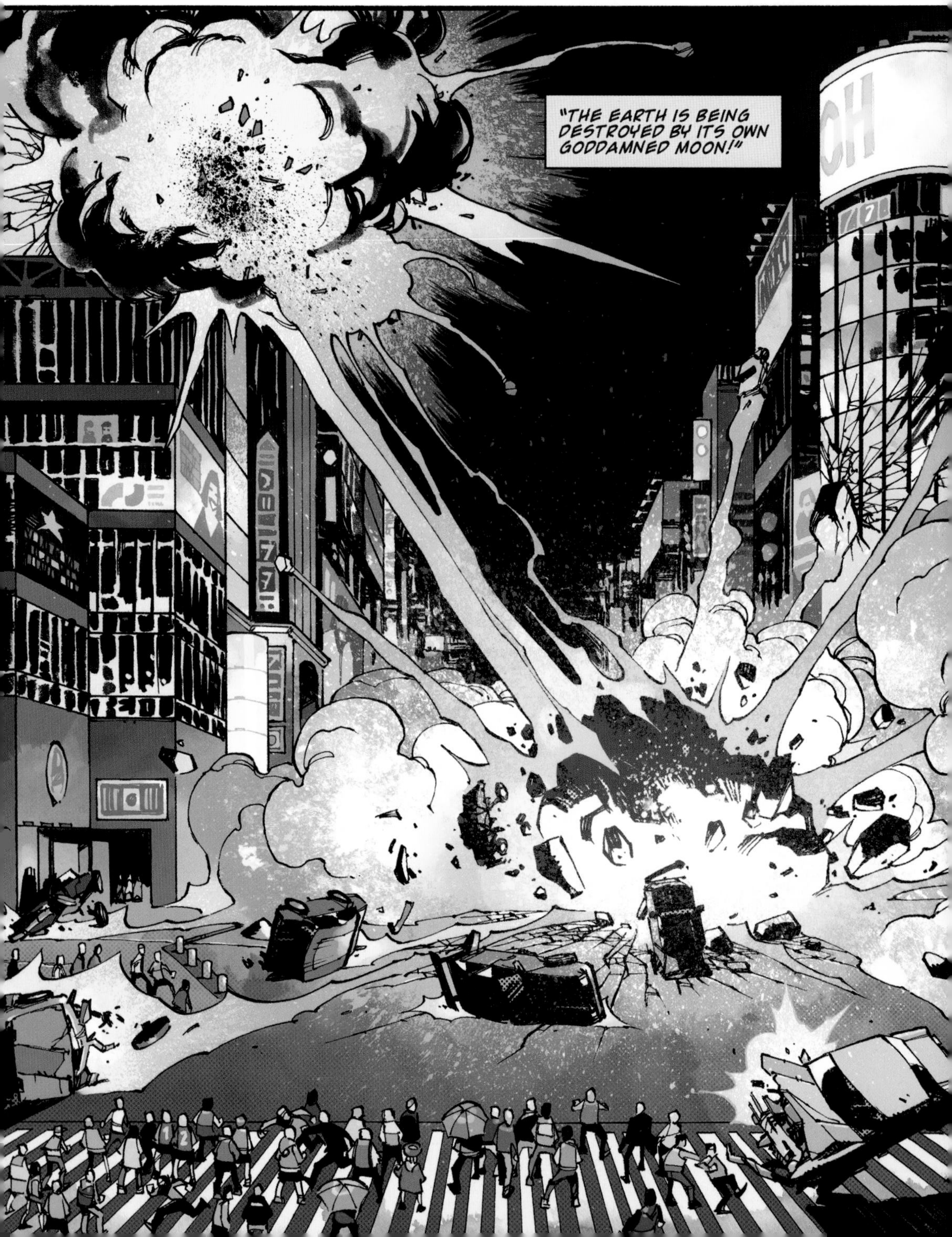
"THE EARTH IS BEING DESTROYED BY ITS OWN GODDAMNED MOON!"

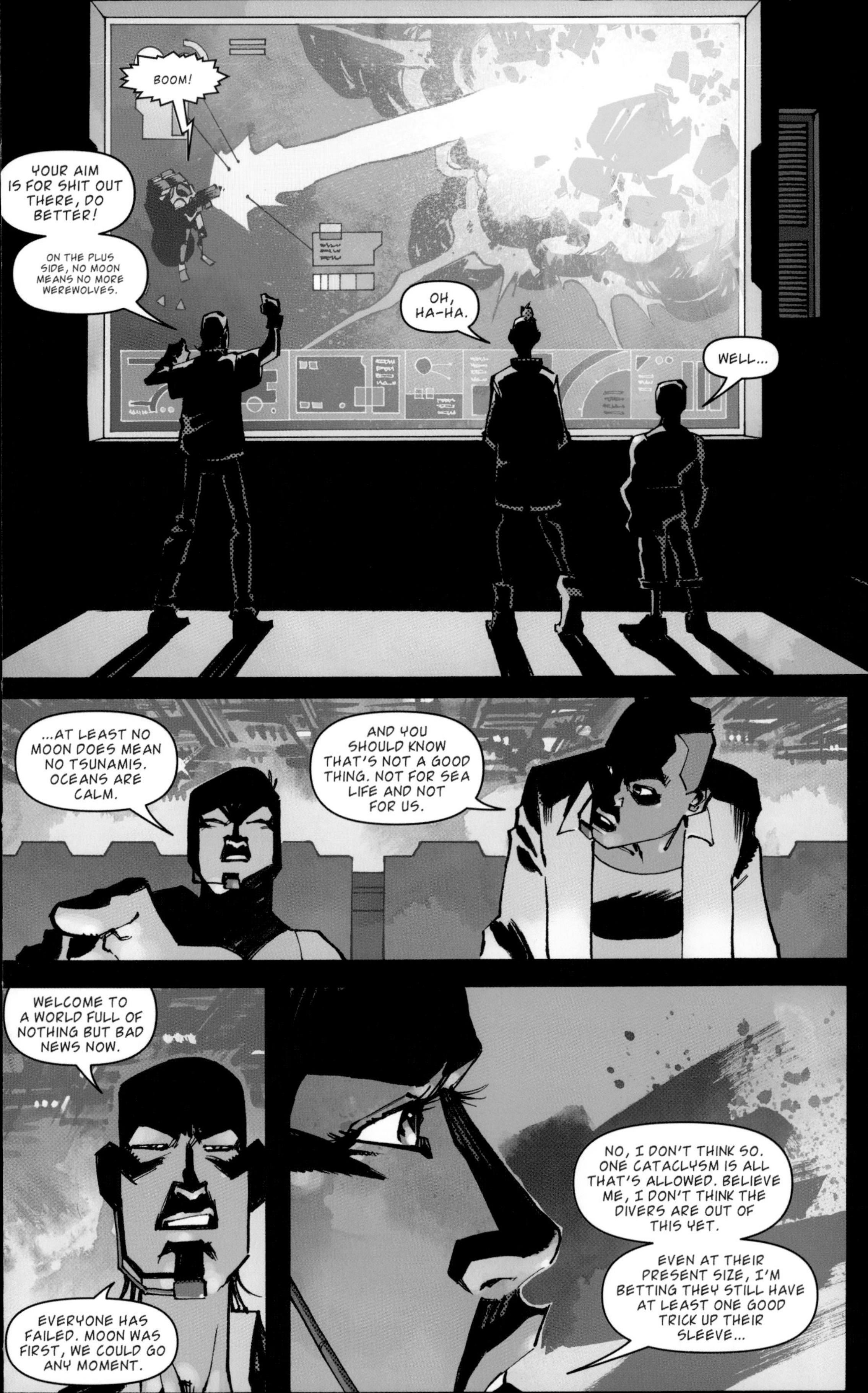
BOOM!
YOUR AIM IS FOR SHIT OUT THERE, DO BETTER!
ON THE PLUS SIDE, NO MOON MEANS NO MORE WEREWOLVES.
OH, HA-HA.
WELL...
...AT LEAST NO MOON DOES MEAN NO TSUNAMIS. OCEANS ARE CALM.
AND YOU SHOULD KNOW THAT'S NOT A GOOD THING. NOT FOR SEA LIFE AND NOT FOR US.
WELCOME TO A WORLD FULL OF NOTHING BUT BAD NEWS NOW.
EVERYONE HAS FAILED. MOON WAS FIRST, WE COULD GO ANY MOMENT.
NO, I DON'T THINK SO. ONE CATACLYSM IS ALL THAT'S ALLOWED. BELIEVE ME, I DON'T THINK THE DIVERS ARE OUT OF THIS YET.
EVEN AT THEIR PRESENT SIZE, I'M BETTING THEY STILL HAVE AT LEAST ONE GOOD TRICK UP THEIR SLEEVE...

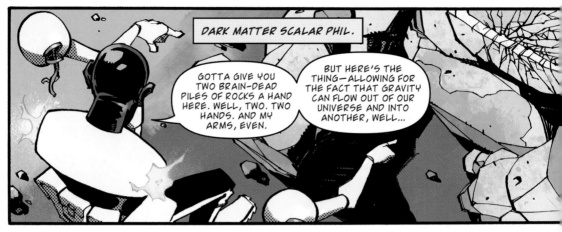

DARK MATTER SCALAR PHIL.

GOTTA GIVE YOU TWO BRAIN-DEAD PILES OF ROCKS A HAND HERE. WELL, TWO. TWO HANDS. AND MY ARMS, EVEN.

BUT HERE'S THE THING—ALLOWING FOR THE FACT THAT GRAVITY CAN FLOW OUT OF OUR UNIVERSE AND INTO ANOTHER, WELL...

RED AND BLACK...

IT WON'T COME OFF, I CAN'T GET MY SHADOW OFF ME. IT'S DEAD AND IT WON'T COME OFF!

HEY, COME HERE—I'VE GOT SOMETHING THAT'LL HELP...

BLUE AND PURPLE.

EASY, BIG BOY, EEEEEASSSSYYY...

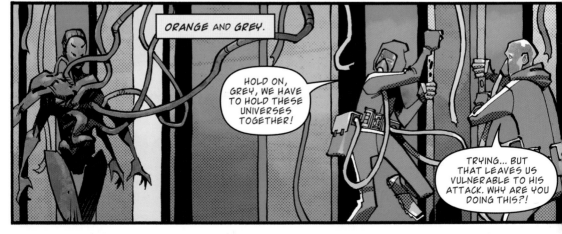

ORANGE AND GREY.

HOLD ON, GREY, WE HAVE TO HOLD THESE UNIVERSES TOGETHER!

TRYING... BUT THAT LEAVES US VULNERABLE TO HIS ATTACK. WHY ARE YOU DOING THIS?!

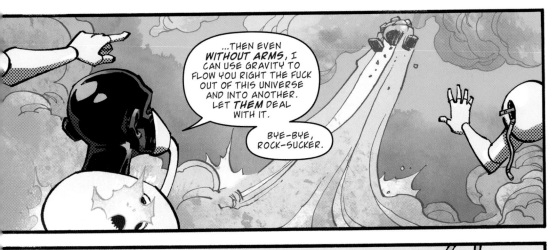

...THEN EVEN *WITHOUT ARMS*, I CAN USE GRAVITY TO FLOW YOU RIGHT THE FUCK OUT OF THIS UNIVERSE AND INTO ANOTHER. LET *THEM* DEAL WITH IT.

BYE-BYE, ROCK-SUCKER.

...AND *WHITE*.

WHAT IS *THAT* DOING HERE?!

HE'S HERE TO HELP. BUT THERE'S BAD NEWS WITH THE GOOD.

HAHA, HE'S... LICKING US?!

SO... MUCH... SLOBBER!

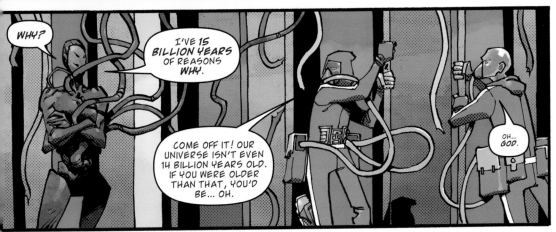

WHY?

I'VE *15 BILLION YEARS* OF REASONS *WHY*.

COME OFF IT! OUR UNIVERSE ISN'T EVEN 14 BILLION YEARS OLD. IF YOU WERE OLDER THAN THAT, YOU'D BE... OH.

OH... GOD.

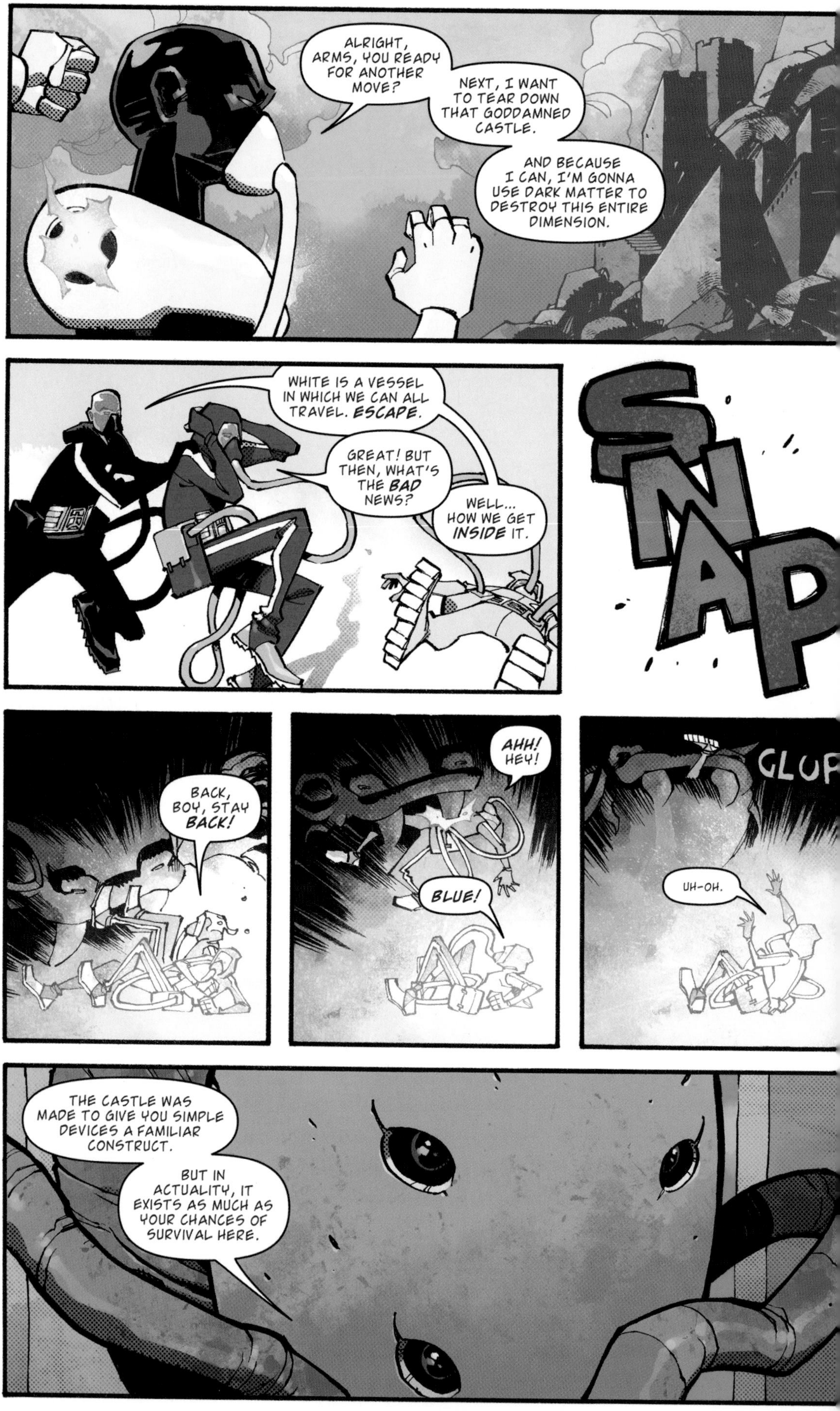
ALRIGHT, ARMS, YOU READY FOR ANOTHER MOVE?
NEXT, I WANT TO TEAR DOWN THAT GODDAMNED CASTLE.
AND BECAUSE I CAN, I'M GONNA USE DARK MATTER TO DESTROY THIS ENTIRE DIMENSION.
WHITE IS A VESSEL IN WHICH WE CAN ALL TRAVEL. ESCAPE.
GREAT! BUT THEN, WHAT'S THE BAD NEWS?
WELL... HOW WE GET INSIDE IT.
SNAP
BACK, BOY, STAY BACK!
AHH! HEY!
BLUE!
GLUP
UH-OH.
THE CASTLE WAS MADE TO GIVE YOU SIMPLE DEVICES A FAMILIAR CONSTRUCT.
BUT IN ACTUALITY, IT EXISTS AS MUCH AS YOUR CHANCES OF SURVIVAL HERE.

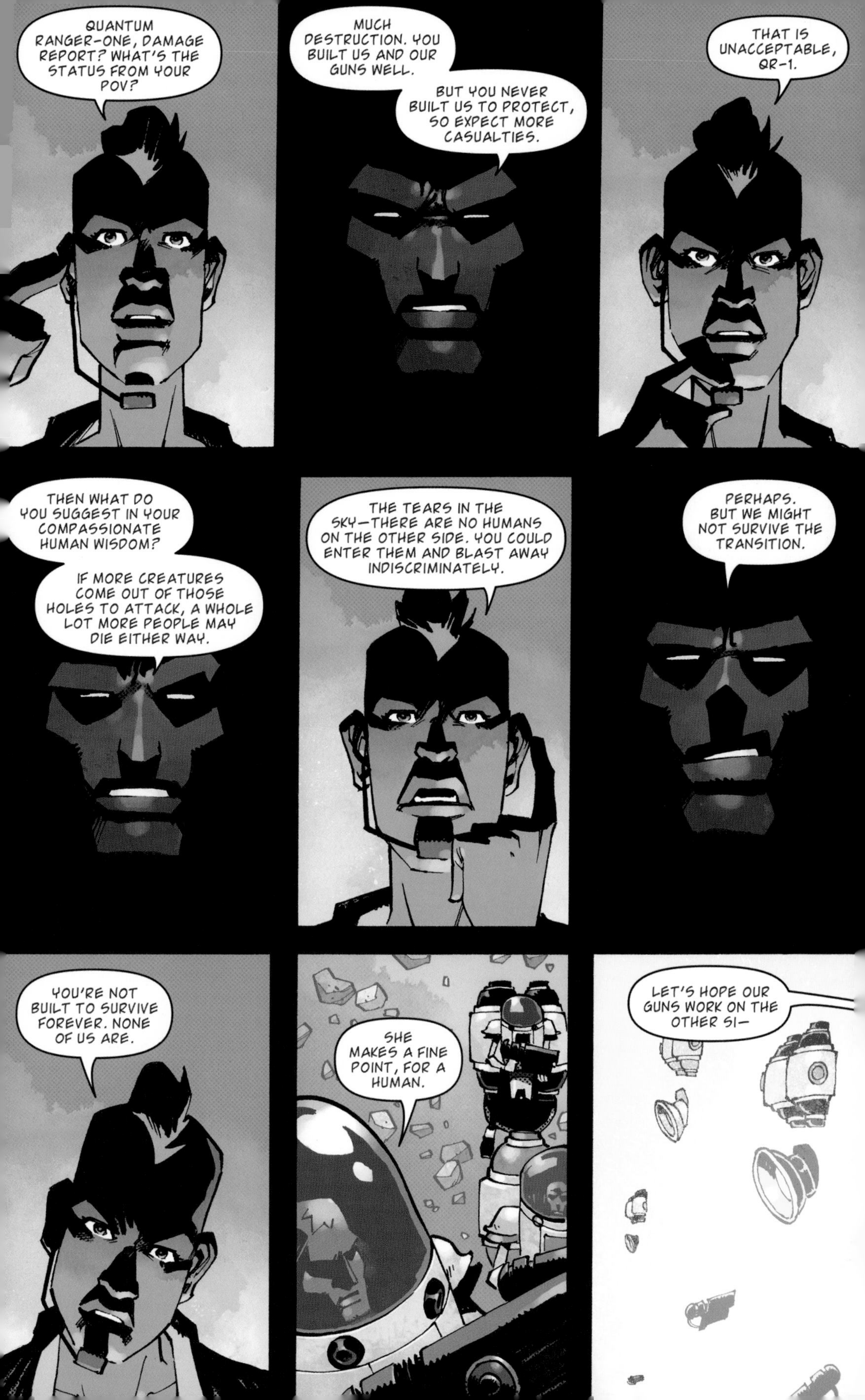
QUANTUM RANGER-ONE, DAMAGE REPORT? WHAT'S THE STATUS FROM YOUR POV?
MUCH DESTRUCTION. YOU BUILT US AND OUR GUNS WELL.
BUT YOU NEVER BUILT US TO PROTECT, SO EXPECT MORE CASUALTIES.
THAT IS UNACCEPTABLE, QR-1.
THEN WHAT DO YOU SUGGEST IN YOUR COMPASSIONATE HUMAN WISDOM?
IF MORE CREATURES COME OUT OF THOSE HOLES TO ATTACK, A WHOLE LOT MORE PEOPLE MAY DIE EITHER WAY.
THE TEARS IN THE SKY—THERE ARE NO HUMANS ON THE OTHER SIDE. YOU COULD ENTER THEM AND BLAST AWAY INDISCRIMINATELY.
PERHAPS. BUT WE MIGHT NOT SURVIVE THE TRANSITION.
YOU'RE NOT BUILT TO SURVIVE FOREVER. NONE OF US ARE.
SHE MAKES A FINE POINT, FOR A HUMAN.
LET'S HOPE OUR GUNS WORK ON THE OTHER SI—

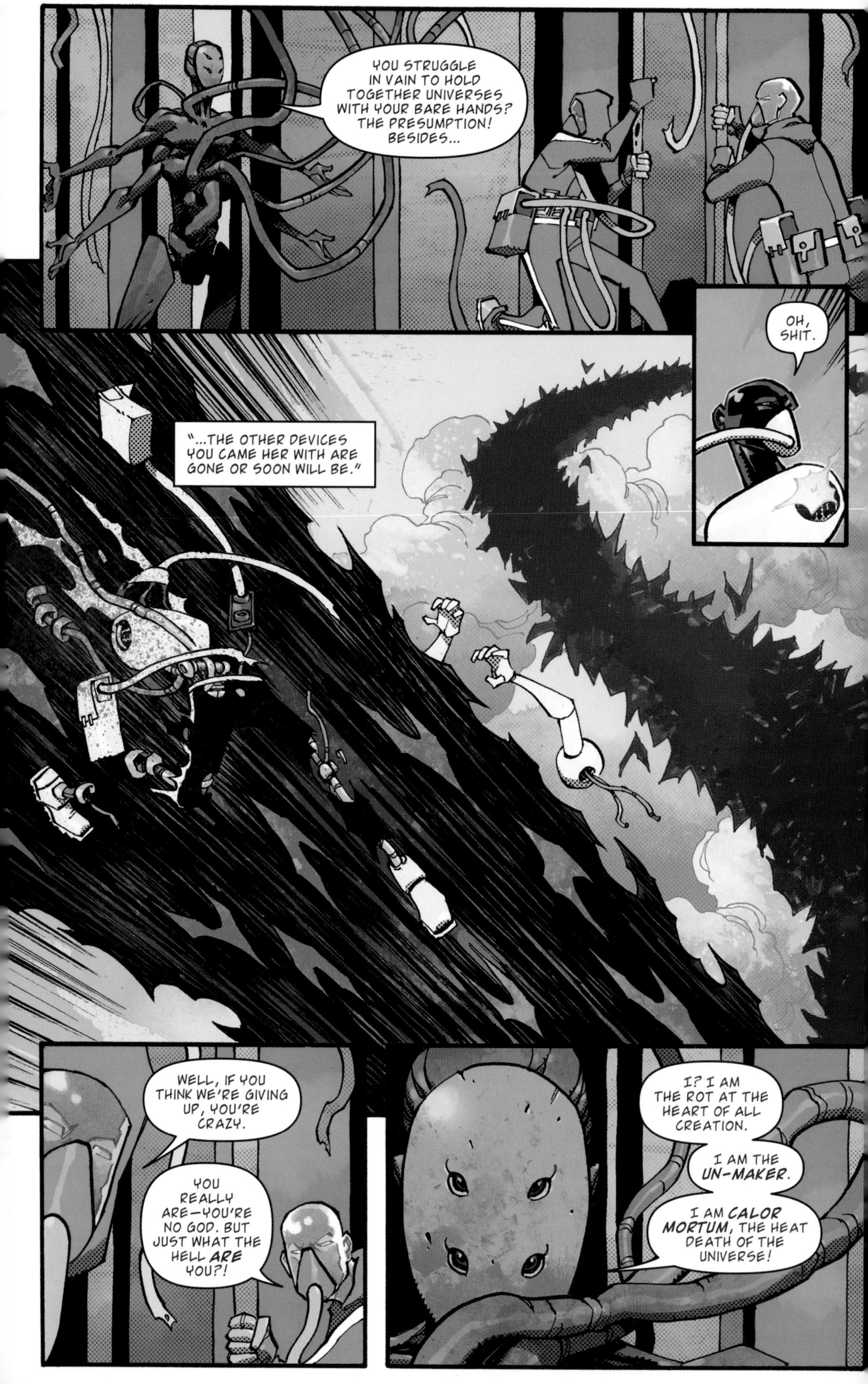
YOU STRUGGLE IN VAIN TO HOLD TOGETHER UNIVERSES WITH YOUR BARE HANDS? THE PRESUMPTION! BESIDES...
OH, SHIT.
"...THE OTHER DEVICES YOU CAME HER WITH ARE GONE OR SOON WILL BE."
WELL, IF YOU THINK WE'RE GIVING UP, YOU'RE CRAZY.
YOU REALLY ARE—YOU'RE NO GOD. BUT JUST WHAT THE HELL **ARE** YOU?!
I? I AM THE ROT AT THE HEART OF ALL CREATION.
I AM THE ***UN-MAKER***.
I AM ***CALOR MORTUM***, THE HEAT DEATH OF THE UNIVERSE!

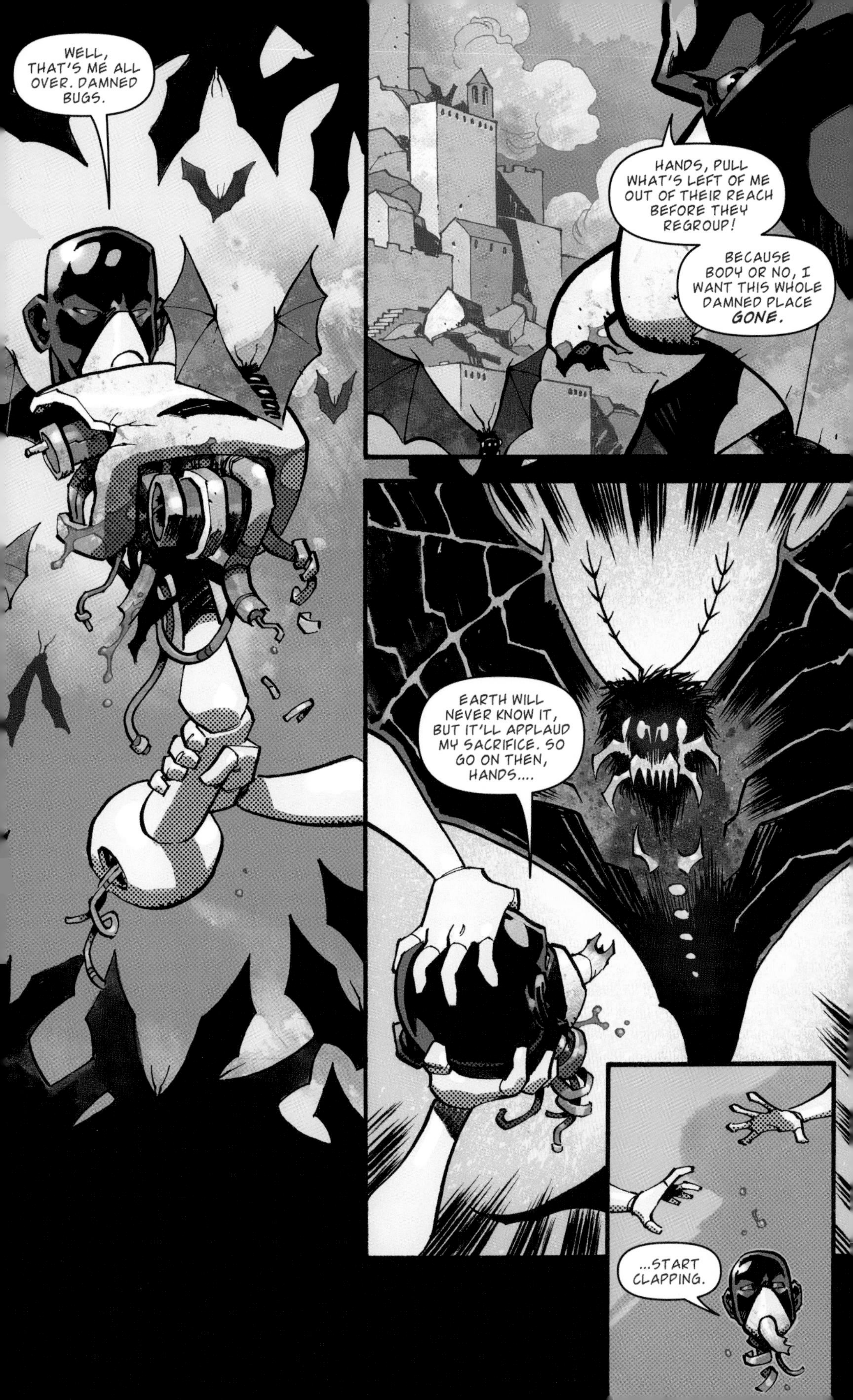
WELL, THAT'S ME ALL OVER. DAMNED BUGS.
HANDS, PULL WHAT'S LEFT OF ME OUT OF THEIR REACH BEFORE THEY REGROUP!
BECAUSE BODY OR NO, I WANT THIS WHOLE DAMNED PLACE GONE.
EARTH WILL NEVER KNOW IT, BUT IT'LL APPLAUD MY SACRIFICE. SO GO ON THEN, HANDS....
...START CLAPPING.

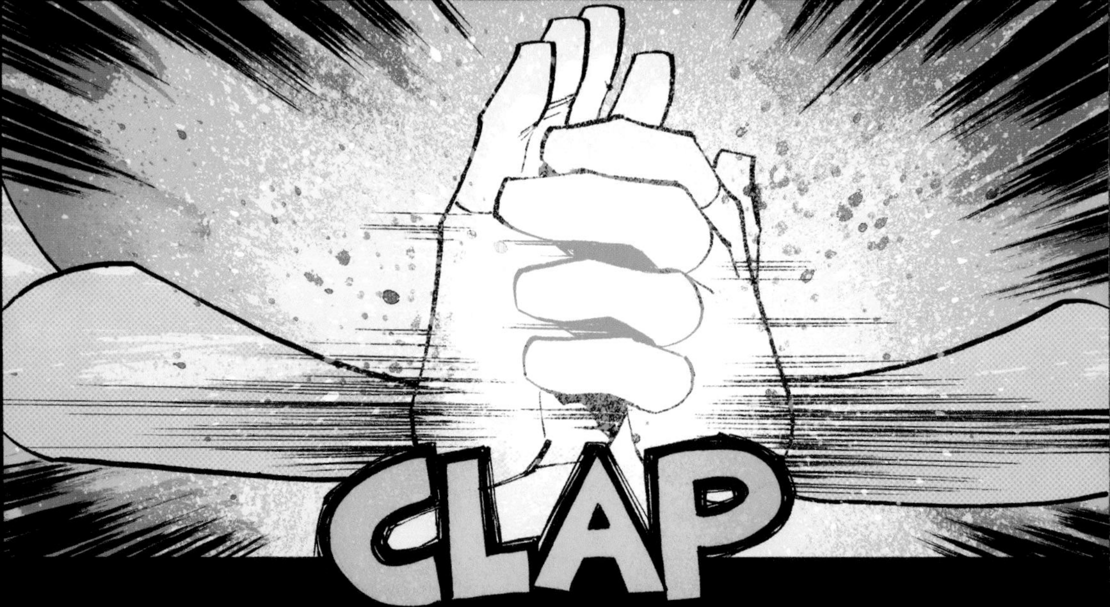
CLAP

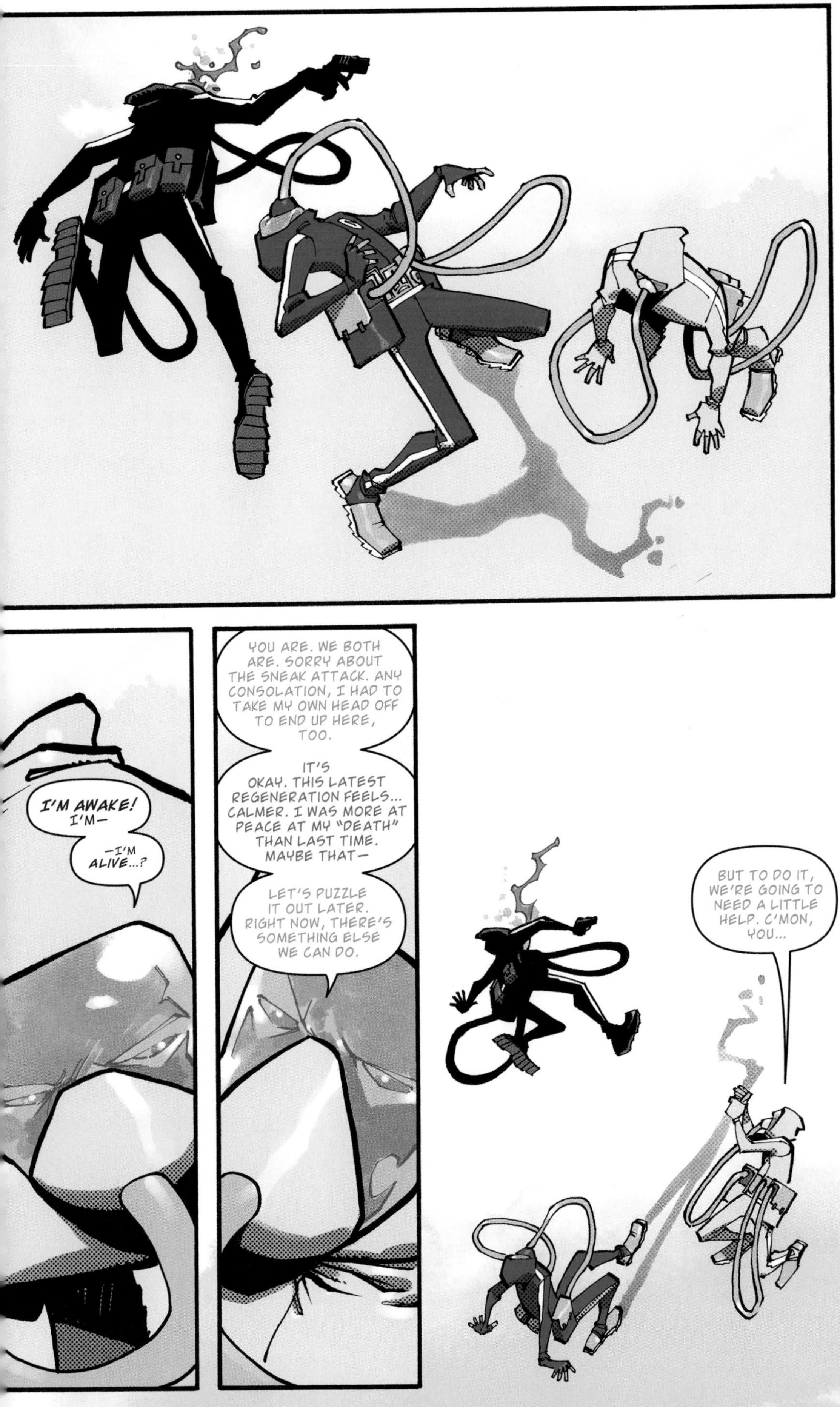
I'M AWAKE! I'M—
—I'M ALIVE...?
YOU ARE. WE BOTH ARE. SORRY ABOUT THE SNEAK ATTACK. ANY CONSOLATION, I HAD TO TAKE MY OWN HEAD OFF TO END UP HERE, TOO.
IT'S OKAY. THIS LATEST REGENERATION FEELS... CALMER. I WAS MORE AT PEACE AT MY "DEATH" THAN LAST TIME. MAYBE THAT—
LET'S PUZZLE IT OUT LATER. RIGHT NOW, THERE'S SOMETHING ELSE WE CAN DO.
BUT TO DO IT, WE'RE GOING TO NEED A LITTLE HELP. C'MON, YOU...

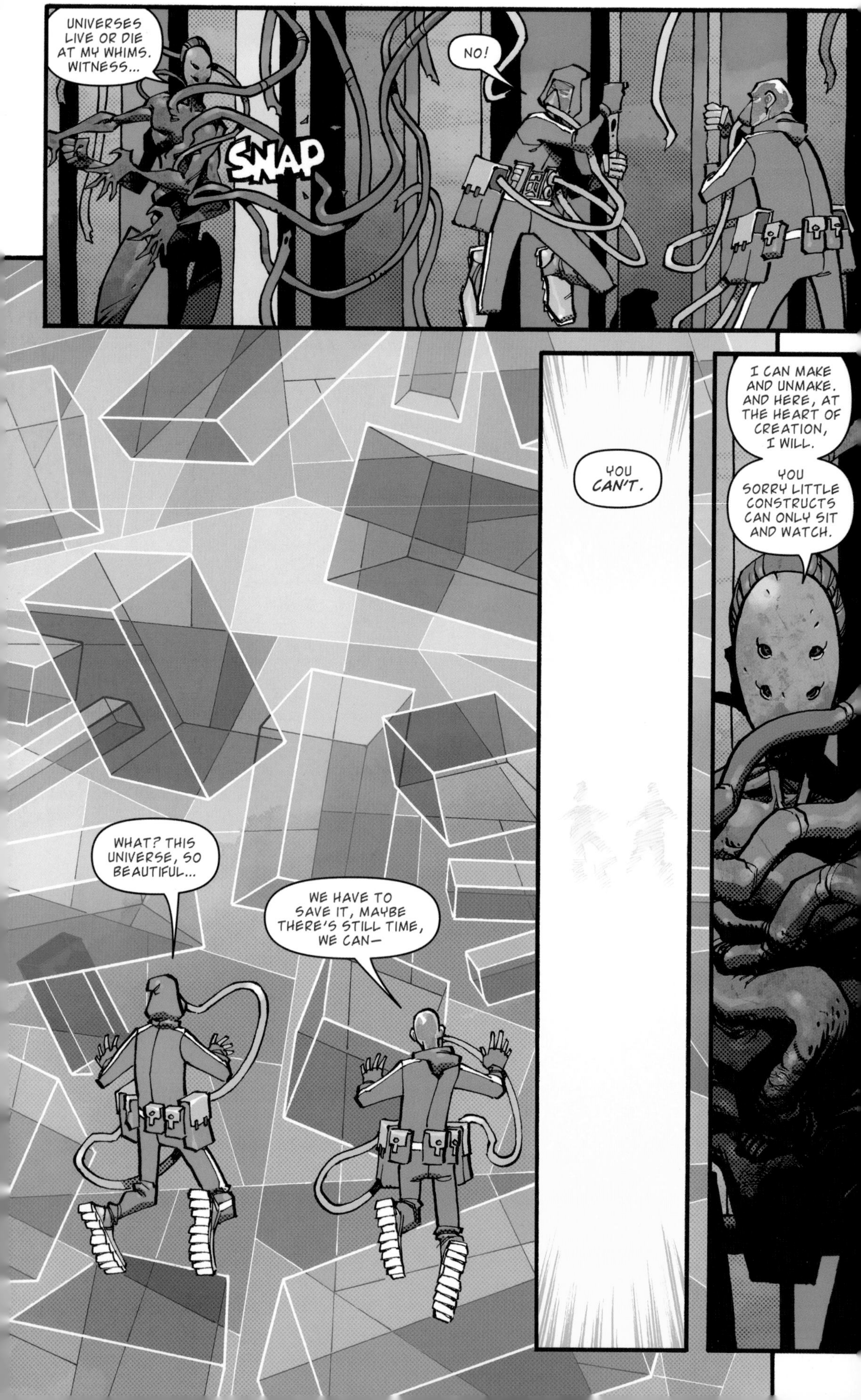

UNIVERSES LIVE OR DIE AT MY WHIMS. WITNESS...
NO!
SNAP
WHAT? THIS UNIVERSE, SO BEAUTIFUL...
WE HAVE TO SAVE IT, MAYBE THERE'S STILL TIME, WE CAN—
YOU CAN'T.
I CAN MAKE AND UNMAKE. AND HERE, AT THE HEART OF CREATION, I WILL.
YOU SORRY LITTLE CONSTRUCTS CAN ONLY SIT AND WATCH.

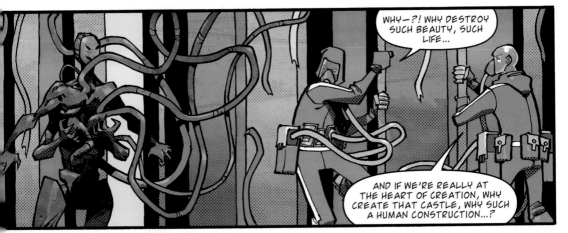

WHY—?! WHY DESTROY SUCH BEAUTY, SUCH LIFE...

AND IF WE'RE REALLY AT THE HEART OF CREATION, WHY CREATE THAT CASTLE, WHY SUCH A HUMAN CONSTRUCTION...?

"CASTLE." IT IS NOT A CASTLE. IT IS EVIDENCE THAT YOU ARE ONLY ABLE TO PERCEIVE THINGS IN A TOO-LIMITED WAY.

CAN YOU SEE RADIO WAVES? GAMMA WAVES? SOUNDWAVES? OF COURSE NOT. YOU ARE LIMITED TO THE POINT OF RIDICULOUSNESS.

YOU ARE FLAWED, UNABLE TO EXPERIENCE THIS UNIVERSE AS IT EXISTS. YOU ARE THE PRIMARY SENTIENT BEINGS IN MANY DIMENSIONS.

YOU ARE ALL TOO HUMAN— ABSOLUTELY UNDESERVING OF LIFE.

WE'RE... TOO HUMAN?

O GREAT UNMAKER OF THE UNIVERSE, IF WE'RE TOO HUMAN, WHY IS YOUR FORM SO, YOU KNOW, HUMANOID?

SURE, YOU'VE GOT SOME TENTACLES AND ALL, BUT OVERALL, SEEMS LIKE A DESIGN LACKING IN IMAGINATION.

AS I STATED, YOUR LIMITED CAPACITY TO PERCEIVE THE UNIVERSE SEES ME IN THIS FORM, BUT THIS FORM IS NOT ME.

BUT ALSO, I WANTED TO EXPERIENCE BEING SIMILARLY HUMANOID AS I KILL YOU ALL.

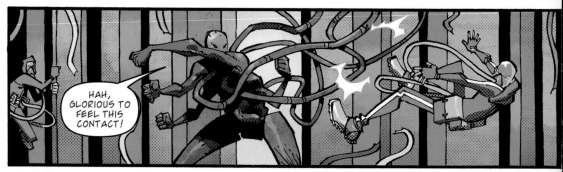

HAH, GLORIOUS TO FEEL THIS CONTACT!

ENDLESS ARE THE LIVES I HAVE SNUFFED WHEN I DAMAGE THESE DIMENSIONAL STRINGS, AND YET...

AND YET SMASHING THE TWO OF YOU PROMISES ME EVEN GREATER, MORE PERSONAL JOY THAN— HEY! WHAT?

WHAT THE?!

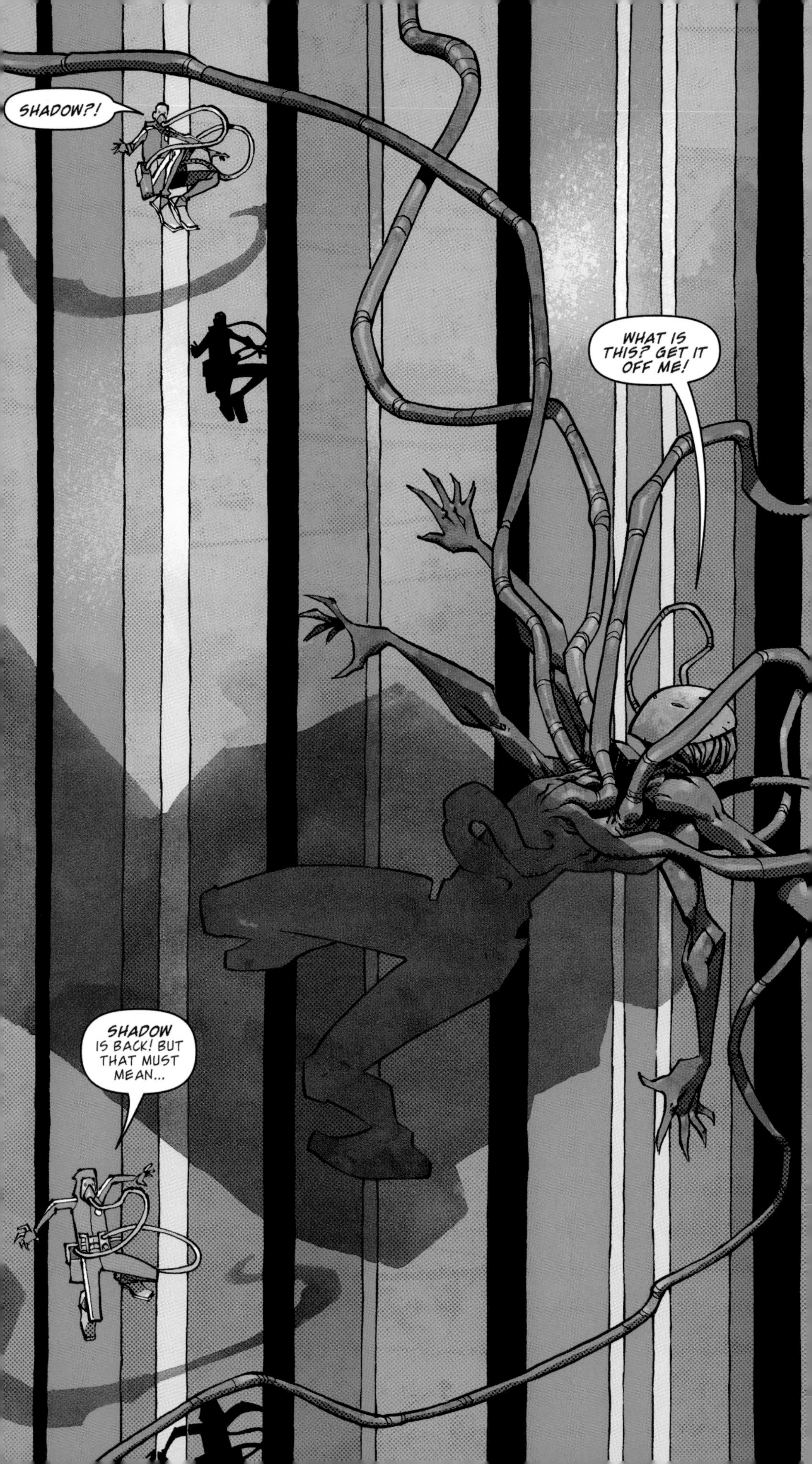
SHADOW?!
WHAT IS THIS? GET IT OFF ME!
SHADOW IS BACK! BUT THAT MUST MEAN...

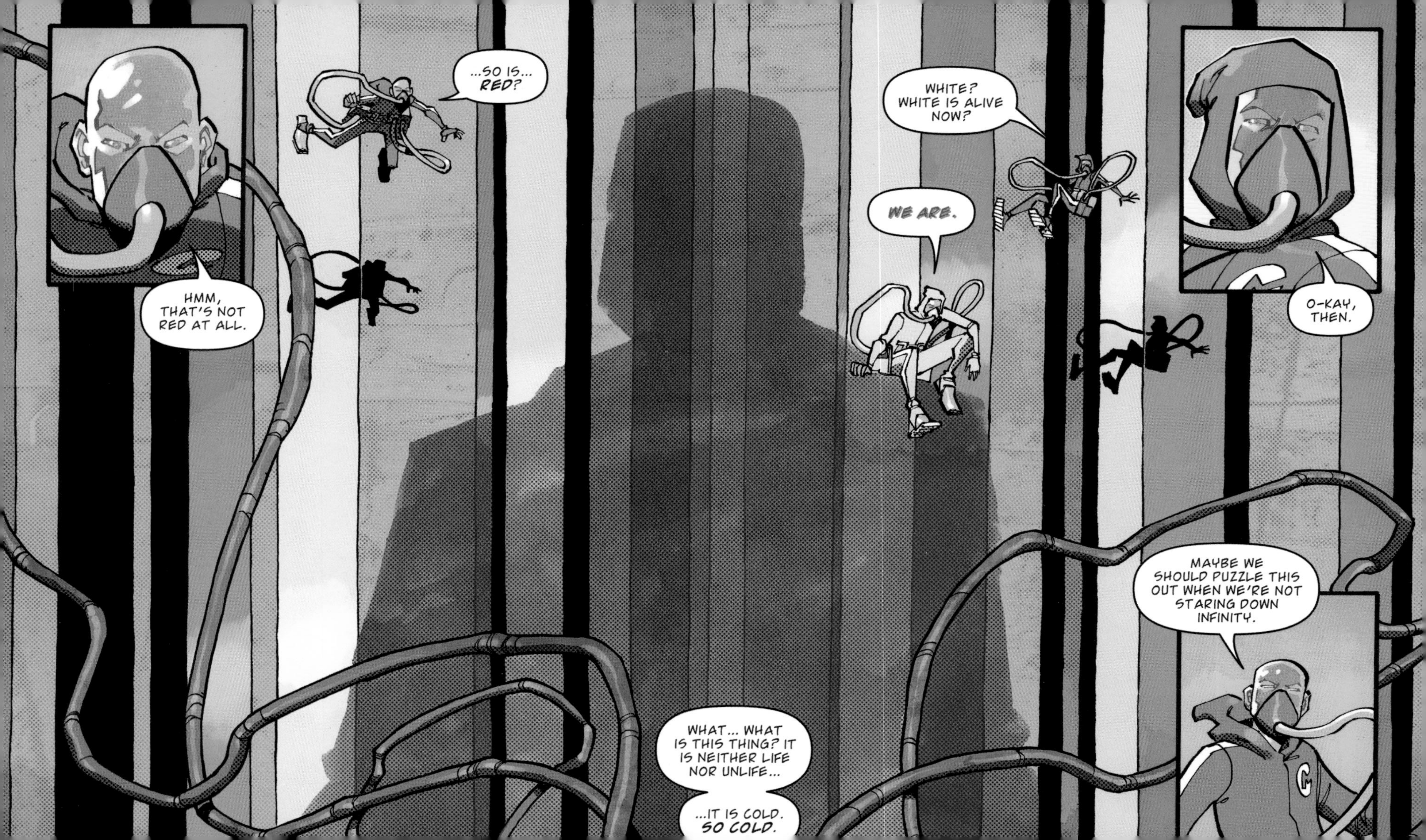
HMM, THAT'S NOT RED AT ALL.
...SO IS... **RED?**
WHITE? WHITE IS ALIVE NOW?
WE ARE.
O-KAY, THEN.
WHAT... WHAT IS THIS THING? IT IS NEITHER LIFE NOR UNLIFE...
...IT IS COLD. **SO COLD.**
MAYBE WE SHOULD PUZZLE THIS OUT WHEN WE'RE NOT STARING DOWN INFINITY.

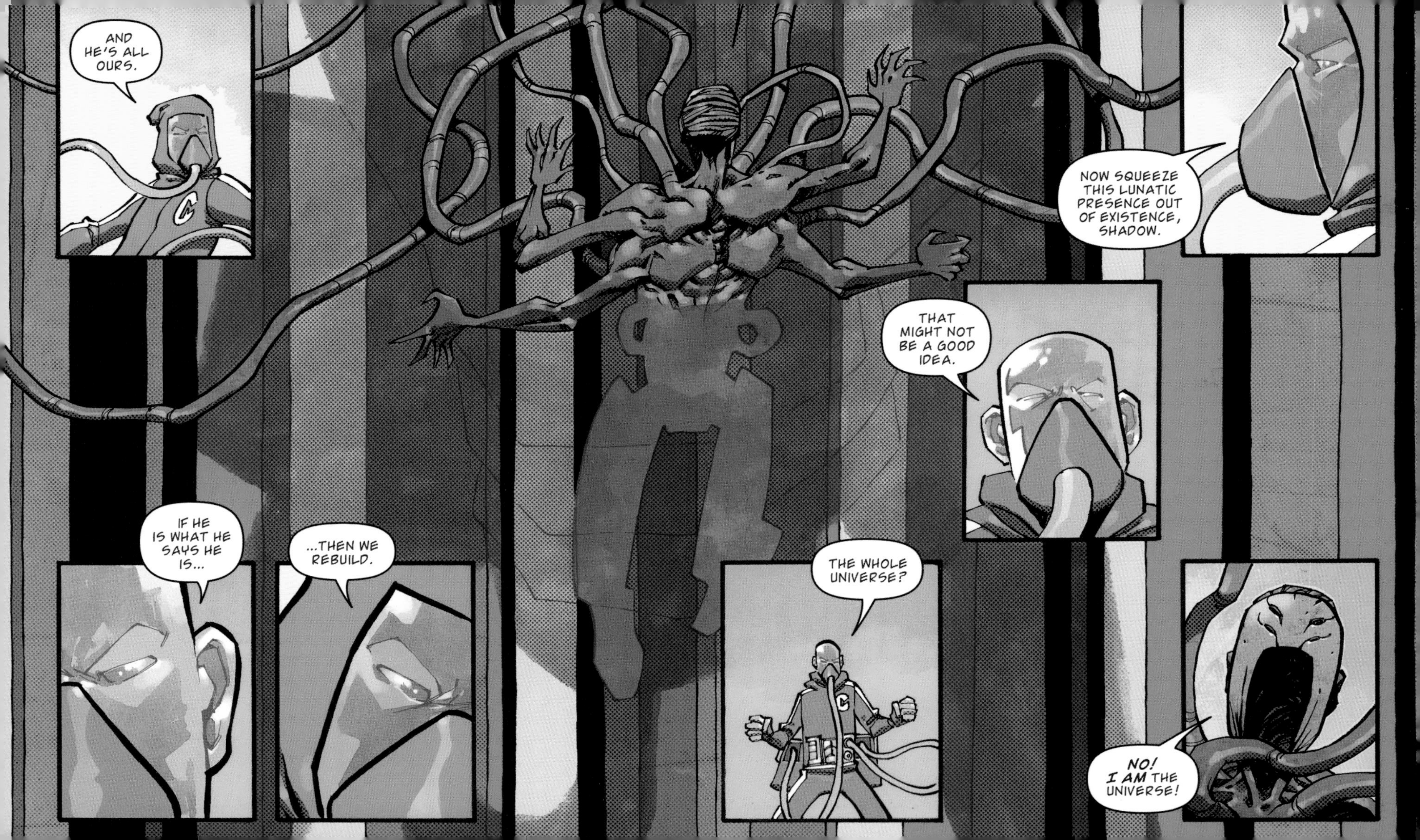
AND HE'S ALL OURS.
NOW SQUEEZE THIS LUNATIC PRESENCE OUT OF EXISTENCE, SHADOW.
THAT MIGHT NOT BE A GOOD IDEA.
IF HE IS WHAT HE SAYS HE IS...
...THEN WE REBUILD.
THE WHOLE UNIVERSE?
NO! I AM THE UNIVERSE!

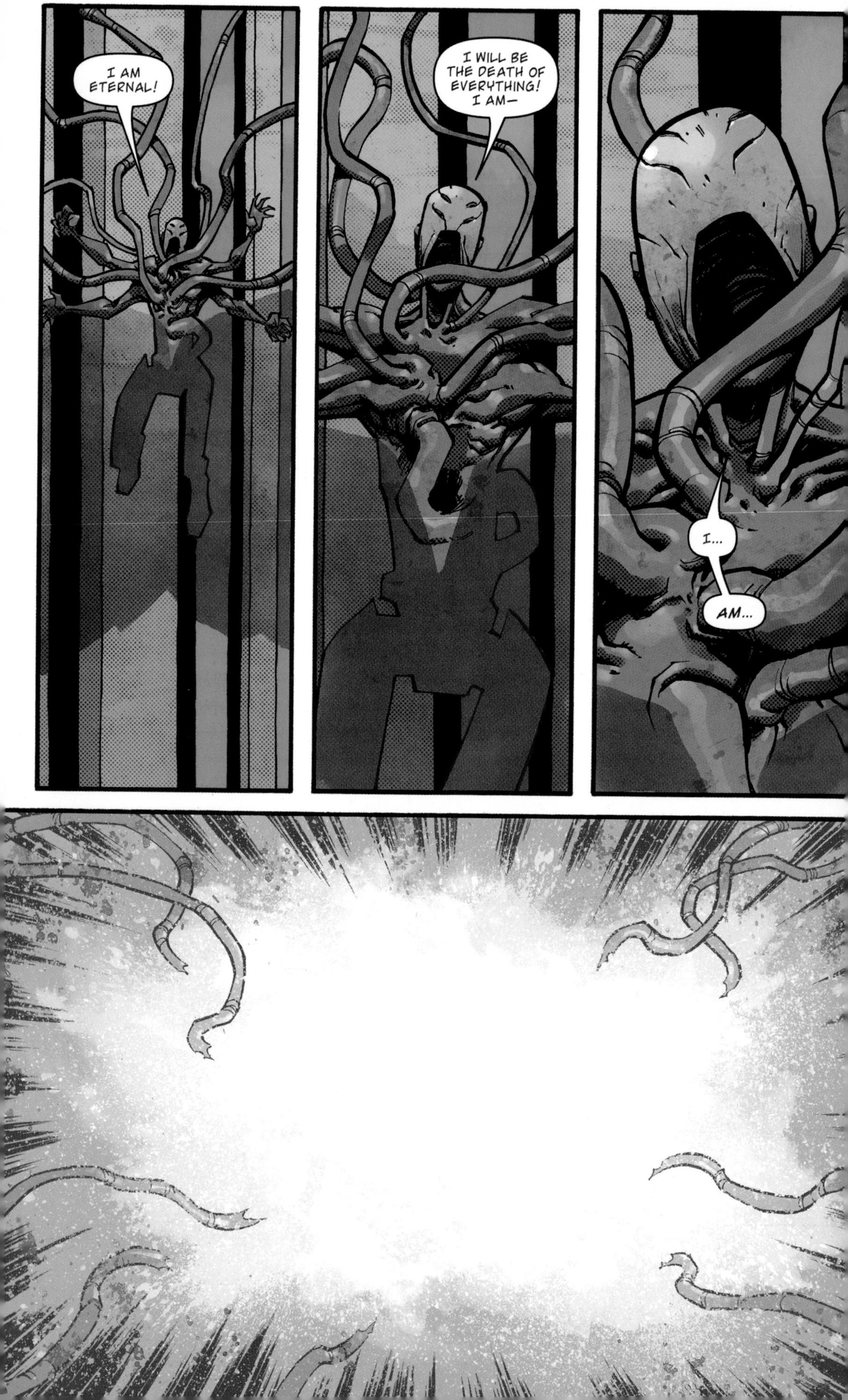
I AM ETERNAL!
I WILL BE THE DEATH OF EVERYTHING! I AM—
I...
AM...

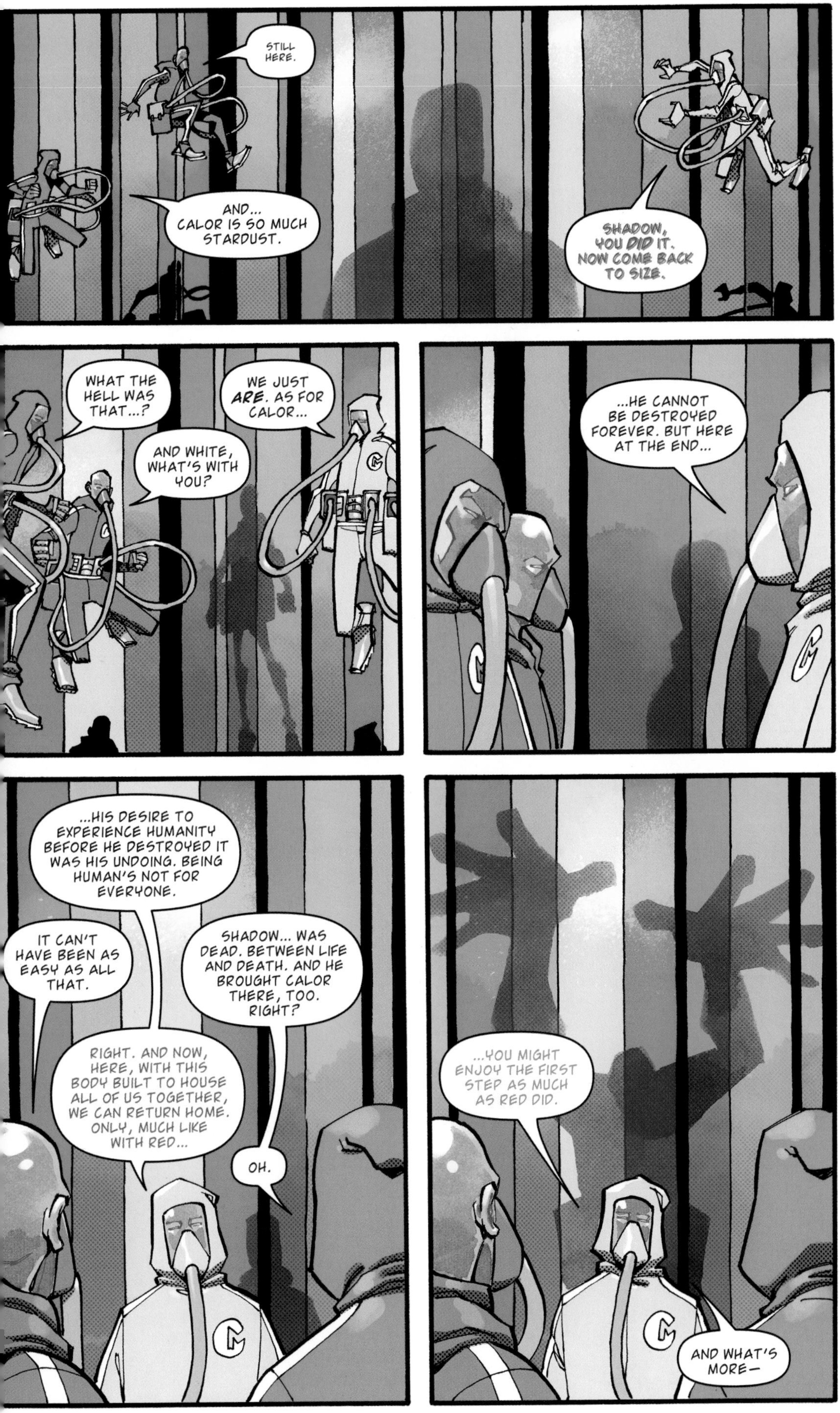
STILL HERE.
AND... CALOR IS SO MUCH STARDUST.
SHADOW, YOU DID IT. NOW COME BACK TO SIZE.
WHAT THE HELL WAS THAT...?
AND WHITE, WHAT'S WITH YOU?
WE JUST ARE. AS FOR CALOR...
...HE CANNOT BE DESTROYED FOREVER. BUT HERE AT THE END...
...HIS DESIRE TO EXPERIENCE HUMANITY BEFORE HE DESTROYED IT WAS HIS UNDOING. BEING HUMAN'S NOT FOR EVERYONE.
IT CAN'T HAVE BEEN AS EASY AS ALL THAT.
SHADOW... WAS DEAD. BETWEEN LIFE AND DEATH. AND HE BROUGHT CALOR THERE, TOO. RIGHT?
RIGHT. AND NOW, HERE, WITH THIS BODY BUILT TO HOUSE ALL OF US TOGETHER, WE CAN RETURN HOME. ONLY, MUCH LIKE WITH RED...
OH.
...YOU MIGHT ENJOY THE FIRST STEP AS MUCH AS RED DID.
AND WHAT'S MORE—

—YOU MIGHT FIND THINGS A BIT DIFFERENT ONCE WE DO MAKE IT BACK.

WELL, YES, I ASSUME SO. THE DAMAGE CALOR CAUSED TO THE... THE VERY STRINGS THAT BIND OUR UNIVERSE HAS TO HAVE HAD CATASTROPHIC EFFECTS ACROSS MULTIPLE DIMENSIONAL REALITIES.

YES, THE UNTYING OF THESE STRINGS HAS TO HAVE UNTETHERED THE VERY STUFF OF WHICH THE UNIVERSE IS MADE.

DARK MATTER FILLING THE CRACKS...

PLANETARY BODIES AT RISK OF IMPLOSION OR, EVEN WORSE, EXPLOSION.

Y-YOU MEAN LIKE... LIKE A SECOND BIG BANG?

"THIRD" BIG BANG, YOU MEAN. UNLESS YOU SUBSCRIBE TO THE MYTHS TOLD TO THE GENERAL POPULACE ON EARTH.

WHATEVER NUMBER! THE POINT IS, THERE MIGHT NOT BE ANY KIND OF UNIVERSE FOR US TO EVEN RETURN TO, R-RIGHT...?

YOU SURE AREN'T MAKING ME THINK WE MADE A DIFFERENCE DOWN HERE.

OF COURSE WE DID. WE PREVENTED THE HEAT—DEATH OF THE UNIVERSE. WE STOPPED... DEATH, OR ENTROPY, OR GOD, OR WHATEVER CALOR WAS...

IS. HE'S STILL OUT THERE, ISN'T THAT WHAT YOU SAID?

SURE. IN THE SAME WAY, SAY, PESTILENCE IS.

SENTIENT PESTILENCE. WE'VE MADE ENEMIES WITH SENTIENT PESTILENCE. KILL ME NOW.

AGAIN? DON'T YOU EVER LEARN?

N-NO, DON'T! I DON'T CARE IF I'LL BE REBORN AGAIN. I DON'T CARE THAT I'LL BE BETTER NEXT TIME. JUST DON'T—

HMM. HEY, GUYS...

I'M SERIOUS, DO NOT!

GUYS! LISTEN—RED JUST PUT AN IDEA IN MY HEAD. IF WE CAN BE REBORN—WITH WHAT HAS BEEN LOST TODAY, MAYBE WE CAN DIRECT THE UNIVERSE TO, YOU KNOW, REBOOT THINGS BACK ON EARTH'S DIMENSION.

A REBOOT? SORRY, NO, REALITY DOESN'T WORK LIKE THAT. THERE ARE NO EASY WAYS OUT. AT LEAST, THERE SHOULDN'T BE,

CORRECT. EVEN IF WHAT WE ALL KNOW IS NOW DAMAGED AND DIFFERENT THAN WE'D LIKE.

BUT CAN'T WE AT LEAST *TRY*, FOCUS OUR ENERGIES...?

SORRY, NO. BETTER OR WORSE, OUR UNIVERSE IS WHAT IT IS NOW. WE'LL ALL JUST HAVE TO ACCEPT THE CONSEQUENCES OF WHAT WE'VE DONE.

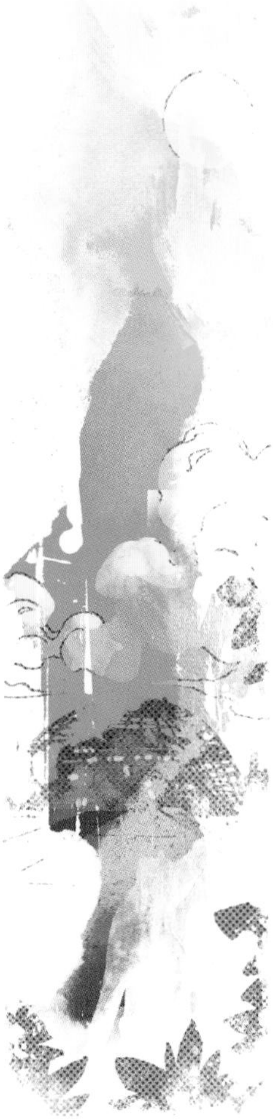

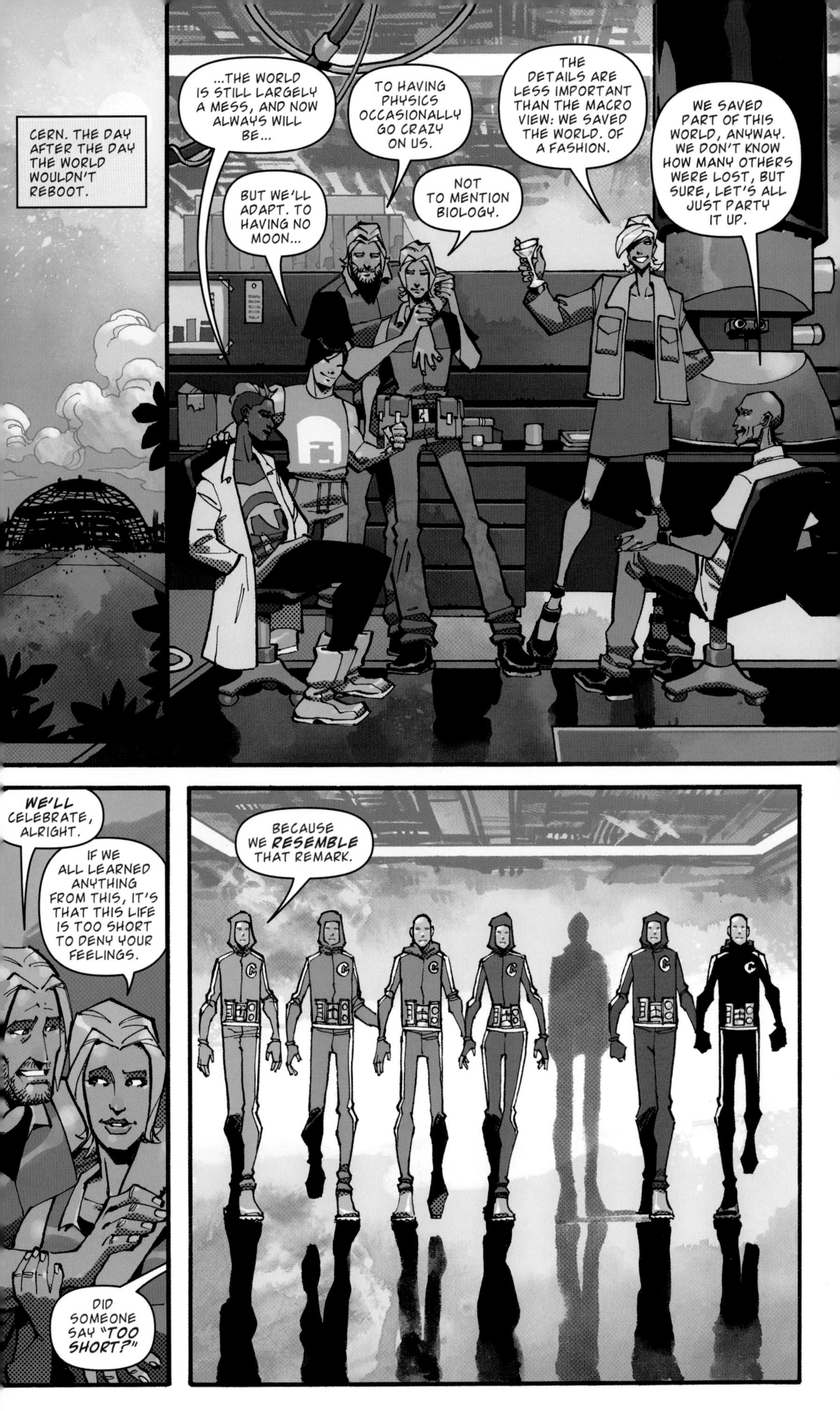

CERN. THE DAY AFTER THE DAY THE WORLD WOULDN'T REBOOT.
...THE WORLD IS STILL LARGELY A MESS, AND NOW ALWAYS WILL BE...
BUT WE'LL ADAPT. TO HAVING NO MOON...
TO HAVING PHYSICS OCCASIONALLY GO CRAZY ON US.
NOT TO MENTION BIOLOGY.
THE DETAILS ARE LESS IMPORTANT THAN THE MACRO VIEW: WE SAVED THE WORLD. OF A FASHION.
WE SAVED PART OF THIS WORLD, ANYWAY. WE DON'T KNOW HOW MANY OTHERS WERE LOST, BUT SURE, LET'S ALL JUST PARTY IT UP.
WE'LL CELEBRATE, ALRIGHT.
IF WE ALL LEARNED ANYTHING FROM THIS, IT'S THAT THIS LIFE IS TOO SHORT TO DENY YOUR FEELINGS.
DID SOMEONE SAY "*TOO SHORT?*"
BECAUSE WE ***RESEMBLE*** THAT REMARK.

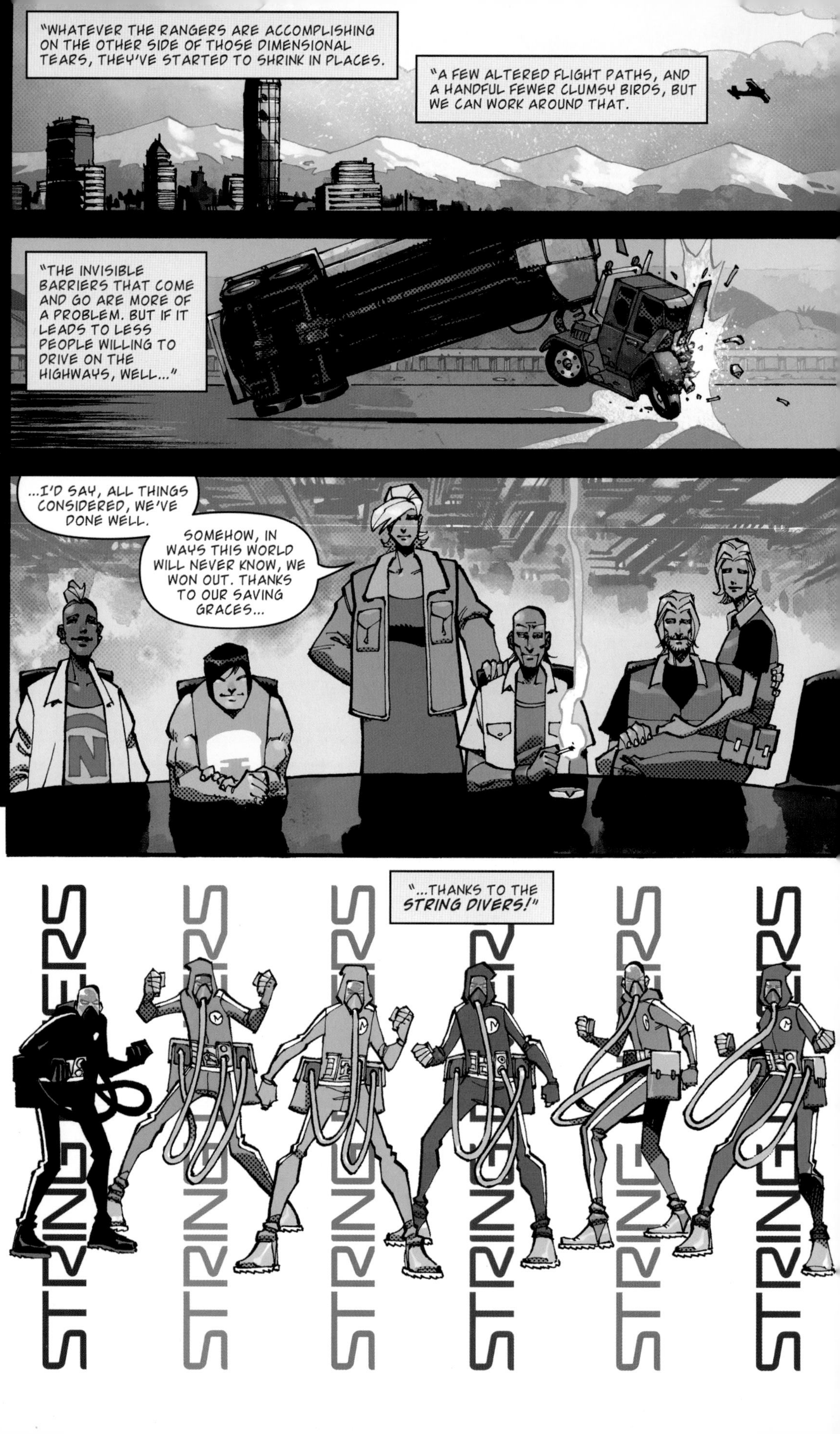
"WHATEVER THE RANGERS ARE ACCOMPLISHING ON THE OTHER SIDE OF THOSE DIMENSIONAL TEARS, THEY'VE STARTED TO SHRINK IN PLACES.
"A FEW ALTERED FLIGHT PATHS, AND A HANDFUL FEWER CLUMSY BIRDS, BUT WE CAN WORK AROUND THAT.
"THE INVISIBLE BARRIERS THAT COME AND GO ARE MORE OF A PROBLEM. BUT IF IT LEADS TO LESS PEOPLE WILLING TO DRIVE ON THE HIGHWAYS, WELL..."
...I'D SAY, ALL THINGS CONSIDERED, WE'VE DONE WELL.
SOMEHOW, IN WAYS THIS WORLD WILL NEVER KNOW, WE WON OUT. THANKS TO OUR SAVING GRACES...
"...THANKS TO THE STRING DIVERS!"
STRINGERS

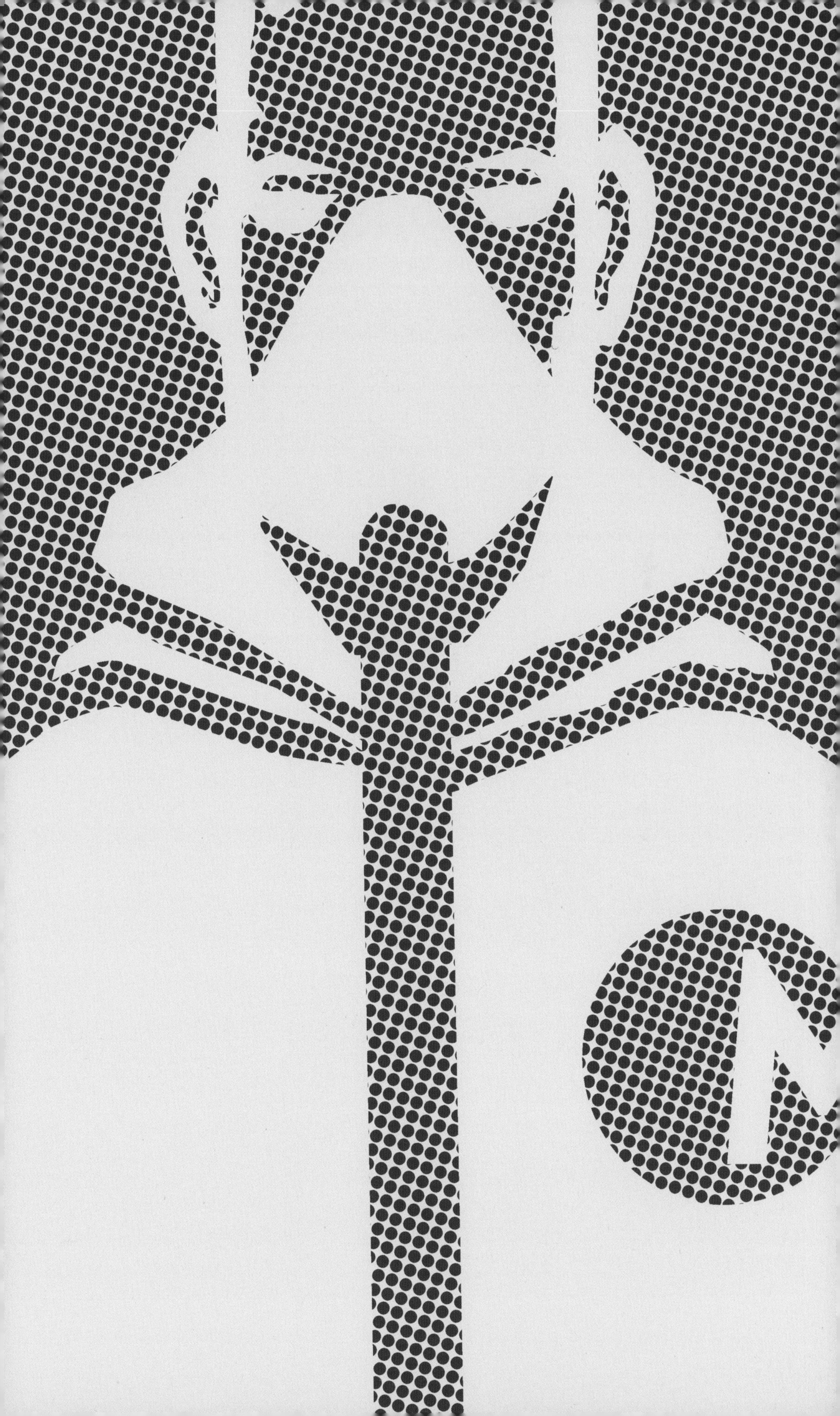

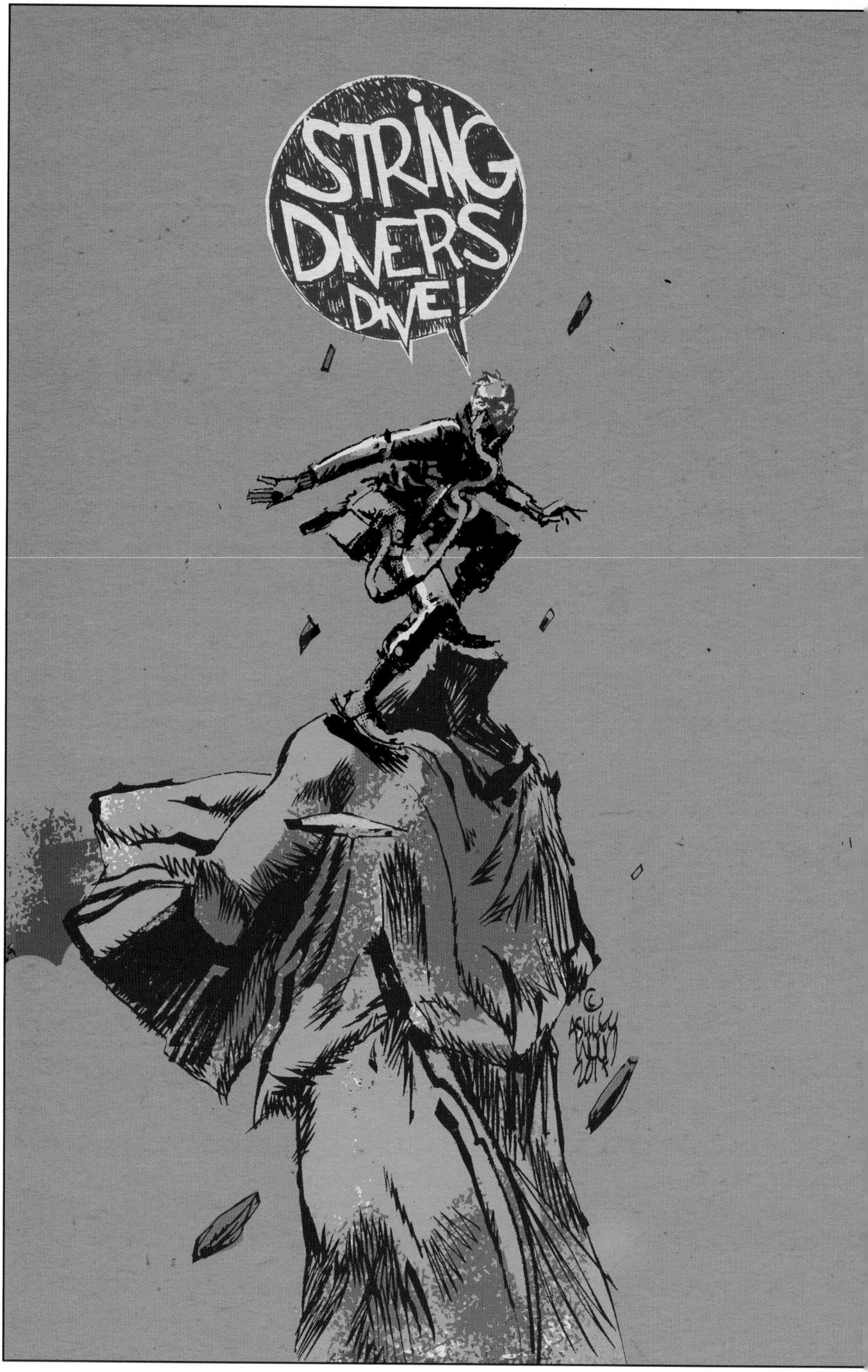
STRING DIVERS DIVE!

ART BY ASHLEY WOOD

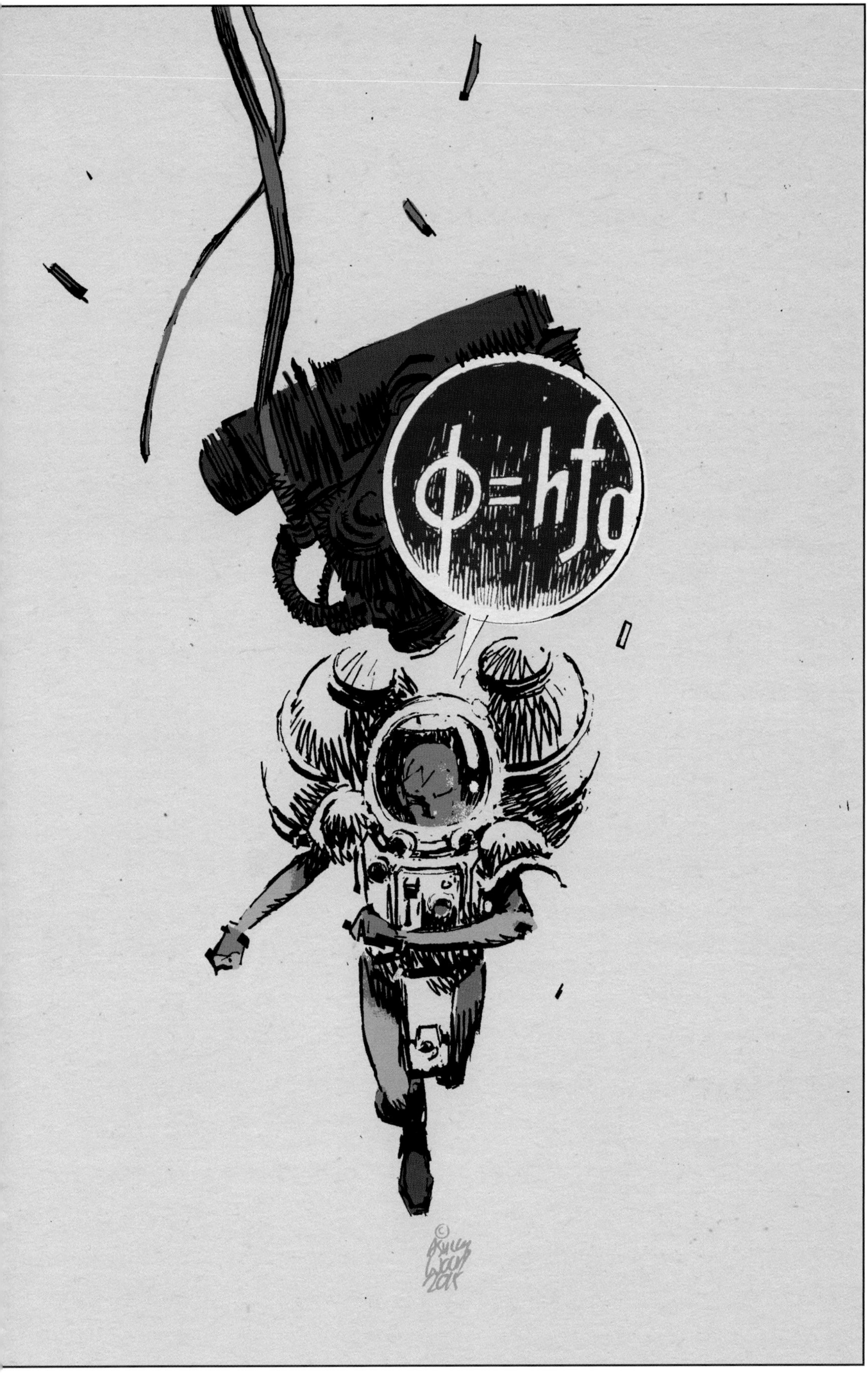

ϕ=hf0

ART BY ASHLEY WOOD

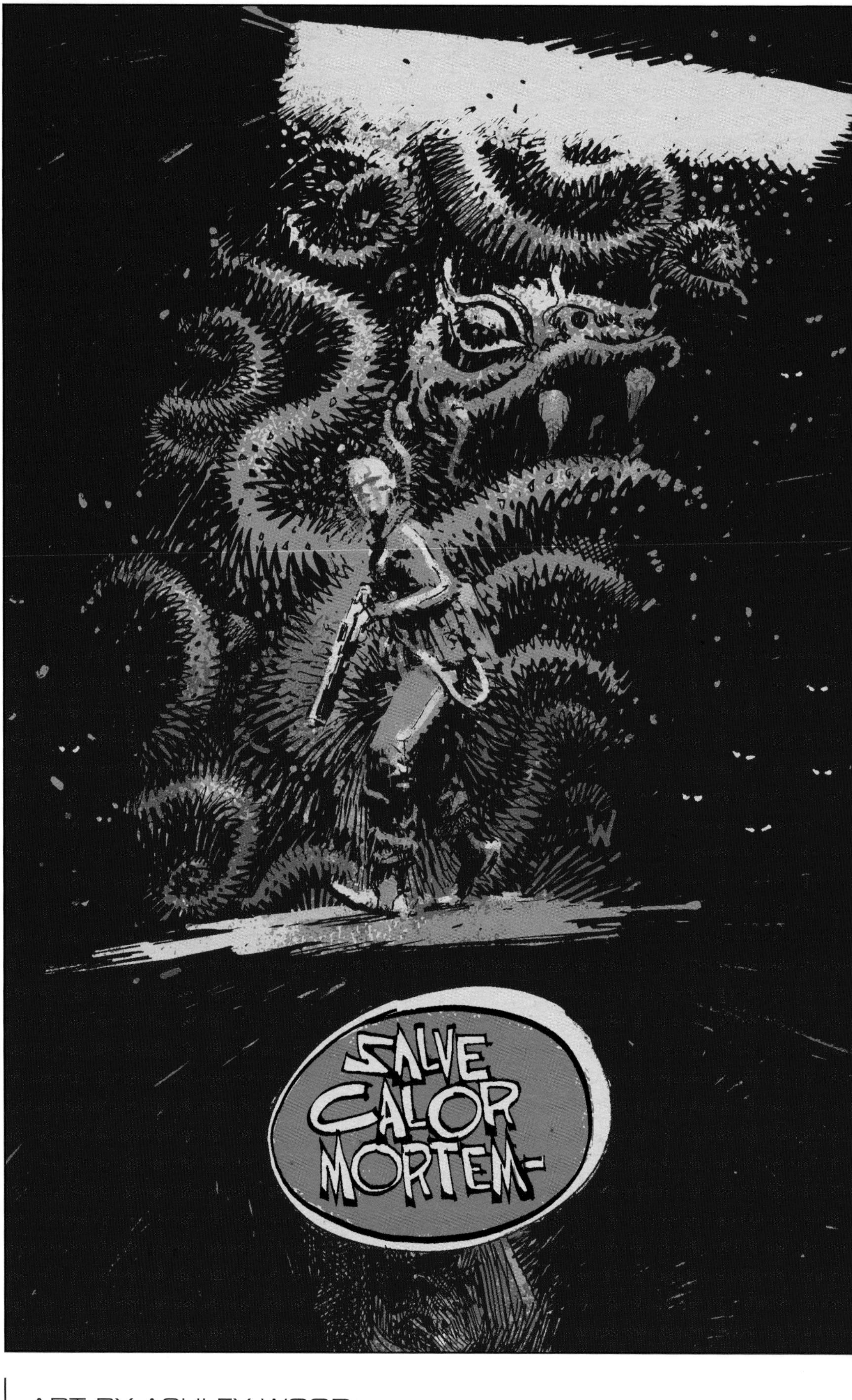
SALVE CALOR MORTEM-

ART BY ASHLEY WOOD

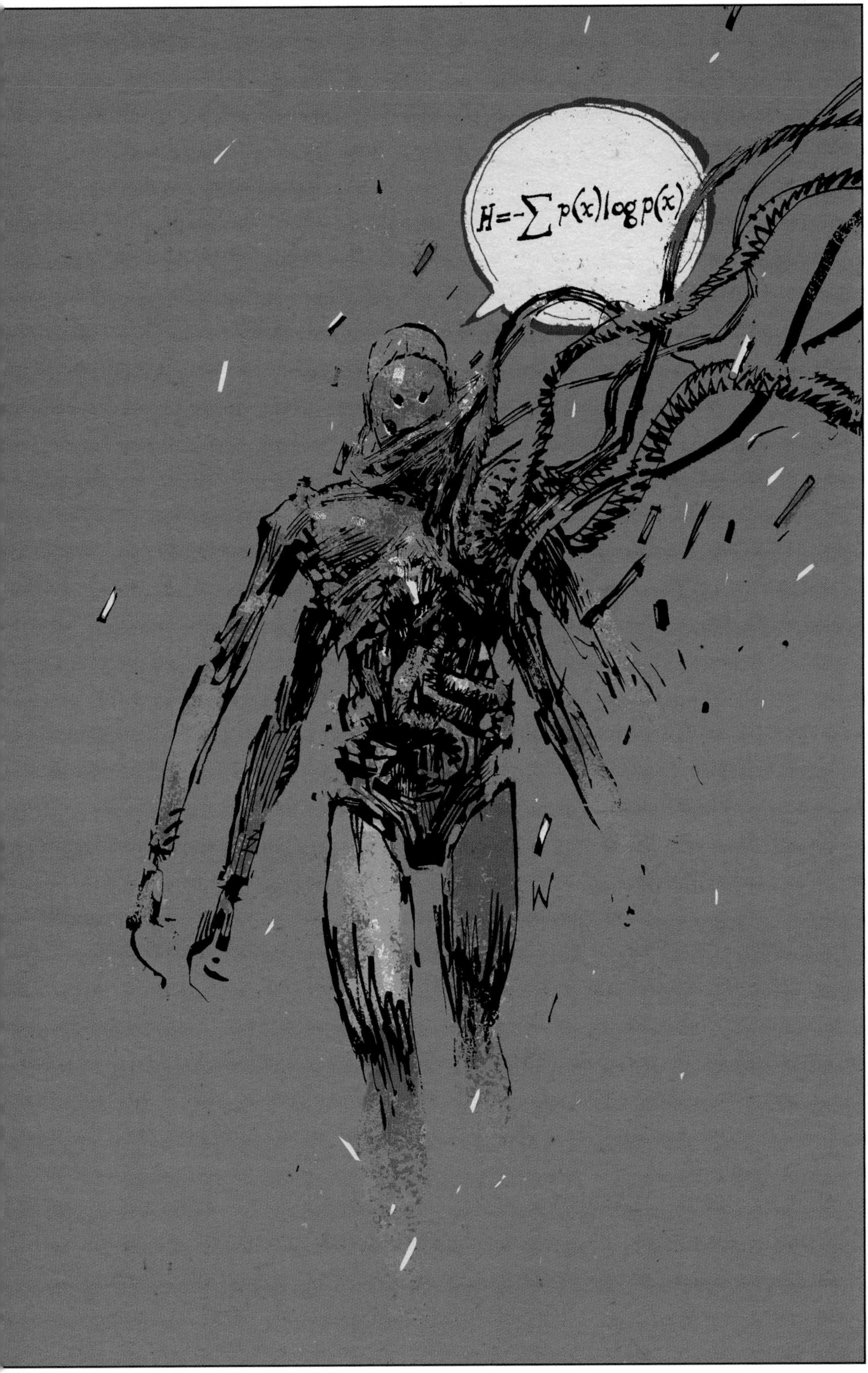
$H=-\sum p(x)\log p(x)$

ART BY ASHLEY WOOD

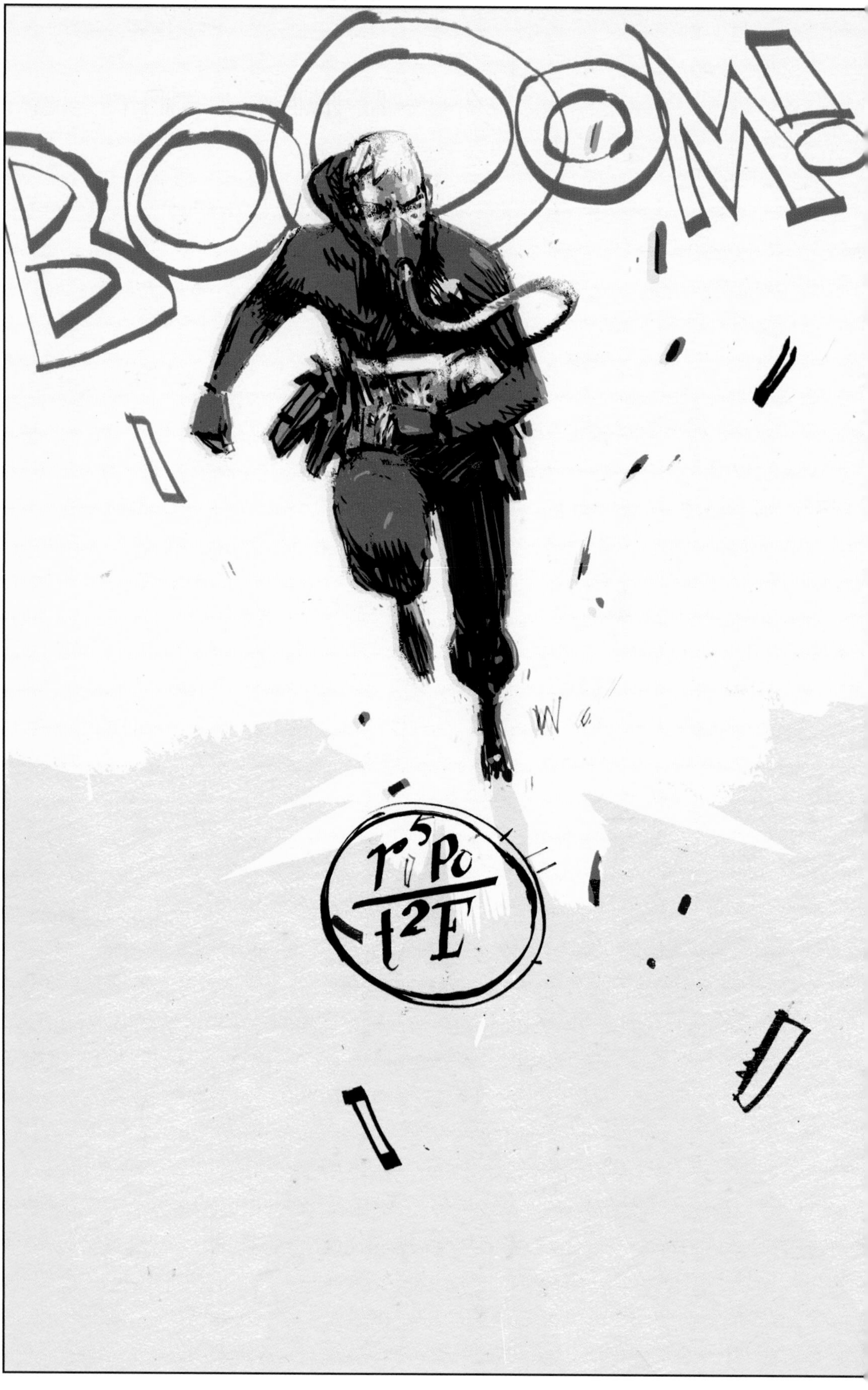
BOOOOM!
$\frac{r^5 Po}{t^2 E}$

ART BY ASHLEY WOOD

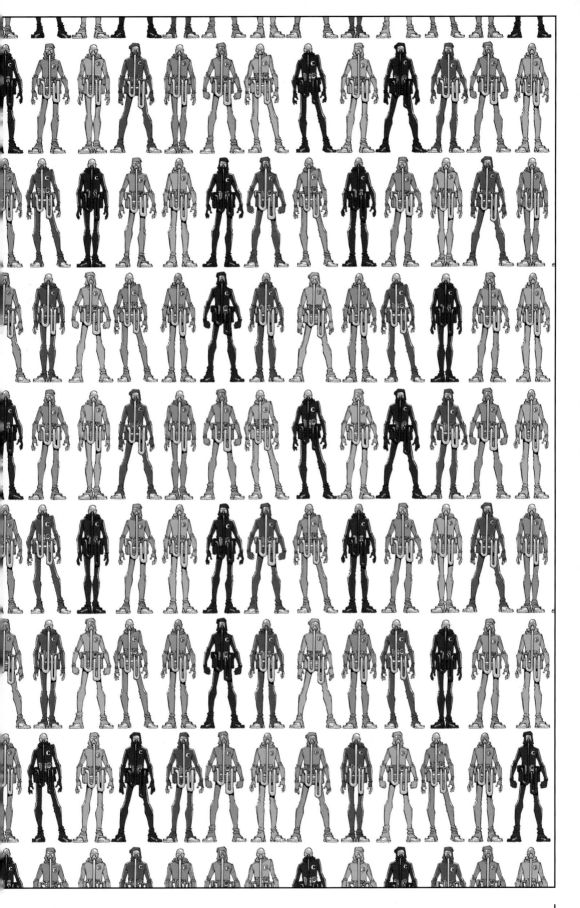

ART BY NELSON DÁNIEL

PROJECT STRING

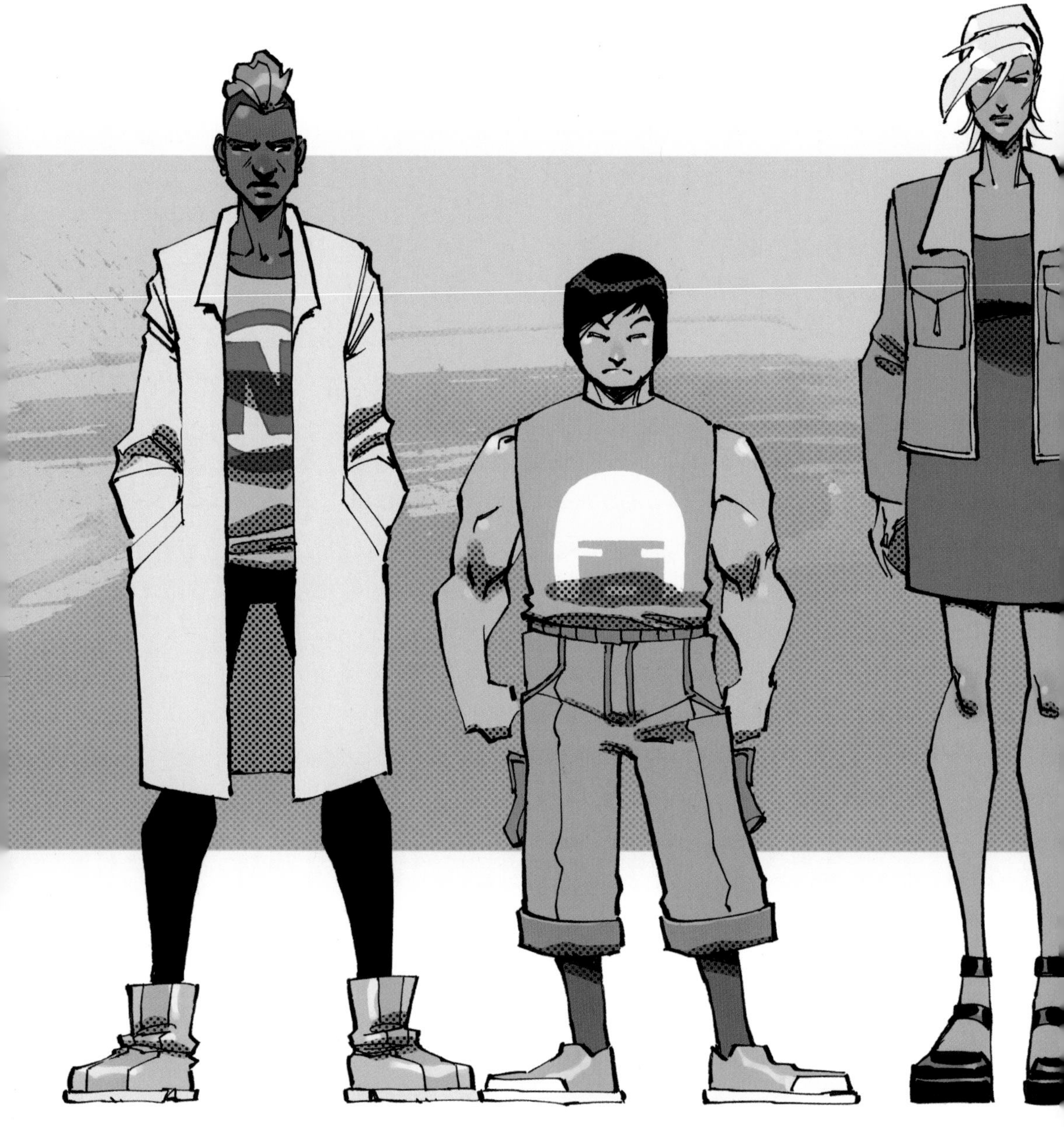

SHAUNTÉ MASON
MICRO-TECH

LEONARD OTO
ENGINEER/ROBOTICIST

ANNE-SYLVIE LaGRANGE
DIRECTOR GENERAL

DIVERS

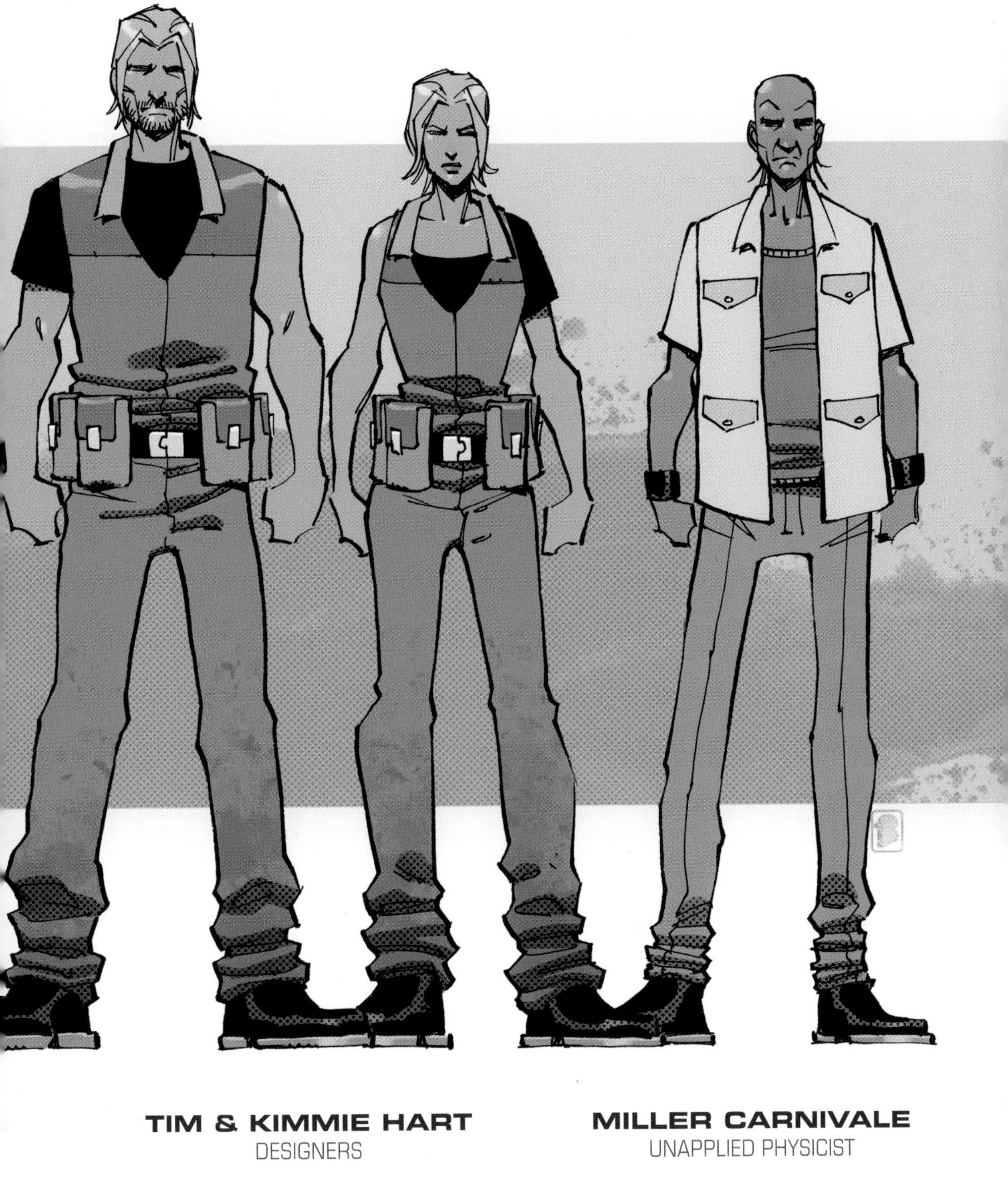

TIM & KIMMIE HART
DESIGNERS

MILLER CARNIVALE
UNAPPLIED PHYSICIST

For ages 3 and up
STRING DIVERS
IDW
3A
ASHLEY WOOD
Creator-Art Director class

//

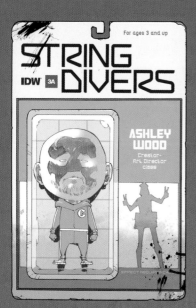

Name: ASHLEY WOOD

Location: AUS / HK

Specialty: Auteur

Published Works: Too many to list, google it!

Statement: Why not!

Future projects to watch for: Ashley Wood

For ages 3 and up
STRING DIVERS
IDW
3A
CHRIS RYALL
Storyteller class
EFFECT REQUIRES CAUSE

//

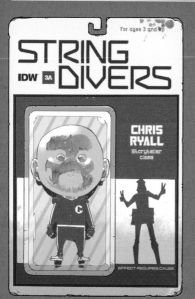

Name: CHRIS RYALL

Location: San Diego, CA

Specialty: Writer/co-creator of *ZvR*, *Groom Lake*, *The Colonized*, *The Hollows*, *Onyx*

Published Works: The above titles, plus many other comics; recent works include *String Divers* and *Dirk Gently's Holistic Detective Agency*

Statement: "I'm looking forward to handing over the keys to the *ZvR* franchise to my new *ZvR* writer/10-year-old daughter, Lucy."

Future projects to watch for: *Rom the Space Knight*

For ages 3 and up
STRING DIVERS
IDW
3A
NELSON DANIEL
Storyteller class
EFFECT REQUIRES CAUSE

//

Name: NELSON DÁNIEL

Location: Santiago, Chile

Specialty: Pencils, inker, colorist, dancer, model, actress, I mean artist

Published Works: Artist on *String Divers*, *Judge Dredd*, *Road Rage*, *The Cape 1969*. Colorist on *Wild Blue Yonder* and *Little Nemo Return To Slumberland*.

Statement: All day!

Future projects to watch for: *Ghostbusters Deviations* in March and *Dungeons & Dragons* in April.